A Values Approach to Health Behavior

Roger L. Sweeting, PhD
Penn State Erie—The Behrend College

Human Kinetics Books
Champaign, Illinois

Library of Congress Cataloging-in-Publication Data

Sweeting, Roger L., 1937-
    A values approach to health behavior / by Roger L. Sweeting.
      p. cm.
    Bibliography: p.
    Includes index.
    ISBN 0-87322-255-5
    1. Health behavior. 2. Health education. I. Title
RA776.9.S94 1990
613'.0434--dc20   89-11157
                                                     CIP

ISBN: 0-87322-255-5

Developmental Editors: Holly Gilly and Lisa Busjahn
Copyeditor: Wendy Nelson
Assistant Editors: Julia Anderson and Valerie Hall
Proofreader: Dianna Matlosz
Production Director: Ernie Noa
Typesetter: Brad Colson
Text Design: Keith Blomberg
Text Layout: Tara Welsch
Cover Design: Jack Davis
Cover Models: Deanna Collins, Trini Fruhling, David Nesbitt
Cover Photo: Will Zehr
Illustrations: Tim Offenstein
Printer: Versa Press

Printed in the United States of America

10 9 8 7 6 5 4 3 2 1

Human Kinetics Books
A Division of Human Kinetics Publishers, Inc.
Box 5076, Champaign, IL 61825-5076
1-800-DIAL-HKP
1-800-334-3665 (in Illinois)

Contents

Preface

Socrates once said, "The unexamined life is not worth living." This book centers around the process of self-examination and addresses your beliefs, attitudes, values, and self-concept as they relate to your health behavior.

Many books have been written about health education, health promotion, disease prevention, wellness, healthy lifestyles, and quality of life. The unique feature of this book is that it considers each of these issues with personal values as the focal point.

Values have been variously defined as standards of personal behavior, guides to action, preferred end-states of existence, preferred modes of conduct, and whatever makes life truly worth living. Although nearly all of us profess to value our own health, conflicts in values sometimes cause us to act in ways that are detrimental to our health.

Many of the values concepts that follow are founded on the writings of Milton Rokeach, who contends that human behavior is unlikely to change unless preceded by changes in attitudes, values, and self-concept. Other behavioral theories are presented to help the reader understand the gap that so often exists between what we *know* about health and what we *do* about health.

The organizational framework of this book is adapted from Darwin Dennison's (1984) Activated Health Education Model. The three basic premises of Activated Health Education are that the learner must become actively involved in the learning process, be made aware of concepts and facts, and be held responsible for personal health behavior.

A series of self-examination statements appears at the beginning of each chapter. These are intended to actively involve you, the reader, in the learning process. This self-examination of knowledge, beliefs, attitudes, values, and self-concept will prepare you for the information presented in that chapter. There are no "right answers," and there is no "perfect score"; use the statements to set the mood for your personal reflection.

Each chapter continues with a section titled "Defining Terms and Concepts" that is meant to clear up a few semantic problems. This is followed by a discussion of empirical, epidemiological, and controlled-study evidence that supports healthy behavior related to that topic. Ultimately however, it is you who must assume responsibility for choosing among behavioral alternatives. Each chapter closes with a section called "Examining Your Values," designed to help you choose behaviors consistent with your values.

The development of this approach to teaching about behavioral health issues, and a text suitable to such an approach, was more than 5 years in its evolutionary stages. I had been teaching a course titled "Values and Health Behavior," but there was no appropriate text according to the publishers and health educators I contacted. I wrote two abbreviated versions for local use, with helpful feedback from students. Then, while attending the 1986 convention of the American Alliance for Health, Physical Education, Recreation and Dance in Cincinnati, I searched (without success) for a value-oriented health text and became convinced that there was still nothing comparable on the market. The people at Human Kinetics Publishers agreed with me, and 1 year later we entered into an agreement as to the kind of text we wanted to bring to interested readers.

I then took a year of sabbatical from college teaching, during which time I crisscrossed the country, traveling more than 15,000 miles, visiting health educators and depositories of information from Eugene to Atlanta, from Austin to Ann

Arbor. What I found was a plethora of information on behavioral health issues, and many health educators who were intrigued with the idea of approaching those issues from a values perspective and who were quite willing to provide their own insights and biases. If the product proves as valuable to you as the process was for me, it will be well worth the price for both of us.

This book was written for a college course, but its intended use is more broadly conceived. Anyone who values good health is a potential reader. It should be particularly useful to any of you who continue to struggle with behavioral health problems, such as lack of exercise, weight control, smoking, alcohol or drug abuse, and stress. Parents, spouses, and "significant others" of those with behavioral health problems are especially likely to gain insight into what they should and should not do in support of their loved ones. Additionally, leaders and members of self-help groups are expected to find in the pages that follow potential solutions to many of their problems.

For health educators and other group leaders who decide to use this book as a text, I have written *A Values Approach to Health Behavior: Instructor's Guide*. This guide contains an introductory section outlining teaching strategies appropriate for values-oriented materials. There is a chapter paralleling each chapter topic in the text, each containing two types of information: additional studies supporting and elucidating concepts presented in this book, and specific examples of how to apply brainstorming, rank-ordering, debating, role-playing, and other teaching strategies to each topic. It should be quite useful for generating discussion and increasing student involvement in classes, particularly when you are teaching health issues from a values perspective for the first time.

Many of my students have assured me that they find the values approach to health education unique, enjoyable, and particularly meaningful. My own perception is that it becomes increasingly suitable as students become older and more mature. In addition, those whose days of formal education have ended, but who believe that true education is a lifelong process, should find it richly rewarding. May it bring an added dimension of health and happiness to your lives.

Acknowledgments

I am particularly indebted to the Pennsylvania State University for providing me with a sabbatical leave for the 1987-88 academic year to research and write this book. Professional colleagues too numerous to mention shared their time and comments with me; I am grateful to each of them. Friends and relatives throughout the country provided a network of social support that proved invaluable during trying times. Dr. James White, a consulting psychologist who wrote his doctoral dissertation on the subject of values, was especially helpful serving as friend, listening post, and source of information. Ultimately, however, I must admit that I was writing to my own children—three healthy young adults—and their peers, who grapple daily with values-related decisions that affect their health behavior. Steve, Greg, and Sue, this book is dedicated to you.

CHAPTER 1
Values and Behavior

If you tell me the way you see it rather than the way it is, then this helps me to fully discover the way I see it.

—Hugh Prather

Self-Examination Statements

Instructions: Read each statement, then circle the **x** in the column at the left that most closely describes your belief about that statement. (Use a pencil. After reading this chapter you may wish to come back and change some of your responses on the basis of new information or attitudes.)

SA = strongly agree   **A** = agree   **U** = undecided   **D** = disagree   **SD** = strongly disagree

SA	A	U	D	SD	
x	x	x	x	x	I know myself well and know what kind of person I am.
x	x	x	x	x	I know what kind of person I want to become.
x	x	x	x	x	I have a positive self-concept; I like who I am.
x	x	x	x	x	I believe my values are well-defined.
x	x	x	x	x	I think of myself as an ethical person.
x	x	x	x	x	I think of myself as a moral person.
x	x	x	x	x	I understand the difference between ethics and morals.
x	x	x	x	x	I understand the difference between morals and values.
x	x	x	x	x	I understand the distinction between values and attitudes.
x	x	x	x	x	I can think of at least one significant change I would like to make in my life this year.
x	x	x	x	x	I can think of one specific change I would like to make in my health behavior this year.
x	x	x	x	x	Being healthy ranks high among my values.
x	x	x	x	x	I can think of at least five values that hold higher priority for me than my health.
x	x	x	x	x	I think of myself as a healthy person.
x	x	x	x	x	I generally behave in a healthy manner.

x	x	x	x	x	My health behavior is consistent with my values.
x	x	x	x	x	My health behavior reflects my attitude toward health.
x	x	x	x	x	I consider myself to be knowledgeable about health matters.
x	x	x	x	x	There is nothing seriously wrong with my present health behavior.
x	x	x	x	x	My health behavior is somewhat inconsistent.
x	x	x	x	x	It takes a great deal of effort for me to stay healthy.
x	x	x	x	x	I understand the concept of values clarification.
x	x	x	x	x	I understand the difference between values education and values clarification.
x	x	x	x	x	I use the values clarification process to help me decide how to behave in health-related situations.
x	x	x	x	x	I understand the concept of delayed gratification.
x	x	x	x	x	I prefer the pleasure of the moment to long-term health.
x	x	x	x	x	I understand Kohlberg's theory of moral development.
x	x	x	x	x	I believe I am at stage five or six of Kohlberg's moral decision-making progression.
x	x	x	x	x	My actions are often influenced by what significant others value, rather than by what I value.
x	x	x	x	x	What I do about my health is my business and no one else's.
x	x	x	x	x	I frequently don't apply my knowledge of health by doing what I know would be healthiest.
x	x	x	x	x	I understand the concept of values conflicts.
x	x	x	x	x	Health behavior is a frequent source of values conflicts for me.
x	x	x	x	x	When values conflicts arise, I know how to manage them.
x	x	x	x	x	I sometimes feel guilty about my health behavior.

DEFINING TERMS AND CONCEPTS

It is helpful to begin a discussion by defining important terms that will be used. Three words that are sometimes used interchangeably, but ought not to be, are *intelligence, knowledge,* and *wisdom.*

Intelligence, Knowledge, and Wisdom

I define intelligence as the capacity to learn, knowledge as the body of factual information one has acquired, and wisdom as the application of knowledge. Vera Bej, honored as Pennsylvania's Teacher of the Year in 1987, put it this way: "I want my students to know the facts, but then they have to be able to use them. That is knowledge. Once the facts are applied, and have values put to them—that is wisdom.''

The effect of health education classes on students is usually to increase their knowledge, sometimes to develop positive attitudes toward health, but less often to lead to the adoption of healthy behavior. ''One of the most clearly established findings of health education research is that health-related information is rarely sufficient to initiate or maintain health-related practices'' (Petosa, 1986, p. 23). What causes people to change their behavior, given that knowledge alone appears to be ineffective?

Rokeach's System of Beliefs Theory

Milton Rokeach (1968, 1973, 1979), a social psychologist, has developed a System of Beliefs theory that purports to answer that very question (Figure 1.1). He believes that behavior is a function of attitudes, values, and self-concept. When

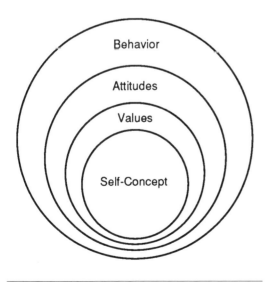

Figure 1.1. A representation of Rokeach's System of Beliefs.

the model is pictured as three-dimensional, it suggests that self-concept is the most difficult to reach and change because it is surrounded by values and attitudes. Behavior occupies the surface of the model, suggesting that it, more than attitudes, values, and self-concept, is easier to observe. For that reason, well-meaning authority figures often try to change behavior by confronting it directly. However, Rokeach has contended that, since behavior is more subject to change than attitudes or values, and self-concept is less subject to change than values or attitudes, lasting behavioral change requires working outward from self-concept, through values and attitudes.

Cognitive Dissonance and Self-Confrontation

Rokeach's System of Beliefs is based on two primary concepts, cognitive dissonance and self-confrontation.

Cognitive dissonance occurs when one or more of the following are present:

- Self-concept is not consistent with one's values.
- Values are not consistent with one's attitudes.
- Attitudes are not consistent with behavior.

Cognitive dissonance is eliminated by developing consistency throughout one's system of beliefs. This can be done by changing any of the four components to make all four components compatible. For example, suppose that you claim to value good health, but that you have an indifferent attitude toward health-related physical fitness and your smoking and eating habits strongly discourage regular and vigorous exercise. These inconsistencies create cognitive dissonance. To ameliorate this inconsistency, you might give good health a lower priority among your values, or you might stop smoking and begin to eat more nutritiously; in either instance, to minimize cognitive dissonance, your attitudes and values should change in the same direction.

Rokeach also espouses self-confrontation rather than confrontation. Most people are likely to resist if someone confronts them about their health behavior and tells them to change it. Most people are also likely to resist when confronted about their attitudes towards health behavior. Figure 1.1 suggests that it is easy to confront others about their behavior because behavior is outermost and therefore easiest to scrutinize. Unfortunately, such confrontation is also counterproductive.

Self-Concept

The Rokeach approach is to ask you to examine your self-concept first rather than your behavior. Two questions are most pertinent: What kind of person are you? What kind of person would you like to be?

To answer these questions, begin by reflecting on your values. If you discover that you are already the kind of person you want to be, and that your values are consistent with your self-concept, you can continue the process of self-examination by considering your attitudes and behavior. However, if you discover an inconsistency between the kind of person you are and the kind of person you want to be, self-confrontation requires you to choose between the two. Having done that, you should reconsider your values for purposes of making them consistent with your chosen self-concept. Again, the choice is yours: Modify your values to accommodate your self-concept, or modify your self-concept to accommodate your values. Applying this same process to your attitudes and behavior will eventually provide you with a consistent system of beliefs, reduce or eliminate any cognitive dissonance that might be present, and complete the process of self-confrontation that Rokeach advocates.

Values, Morals, and Ethics

The terms *values, morals*, and *ethics* are also sometimes used interchangeably but ought not to be. *Values* are related to priorities. Values help us decide what we are for and against, what we believe is good and bad, right and wrong. Usually we value things that we believe make life worth living or add meaning and substance to our lives. Your values are based on your perceptions and judgments and will help you define what you mean by "the good life," what you expect from "a good person," and what you expect from "the best of all possible worlds."

Given $100 a month for discretionary spending, you might choose to join a health club, buy cocaine, buy gifts for loved ones, or give it to your favorite church or charity. Thus, your values also strongly affect your actions. How you behave is a much clearer indicator of your values than what you say or write about your values. How you spend your resources—time, money, energy—can be important indicators of your true values.

Take a few minutes now to rank the 10 things you value most in life, using the left side of Form 1.1. There are no right or wrong answers, but the things, qualities, or conditions you value most should appear highest on your list. For example, judging from the Declaration of Independence, our founding fathers apparently placed their highest value on life, liberty, and the pursuit of happiness. Or how about the proverb that urges us to be "healthy, wealthy, and wise"? I'm sure you're getting the idea!

Solomon (1984) used the analogy of a deck of playing cards to distinguish *morals* from *ethics*. To be ethical is to behave in a civilized manner. Each principle of conduct or action that makes life more civilized is represented by one of the 52 cards in a deck. Just as some cards are valued more highly than others, perhaps

Form 1.1
Rank-Ordering Personal Values

Beginning values	*Ending values*
When you reach this page, rank order the things, qualities, or conditions that you value most in life.	When you reach the end of this chapter, come back and rank order the things, qualities, or conditions that you value most in life.

1. _____

2. _____

3. _____

4. _____

5. _____

6. _____

7. _____

8. _____

9. _____

10. _____

1. _____

2. _____

3. _____

4. _____

5. _____

6. _____

7. _____

8. _____

9. _____

10. _____

because they are aces or trump, certain ethical principles are more valued than others; these are referred to as morals. Morals are considered to be more important because they represent the core values. If honesty were the core value in question, it might be considered unethical to keep found money without making any attempt to find the owner, but it would be considered immoral to steal it from its owner's purse or wallet. Both ethics and morals are based on a system of personal and cultural values. Not all values, however, have ethical or moral connotations of right and wrong. For example, I value my health and my education, irrespective of any moral or ethical consideration.

One traditional theory holds, according to Rachels (1986), that "morality consists in the set of rules, governing how people are to treat one another, that rational people will agree to accept, for their mutual benefit, on the condition that others follow those rules as well" (p. 129). Rachels refers to this as the Social Contract Theory of Morals, after the work of the 18th-century French philosopher Jean Jacques Rousseau.

Frankena (1980) believes that morality is simply giving the moral point of view top priority whenever conflicts in values arise. The moral point of view is consideration for how your actions may affect others.

Combining these views, we can say that, in general, moral action is ethical, rational, and based on one's system of values.

tudes; values are relatively stable, whereas attitudes vary with situations; values determine standards of behavior, but attitudes determine specific behavior; and values express what is desirable, but attitudes may not (e.g., I value physical fitness [I believe it should be desired], but I have a negative attitude toward pistachio ice cream [I don't like its taste—but I have no belief that other people should find it undesirable; others might like its taste]).

The Rokeach Value Survey distinguishes between *terminal values*, or preferred end-states of existence (the items in Form 1.2 are terminal values), and *instrumental values*, or preferred modes of conduct (the items in Form 1.3 are instrumental values). That is, terminal values relate to conditions, while instrumental values relate to behavior. How many of your top 10 values are included in the Rokeach Value Survey?

Rokeach suggested ranking your top and bottom values first, then gradually working from both ends toward the middle. Once you have completed this assignment, you should have a much clearer picture of your personal system of values, which will probably be a reflection of your self-concept. Generally, your values and self-concept together are the basis for developing and maintaining attitudes, a standard for and guide to action, a standard for judging your own moral and ethical behavior, and a standard for influencing the values, attitudes, and behavior of others.

THE ROKEACH VALUE SURVEY

Rokeach developed a value survey, and he explains in his three books on values how he arrived at it. He points out that each of us has thousands of attitudes, but only a few dozen values. Values differ from attitudes in several ways. Values precede and help determine atti-

VALUES CLARIFICATION

You may have found it difficult to identify or rank your personal values. There are many methods for simplifying the task; perhaps the best known is the *values clarification process* developed by Raths, Harmin, and Simon (1974). These authors remind us that the acquisition of values is a lifelong process, and that values are

Form 1.2

Terminal Values

Nineteen values appear in the left-hand column. Your task is to rank order them in the right-hand column, according to their personal importance to you.

A comfortable life (a prosperous life) _____

An exciting life (a stimulating, active life) _____

A sense of accomplishment (lasting contribution) _____

A world at peace (free of war and conflict) _____

A world of beauty (beauty of nature and the arts) _____

Equality (equal opportunity for all) _____

Family security (taking care of loved ones) _____

Freedom (independence, free choice) _____

Happiness (contentedness) _____

Health (physical and mental well-being) _____

Inner harmony (freedom from inner conflict) _____

Mature love (sexual and spiritual intimacy) _____

National security (protection from attack) _____

Pleasure (an enjoyable, leisurely life) _____

Salvation (saved, eternal life) _____

Self-respect (self-esteem) _____

Social recognition (respect, admiration) _____

True friendship (close companionship) _____

Wisdom (a mature understanding of life) _____

Form 1.3
Instrumental Values

Nineteen values appear in the left-hand column. Your task is to rank order them in the right-hand column, according to their personal importance to you.

Ambitious (hardworking, aspiring)   _____

Broadminded (open-minded)   _____

Capable (competent, effective)   _____

Cheerful (lighthearted, joyful)   _____

Clean (neat, tidy)   _____

Courageous (standing up for your beliefs)   _____

Forgiving (willing to pardon others)   _____

Helpful (working for the welfare of others)   _____

Honest (sincere, truthful)   _____

Imaginative (daring, creative)   _____

Independent (self-reliant, self-sufficient)   _____

Intellectual (intelligent, reflective)   _____

Logical (consistent, rational)   _____

Loving (affectionate, tender)   _____

Loyal (faithful to your friends, group)   _____

Obedient (dutiful, respectful)   _____

Polite (courteous, well-mannered)   _____

Responsible (dependable, reliable)   _____

Self-controlled (restrained, self-disciplined)   _____ subject to change. They list seven criteria for identifying values:

- A value must be chosen from among alternatives.
- A value must be chosen after carefully considering the consequences of each alternative course of action.
- A value must be chosen freely, without coercion from others.
- A value must be prized; you should be proud of your choice.
- A value must be publicly affirmed; you must be willing to take a position.
- A value must be acted upon; your action will affirm your position.
- There must be repetition of your action; your action will be consistent and in accord with your other values.

Raths and his colleagues believed that anything that failed to meet all seven criteria was a *values indicator* rather than a true value. For example, an adolescent who hides a smoking or drinking habit from his parents probably values the resultant peer-group approval. The tobacco or alcohol is only an indicator of the value placed on affiliation or friendship.

This list of criteria is not without its critics. One primary criticism is that it teaches people *how* to value without teaching them *what* to value. Others object to its implication that values are relative or just a matter of opinion (that there are no right or wrong values, and that one set of values is just as good as another). Still other critics have objected to the last three criteria on the list, believing that it is unnecessary, and sometimes even unwise, to publicly affirm or act on one's values. For example, if you were compelled to publicly affirm every one of your personal values, especially in the presence of strangers, you would probably feel it was an invasion of privacy; if you value courage and act on that value by going over Niagara Falls in a barrel, you could well meet with an early death!

Although there is an element of truth in each of these criticisms, the values clarification process has considerable merit in my judgment, and you can use it to determine how well the values you listed earlier measure up to these criteria.

VALUES EDUCATION

The proponents of values education, unlike those of values clarification, believe that most people need some guidance about *what* to value, in addition to clarifying the process of valuing. Simmons (1982) describes values education as "a high commitment to those values enhancing empathic and compassionate living—freedom and equality" (p. 96). For Frankena (1980), moral education is the development of a value system that is rationally defensible from a moral point of view, that is, learning to do what is right and what is good, and considering the consequences for persons other than yourself. He concluded that beneficence (kindness) and justice are the two core values around which human existence revolves.

Maslow (1970) describes the highest values as "being-values" or B-values, among which are the following:

- Truth
- Justice
- Equality
- Goodness
- Kindness

It was his contention that persons who value these qualities are self-actualizing, a desirable state that will be more fully described in the next chapter.

Aristotle wrote that happiness is the highest value, and that happiness is based on "reasoned action." For him, happiness was dependent not on short-term pleasures but on the long-range satisfaction that comes from living a good life, one in which wisdom prevails.

Much of Rokeach's research was based on his belief that valuing freedom (for oneself) much more highly than equality (comparable freedom for others) leads to injustices. You may want to go back and see how you ranked these two key values, freedom and equality. If fairness is an important part of your self-concept, you should have accorded them similar value.

Proponents of values education emphasize developing a consistent system of beliefs through learning what we value and what we ought to value. Morrill (1980) advocated a process combining the following:

- Values analysis
- Values consciousness
- Values criticism

Values analysis requires you to study values relevant to a particular situation without choosing among them or applying them to your personal life. Values consciousness involves your becoming more aware of your own values in particular situations. Values criticism requires you to constructively criticize your own values before taking action on them. Morrill concludes that values education is a process of becoming more aware of your values and learning to act on them. It is my intent that this book will help you to achieve that end, to become more aware of your values as they relate to your health behavior, and to learn to act on them.

By applying Morrill's suggestions you will also be using Dennison's Activated Health Education Model, which was mentioned in the preface. Dennison described the model as one based on values clarification, social learning theory, and behavioral self-management. It includes: an experimental phase, during which an individual actively compares personal values and attitudes to societal norms; an awareness phase, during which one's base of knowledge is expanded; and a responsibility phase, during which congruence of values and behavior is sought. As with Morrill's values education, the responsibility phase requires that knowledge be translated into healthy behavior.

Kohlberg's Six Stages of Moral Development

Kohlberg (1981) outlined his theory of moral development, which I think of as another form of values education. According to his theory, there are three levels of moral development: preconventional, conventional, and post-conventional. Each has two stages. In the earliest developmental stage a child acts so as to avoid punishment, as a two-year-old might adhere to toilet training in order to avoid a spanking. Action during stage two is motivated primarily by anticipated rewards and immediate gratification; a five-year-old might finish her vegetables in order to get dessert or be allowed to go outside and play. In the third stage we are more likely to base our decisions and actions on a desire for the approval of peers; twelve-year-olds often make smoking or no-smoking decisions on this basis. At stage four we become more concerned about laws and the opinions of authority figures; feelings of guilt and fear will often influence our judgments. When we drive within the speed limit for fear of getting a ticket, or report to work early because we want the boss to think well of us, we are at stage four. It is not uncommon for adults to remain at this level for most of their decision-making throughout life. With education, however, people often learn to operate at stage five or six, which Kohlberg believes is in the best interests of society. In stage five, decisions are based on one's personal honor and self-respect, as when parents agree to coach youth sports teams or chaperone the high school dance. It is a recognition that society benefits if each of us does our fair share. At stage six, decisions are based on morals, values, principles of right action, conscience, and respect for others. Devoting one's life to the care of a loved one who is incapable of self-care is an example of such a decision.

For Kohlberg, justice is the critical core value at the highest stage of moral development. He contends that every individual starts in stage one and passes sequentially through the other stages, although not all of us reach the highest stage(s). Although we cannot skip stages, Kohlberg believes that our moral development can be facilitated through discussion of value-laden situations, to see how decisions are made by people whose reasoning is one stage above our own level.

Would you agree that Kohlberg's approach is a form of values education? Which stage of moral development best describes your present decision-making process? Can you think of acquaintances who are obviously operating at a different (either higher or lower) stage of moral development than your own? Can you envision yourself operating at the next higher level? How can you apply Morrill's principles of analysis, consciousness, and criticism to your own values, so as to expedite your moral development?

As an example of the sort of value-laden situation Kohlberg suggests for discussion, here is a variation of Kohlberg's "Heinz's dilemma":

> Your mother is suffering from an illness that causes excruciating pain, and she will die without a specific medication that is available but prohibitively (unfairly so) priced. Your choices are to steal the medicine, thereby easing your mother's pain and perhaps saving her life, or to do nothing while she suffers and dies. You have already borrowed more money than you can repay, so getting a loan to buy the medicine is impossible. What course of action do you take? What is your justification? Which level of moral development does this represent?

VALUING HEALTH AND VALUES CONFLICTS

Before reading on, return to your original list of rank-ordered values (page 5) and see where you ranked health, if at all. Then look at your Rokeach Value Survey of terminal values, and note where you ranked health. Now think about what you have read in this chapter thus far. In describing the views of Rokeach, Maslow, Kohlberg, Frankena, Solomon, Rachels, and Aristotle, we mentioned almost nothing about health! Does that mean that health is unimportant? Does it mean that those who understand values do not value health? The answer to these questions is "no," but it may mean that you need to keep the importance of good health in proper perspective.

Health as an Instrumental and Terminal Value

As many writers have pointed out, health ought to be thought of as a means to an end and not as an end in itself. If that is true, perhaps health is both an instrumental and a terminal value; that is, healthy behavior, a preferred mode of conduct, leads to good health, a preferred end-state of existence. Rokeach excluded health from his original Value Survey, explaining that health, like life itself (also excluded from his Value Survey), was of such obvious and universal importance as to make its inclusion unnecessary.

Leichtman and Japikse (1985) wrote, "Health is not an end unto itself. Health merely enables us to live with purpose and to achieve loftier goals" (pp. 68-69). A study of North American values reported by Naroll (1983) seems to concur, as respondents ranked health a consensus 14th among their values. Conversely, a study by Petersen-Martin and Cottrell (1987) reported that health ranked number one among the values of the community college students they polled (median rank), 43 percent of whom placed it among their top four terminal values on the Rokeach scale. Brown, Muhlenkamp, Fox, and Osborn (1983) reported that over 50 percent of their middle-class adult subjects ranked health first or second among their terminal values. Likewise, Lau, Hartman, and Ware (1986) found that health was the consensus number one value of their college-age subjects. How do you account for these seeming inconsistencies?

There are several plausible explanations. One involves who collects the data, for whom, and under what circumstances. For example, I would expect the people reading this book to value health more highly than the national norm, because there is a good likelihood that you are predisposed toward health values. Further, I would expect respondents to a health-related survey to value health more highly than respondents to a survey being conducted by a philosopher (Frankena), psychologist (Maslow), or anthropologist (Naroll). Social scientists are well aware of the effects of biased rather than random sampling, and of the tendency for respondents to report what they think the researcher wants to hear. For these reasons I encourage you to be more interested in the process by which you decided how highly you value health than where you ranked it, and that you now concern yourself with how your expressed value of health will influence your health behavior.

Health as a Need, Met or Unmet

Maslow's hierarchy of human needs, which will be discussed at greater length in chapter 2, offers another possible explanation of the apparent inconsistency in health values among various groups of people. This explanation was alluded to by Lau and colleagues, who hypothesized that healthy people take good health for granted, whereas those whose health is threatened value health more highly. Maslow believed that unmet needs are more highly valued than met needs, in which case unhealthy people would be expected to value health more than would persons in good health. However, his hypothesis that, other factors being equal, self-actualized people are psychologically healthier and more attuned to healthy behavior than others, may help explain why Brown's middle-class subjects and Lau's college students valued health more highly than Naroll's general population.

Rank-Order Measurement and Values Conflicts

Another explanation of the seeming inconsistency is that rank-order of values does not necessarily indicate strength of values. (The Rokeach Value Survey has been criticized for its inability to measure *strength* in addition to *order* of values.) For some people, two or three values are very dominant and the next three are relatively unimportant but still achieve a ranking of four, five, or six; other people may have a dozen or more values of virtually equal strength, but rank ordering requires that one must artificially be 1st and another 10th. Thus it is possible that I might not even include health in my top 10 values, and yet value it more strongly than you, who ranked it 5th.

When a person has many values of roughly equal strength, there is a greater likelihood of values conflicts. People sometimes feel guilty about claiming to value health, yet behaving in a way that appears inconsistent with that claim. There is a perfectly logical explanation for this as well, and it has to do with the nature of values conflicts.

Having asked hundreds of college students to rank-order their values, I know that the values mentioned most frequently include family, friends, faith, freedom, health, happiness, education, money, and success. Each pair of these represents a potential source of values conflicts. Is there anyone among you who has not experienced a conflict between being loyal to family and being loyal to friends? Parents and peers typically have different values; the more you value your association with each of them, the more difficult it may be to resolve that conflict.

For college students, the conflict mentioned most often is between their value of health and their value of having the social approval of their peers. Peers have a way of promoting eating, drinking, smoking, sexual, and other behavior that is not always consistent with one's expressed value of health. It is my belief that only nonthinking people are totally free from such conflicts. The remainder of this book deals with how to manage these and similar conflicts between values and health behavior.

Finally, we must concern ourselves with conflicts that arise between values and other variables that influence human behavior. These include beliefs, attitudes, intentions, self-efficacy, social norms, locus of control, perceived costs and benefits of taking action, environmental influences, and many others. In chapter 2 you will learn more about these concepts and their interrelationships.

SUMMARY

Ethical behavior is "civilized" behavior, or living within society's rules. Moral behavior gives primary consideration to positively affecting the feelings and well-being of others, a much deeper commitment than merely abiding by the law. Values are a very personal reflection of our individual priorities, of what we deem to be important. Core values—justice, kindness, freedom, honesty—are sometimes called morals.

Rokeach distinguishes between *instrumental values*, behavioral traits like being honest and loving, and *terminal values*, ideal states of existence like happiness or security. He believes that values are more constant than attitudes. Behavior is a function of attitudes, values, and self-concept. Dissonance among these will create a desire for change. Lasting change is more likely to result from self-confrontation than confrontation by an authority figure. Lasting change is also more likely when changes in self-concept precede changes in values and attitudes.

There is disagreement regarding how educators should influence values. Some advocate values clarification, a seven-step process for clarifying values without making value judgments. Others believe in values education, advocating certain values as prerequisites for the American way of life. Either way, the ultimate responsibility for behavior rests with the individual.

Examining Your Values

You are alone in your car at a roadside rest stop in rural South Dakota, reading a book about moral and ethical behavior. Suddenly there is a rap on your window. It is a stranger, asking for $3 to buy gasoline to get to a Western Union station and wire for money. You have six quarters and a $10 bill. What is your response?

1. Will the gender of the stranger affect your decision? If so, are you more likely to give to a same-sex or opposite-sex person?
2. Will the age of the stranger affect your decision? If so, are you more likely to give to a younger or older person?
3. Will the appearance of the stranger affect your decision? If so, are you more likely to give to someone who is relatively attractive or someone who appears needy?
4. Will what the person has to say affect your decision? If so, what does that tell you about your value of kindness?

5. Does justice dictate that you be repaid? If so, what assurance of repayment would you require?
6. What is your self-concept if you decline to help? What is your self-concept if you give six quarters? What is your self-concept if you give $10? Who benefits more if you give $10, you or the stranger?
7. Now go back to your rank-order lists of terminal and instrumental values. Have your values changed? If so, how?

CHAPTER 2
Human Behavior and Health Behavior

The most significant factor for good health is love—for oneself and others.

—Bernard Siegel

Self-Examination Statements

Instructions: Read each statement, then circle the x in the column at the left that most closely describes your belief about that statement. (Use a pencil. After reading this chapter you may wish to come back and change some of your responses on the basis of new information or attitudes.)

SA = strongly agree   **A** = agree   **U** = undecided   **D** = disagree   **SD** = strongly disagree

SA	A	U	D	SD	
x	x	x	x	x	I am familiar with the concept of predisposing factors.
x	x	x	x	x	I believe that I am favorably predisposed toward healthy behavior.
x	x	x	x	x	Skills are more important than knowledge when it comes to healthy behavior.
x	x	x	x	x	I am familiar with the concept of reinforcing factors.
x	x	x	x	x	I grew up in a family that valued good health.
x	x	x	x	x	My family reinforces my desire to maintain good health.
x	x	x	x	x	My friends reinforce my desire to maintain good health.
x	x	x	x	x	I don't believe that I am particularly susceptible to ill health.
x	x	x	x	x	I have never experienced severe illness.
x	x	x	x	x	I would change my behavior if I thought it were going to have a negative impact on my health.
x	x	x	x	x	I would change toward healthier behavior immediately if I knew what to do.
x	x	x	x	x	I would change toward healthier behavior immediately if the benefits were obvious.
x	x	x	x	x	It is easy for me to see the benefits of good health.

x	x	x	x	x	I believe that the major benefit of healthy behavior is longer life.
x	x	x	x	x	I believe that the major benefit of healthy behavior is greater quality of life.
x	x	x	x	x	The primary barrier to healthy behavior is that it is inconvenient and time consuming.
x	x	x	x	x	My value of good health conflicts with my value of an exciting, enjoyable life.
x	x	x	x	x	I am familiar with social learning theory.
x	x	x	x	x	I am familiar with the concept of self-efficacy.
x	x	x	x	x	My positive self-concept helps me to maintain healthy behavior.
x	x	x	x	x	My perception of what others expect me to do is a negative influence on my health behavior.
x	x	x	x	x	My perception of what others are doing is a negative influence on my health behavior.
x	x	x	x	x	If I intend to do something that is healthy, I usually do exactly what I intended.
x	x	x	x	x	Given a choice, I intend to do what is healthy rather than what is unhealthy.
x	x	x	x	x	Given a choice, I usually do what is enjoyable rather than what is healthy.
x	x	x	x	x	I understand the concept of locus of control.
x	x	x	x	x	I believe that I have an internal locus of control.
x	x	x	x	x	An internal locus of control leads to healthier behavior than an external locus of control.
x	x	x	x	x	I believe that good health is largely a matter of luck or chance.
x	x	x	x	x	I rely primarily on medical personnel to keep me healthy.
x	x	x	x	x	Single people are typically healthier than married people.
x	x	x	x	x	Higher socioeconomic status is usually related to healthier behavior.
x	x	x	x	x	Higher levels of education correlate with healthier behavior.
x	x	x	x	x	I am familiar with the concept of self-actualization.
x	x	x	x	x	I believe that self-actualization is related to healthy behavior.
x	x	x	x	x	For me, good health means feeling safe and secure from serious illness or disease.
x	x	x	x	x	I understand the basic ideas of attribution theory.
x	x	x	x	x	I attribute at least some of my negative health habits to the influence of advertising.
x	x	x	x	x	I attribute at least some of my negative health habits to the mass media— movies, TV, radio, magazines, and so on.

DEFINING TERMS AND CONCEPTS

Developing a healthy lifestyle is analogous to putting together a jigsaw puzzle. In chapter 1 we identified values as a prominent piece of the puzzle. Using the Rokeach System of Beliefs, we also identified self-concept and attitudes as pieces that are closely related to values. In this chapter we will take a look at some of the other pieces that interlock with these three.

Before considering further factors that influence health behavior, we should step back and try to visualize the completed picture. Toward this end, we need to define what is meant by *health* and *health education*.

Health

According to the World Health Organization's classic definition, health is not merely the absence of disease, but complete physical, mental, and social well-being. The American Journal of Health Promotion, in its premier issue, defined optimal health as a balance of physical, emotional, social, intellectual, and spiritual health (O'Donnell, 1986). We will discuss the physical dimensions in the chapter on exercise and fitness (chapter 5) and the emotional dimension in the chapter on stress management (chapter 11). This chapter will elaborate on the social and intellectual dimensions. Although some people might question the inclusion of the "spiritual" as a dimension of health, Chapman (1987) explains that this dimension need not be God-centered and offers this definition:

> Optimal spiritual health is defined as the ability to develop one's spiritual nature to its fullest potential. This includes our ability: to discover, articulate and act on our own basic purpose in life; to learn how to

give and receive love, joy and peace; and to contribute to the improvement of the spiritual health of others. (p. 17)

I am persuaded that this is a legitimate aspect of health and wellness, irrespective of one's religious beliefs.

Health Education

As reported by Ford and Ford (1981), the consensus of presenters at the International Union of Health Education was that "the goal of health education ought to be the process and practice of *informing, influencing*, and *assisting* individuals to assume greater responsibility for their own health" (p. 85). Hochbaum (1982) wrote, "The goal of all health education is, of course, to achieve adoption and maintenance of healthful living practices" (p. 15). According to Green and Lewis (1986), "The term health education describes any combination of learning experiences designed to predispose, enable, and reinforce voluntary adaptations of behavior conducive to well-being" (p. xvii). The operational word is "voluntary."

All agree on the desirability of healthy behavior as a goal, but there is disagreement about how individuals should achieve it. The *active* or *directed* approach is for a person or group to guide, direct, control, persuade, motivate, and manipulate an individual's health behavior. The *voluntary* approach is to rely on the judgment of the individual, recognizing that no one is obliged to value or seek good health.

Let me state my own preference at this point. A directed approach may be appropriate for a child, whose system of values is not yet well established, but the voluntary approach seems more appropriate for the adult readers of this book. You are urged to use the values clarification process, which requires that alternative courses of action be available and that you choose a course of action after considering the likely consequences of each alternative. You are also advised to apply Morrill's values education concepts (values analysis, consciousness, and criticism) mentioned in chapter 1.

There are several strategies for using health education to influence health behavior:

- One is to provide *information*, the most current and scientific information available, then let the learner decide to what extent it ought to be applied. Unfortunately, this approach has not been particularly effective. One of the most clearly established findings of health education research is that health-related information is rarely sufficient to initiate or maintain health-related practices (Kolbe, 1985; Norman, 1986; Parcel, 1984).
- Another approach (Conroy, 1979) is to attempt to influence *attitudes* and *values* that affect health behavior.
- A third approach (Petosa, 1986), which seems to be gaining favor, is to assist the learner in acquiring *skills* that improve self-concept, self-control, and decision-making, and lead to healthier behavior.

All three approaches to health education have been incorporated into this book.

One more point should be made about modern health education. Health educators are painfully aware of their collective reputation for denying pleasure. It has sometimes seemed that anything that added a little spice to life was denounced as "bad for your health." The current trend is to "accentuate the positive" by stressing how certain behaviors can lead to enhanced quality of life, as with Maslow's inclusion of health among self-actualizing qualities. I strongly endorse this approach.

Precede Model

Lawrence Green, a leader in the field of public health education, has developed a model for planning and promoting good health (Green, Kreuter, Deeds, & Partridge, 1980; Green & Lewis, 1986), a simplified version of which appears in Table 2.1. He maintains that good health improves quality of life and is dependent on one's environment and lifestyle or behavior. He divides the factors that affect environment and behavior into three categories: predisposing, enabling, and reinforcing factors. Among the predisposing factors are values, attitudes, and knowledge; their roles in healthy behavior were discussed in chapter 1. Enabling factors include resources and skills. This book is a resource, as is your local fitness club, a weight-control support group, or a local chapter of Alcoholics Anonymous. Examples of enabling skills are learning CPR, learning to swim, or learning to monitor your blood pressure or cholesterol consumption.

Reinforcing factors are an important added dimension. The people you live and work with can be a positive or negative influence on your health. Their attitudes and behavior will rein-

Table 2.1 Green's Simplified Precede Model

Predisposing factors (e.g., values, attitudes)		Lifestyle		Quality
Enabling factors (e.g., skills, resources)	>	and	>	Good health > of
Reinforcing factors (e.g., social norms)		environment		life

force your attitudes and behavior, provided you have similar values. There is a grain of truth to the old quip about good health being dependent on choosing your parents carefully (heredity), but there is much more truth to the notion that you should choose your friends carefully. Peer pressure among adolescents is generally thought of as an unhealthy influence. However, peers can just as readily be a positive influence. Being a positive influence on others, and selecting associates who will reinforce your preferred health values and behaviors, are two of the earmarks of maturity. How effective are you at giving and receiving positive reinforcement for healthy behavior?

HEALTH BELIEF MODEL

Becker (1974) described the following Health Belief Model. Healthy behavior is more likely to occur when the following are present:

- A person perceives that failure to act will make him or her susceptible to illness or disease
- The consequences of failing to act will be serious
- There are perceived benefits to taking action
- The perceived benefits outweigh the perceived costs
- There is a belief that the action will be successful in achieving the desired outcome (self-efficacy)
- One or more cues to action initiate and reinforce the contemplated behavior

This model was developed by Godfrey Hochbaum, Irwin Rosenstock, and others (Rosenstock, 1974), and has been widely used in the public health field to explain health behavior. The model is based on the field theory of psychologist Kurt Lewin, which suggests that human behavior depends primarily on two variables: the value placed by an individual on a particular outcome, and the person's estimate of the likelihood that a given behavior will result in that outcome (efficacy).

Maiman, Becker, Kirscht, Haefner, and Drachman (1977) concluded that there is a "large body of evidence linking these belief dimensions to various types of personal health behavior" (p. 227). How does all of this apply to you? To paraphrase Maiman and Becker (1974), you are more likely to perform a preventive health action if you feel vulnerable to a serious illness or disease, action seems likely to benefit your health, the action seems efficacious, you think you can perform it, the costs or barriers are not too great, you are stimulated to act by an outside source, and you are motivated to act because you value health.

This model helps explain not only why people take preventive health actions but also why people often fail to adopt healthy behavior. If you are a smoker who has unsuccessfully attempted to quit on several occasions, lack of self-efficacy may prevent you from trying again. You may value the effects of regular and vigorous exercise, but the costs in terms of time, effort, and inconvenience may dissuade you from acting on that value. If you are a monogamous heterosexual, you might not feel vulnerable to AIDS, even though you recognize the seriousness of the disease, and might not take precautions against it. These are very real examples of why people fail to act in accord with their knowledge of healthy behavior.

SOCIAL LEARNING THEORY

Bandura (1977, 1986) argued that a person's behavior is largely a function of efficacy expectations and outcome expectations. According to Bandura, a person's behavior is based on:

1. Perceived outcome expectations
2. Perceived self-efficacy

Efficacy expectations are learned from:

1. Personal experience
2. Role models
3. Verbal persuasion

According to this model, you are likely to engage in healthy behavior if you believe that you can successfully perform the behavior required to produce the desired outcome, and if you are convinced that the outcome will benefit you.

Both Bandura's self-efficacy paradigm and Hochbaum's Health Belief Model have their roots in social learning theory—that is, in the view that behavior is not dependent solely on such inner forces as needs and drives, but is affected by environmental and social conditions.

Self-Concept, Self-Esteem, and Self-Efficacy

Self-concept, self-esteem, and self-efficacy are intertwined. *Self-concept* is simply how you see yourself and does not necessarily involve a value judgment. *Self-esteem* is a realistically-based self-respect and does involve a value judgment. If I think of myself as being of normal height and weight, and think of my height and weight as being neither good nor bad, that is part of my self-concept. If I am taller than normal, and like being tall, that may enhance my self-esteem. Self-esteem leads to a positive self-concept. *Self-efficacy* refers to a specific ability to perform a specific task in a specific situation. Seven-footers usually dunk basketballs more easily than five-footers, but five-footers may find it easier to enter and exit low-slung sports cars. Which (if either) of these abilities is more likely to enhance your self-esteem depends on your values.

Tasks that are too easy for you, like brushing your teeth, are efficacious and produce a desired outcome, but do little for your self-esteem. On the other hand, tasks that are too difficult for you (perhaps, doing a reverse twisting somer-sault off the 3-meter board) threaten your self-esteem because you are likely to fail at them so you might fear and avoid such tasks. By starting with tasks that are moderately easy and progressing incrementally to more difficult tasks, you can maintain self-efficacy, increase self-esteem, and develop a positive self-concept.

Strecher, DeVellis, Becker, and Rosenstock (1986) reported on a series of studies that demonstrated the applicability of these principles to health behavior. Their data indicated the following: nonsmokers and former smokers who successfully quit had higher self-efficacy and self-esteem than smokers; subjects who successfully lost weight had higher self-efficacy than those who dropped out of a weight-loss program or failed to lose weight; and women with a high level of self-efficacy were more likely to use contraceptives effectively. How long a person persists at a difficult health behavior, like getting in shape or losing weight, depends to a large extent on the value of the expected outcome, perceived self-efficacy, and how much a failure would threaten self-esteem. If you wish to change your health-related behavior, you are advised to start with simple tasks that generate a high level of success.

Emphasizing Learning Skills

Parcel and Baranowski (1981) have described an application of social learning theory to health behavior that emphasizes learning skills rather than facts. They propose to accomplish "directed behavior change" in four phases:

1. Pretraining
2. Training
3. Initial testing
4. Continued performance

The pretraining phase emphasizes an awareness of values and expectations. "A person learns that a particular behavior leads to a particular outcome, which is or is not valued.

If a person values the outcome, the frequency of the behavior increases'' (p. 15). Successful behavior change requires that the relevant outcome be both expected and valued; one without the other is insufficient.

The training phase consists of social modeling, or learning from a role model. This is consistent with Bandura's self-efficacy paradigm and presumes that observation should precede direct experience. Practicing the skill should then proceed in a controlled environment. The initial testing phase requires that the learner perform the skill in his or her own environment. Success is more likely if the skill is broken down into subtasks. The final phase, continued performance, requires one to apply the new skill in a variety of settings, gradually increasing the level of difficulty to reduce the threat of failure or loss of self-esteem.

Can you think of examples where you might be able to apply this four-phase process of directed behavior change? Consider this hypothetical situation: Over the past year or two you have become increasingly lethargic and overweight. You have considered several alternatives and have decided that, although a jogging program might increase your fitness level and reduce your weight, the costs in terms of effort and inconvenience outweigh the benefits as you perceive them. You think of swimming, however, as a social activity that will be enjoyable and will place you among potential dating partners; and that, almost incidentally, may have health benefits similar to jogging. You decide on swimming and sign up for a class, where you can refine your swimming skills and a friend can serve as a role model. Gradually you test your newfound skills in a nonthreatening situation. As self-efficacy increases, you establish new goals: longer distances, faster times, new strokes. You have new friends, more energy, and greater self-esteem, all as a result of newly acquired skills. By applying concepts from several of the theoretical models addressed in this chapter, you have improved the quality of

your life; coincidentally your health has also improved.

Now see if you can apply the process of directed behavior change to some aspect of your life where change seems advisable.

Attitudes and Intentions

Another aspect of social learning theory that has interested researchers for decades is the relationship between attitudes and behavior. Rokeach hypothesized that attitudes directly influence behavior (see chapter 1). Stewart (1985), after reviewing 50 years of literature on the subject, concluded that the evidence supports the traditional belief that attitudes cause behavior. However, Festinger, Bem, and other theorists have contended that attitudes are as likely to derive from as to cause behavior (Bem, 1970).

Jaccard and Becker (1985) observed that an individual can have attitude conflicts similar to value conflicts. For instance, it is possible to have positive attitudes toward many activities, all of which are incompatible at a given moment with doing any of the others (e.g., working late, socializing with friends, and spending time with family), in which case you are most likely to choose the activity toward which you have the most positive attitude at the moment.

The most enlightening and often-cited information about attitudes and behavior is provided by Ajzen and Fishbein (1977, 1980) and Fishbein and Ajzen (1984). Their earlier work reviewed 17 studies examining the attitude-behavior relationship, all of which agreed that unless there is *correspondence* between an attitude and a behavior, correlations are low and not significant. Ajzen and Timko (1986) elaborated the principle of correspondence as follows: General attitudes correspond to general behaviors, and specific attitudes correspond to specific behaviors, but general attitudes do not correspond to specific behaviors, nor do specific attitudes correspond to general behaviors. (For example, you may have a generally positive attitude about health, but not perform a specific health act like brushing your teeth after meals.) In their study of college students, Ajzen and Timko discovered that a positive attitude about health behavior in general corresponded with a high aggregate measure of health behavior.

Ajzen and Fishbein (1980) offered a model of *reasoned action* (Table 2.2) that draws attention to the unique contribution of intentions in determining behavior. According to this model, behavior is a function of both intent, as determined by attitude toward the behavior, and subjective norms. In turn, attitudes are based on a person's beliefs that the behavior in question leads to desired outcomes (see Bandura's outcome expectancies), and subjective norms are based on one's belief that a significant other or others would behave similarly or approve of the behavior (that is, they are based on a form of peer pressure). "Generally speaking, individuals will intend to perform a behavior when they evaluate it positively and when they believe that important others think they should perform it" (p. 6). Ajzen and Fishbein concluded that intent to behave in a particular way is the best single predictor of behavior.

Pender and Pender (1986) conducted a review of literature related to "reasoned action," then conducted a study in which they applied the theory to health-related behaviors, including intent to exercise regularly, eat a diet designed to maintain a healthy weight, and avoid highly stressful situations. They concluded that there was limited support for the theory of reasoned

action. Subjects who were close to their recommended weight expressed stronger intent to exercise to maintain weight, and positive attitudes toward weight control correlated with stronger expressed intent to eat a diet consistent with weight control. It seems likely that variations in experimental design, specifically the failure of researchers to apply the principle of correspondence, would account for as much of the "limited support" as would shortcomings in the theoretical model itself.

Application of the principle of reasoned action is fairly straightforward. If there is a particular health behavior you would like to practice, but you are having difficulty doing so, you may find it helpful to make a public affirmation of your intent to your friends. (This would be a step in values clarification—see chapter 1.) Likewise, announcing your intent to avoid a particular unhealthy behavior that you wish to discard may similarly strengthen your resolve.

Locus of Control

Another notion from social learning theory is *locus of control*. Its prominence in the health-related literature is owed primarily to Barbara and Kenneth Wallston and their colleagues (Wallston, Wallston, 1978; Wallston, Maides, & Wallston, 1976). They developed a Health Locus of Control (HLC) scale (Wallston, Wallston, Kaplan, & Maides, 1976), and later a Multidimensional Health Locus of Control (MHLC) scale (Wallston, Wallston, & DeVellis,

Table 2.2 Ajzen/Fishbein Model of Reasoned Action

Attitudinal beliefs	>	Attitudes				
			>	Intention	>	Behavior
Normative beliefs	>	Subjective norms				

1978). Their HLC had only two dimensions, internal and external; the MHLC was a refinement that split external locus of control. Their format follows.

A. Internal health locus of control (IHLC)
B. External health locus of control (EHLC)
   1. Powerful others (PHLC)
   2. Chance/luck/fate (CHLC)

If you have an *internal* locus of control, you probably believe that you are largely in control of your own destiny and that the quality of your health is based on what you do to protect and promote it. If you have an *external* locus of control, you probably believe that your health is dependent on doctors and other medical personnel (PHLC) or on some combination of chance, luck, and fate (CHLC). Which of these do you believe is likely to have greater impact on your health status and behavior?

Implications of Internal Locus of Control

The concept of locus of control has been widely applied by health researchers, and some of the results have been notable. The basic assumption has been that people with an IHLC will perform healthy behaviors more consistently and will exhibit a higher standard of health than people with an EHLC. Wallston, Maides, and Wallston (1976) reported that subjects with an internal locus of control and a higher value of health (as measured by a variation of the Rokeach Value Survey) were more apt to seek health-related information. Wallston and Wallston (1978) reported that nonsmokers are more likely to be internals than smokers; college females who are internals and sexually active are more likely than sexually active externals to use contraceptives effectively; and internals can succeed in a self-directed weight-loss program, but externals are more successful when they have the support of a powerful other (such as a group leader).

Lau (1982) reviewed the literature and concluded that "there is little doubt that health-related locus of control is significantly related to a variety of health behaviors and health outcomes" (p. 322). He observed that good health habits associated with an internal locus of control seemed to be more prevalent among people with "middle-class values." After using a modified version of the HLC scale to measure a variety of health-related behaviors (e.g., diet, weight control, exercise, medical and dental checkups), he concluded, "Belief in Self-Control Over Health has a strong positive correlation with actually performing health-care behaviors" (p. 327).

Implications of External Locus of Control

In 1983 Seeman and Seeman reported that their subjects with an external locus of control were less likely to initiate preventive health care, were less optimistic concerning the efficacy of early treatment, rated their own health as poorer, and reported more bed confinement due to illness than internals. Those who were internals and valued health highly were 3 times as likely to perform preventive health behaviors as externals with a low value of health. Smokers were more likely to have an external locus of control than nonsmokers and former smokers.

Effect of Internal and External Control on Health and Values

Abella and Heslin (1984) studied the relationship between health, locus of control, and values. They considered the seven health practices associated with longevity by the Breslow and Enstrom (1980) study—smoking, drinking, exercise, sleeping, weight control, eating breakfast, and eating three meals a day. "It was found that it is the respondent who both values health and has an internal locus of control who is more likely to engage in preventive health behavior" (p. 283). Based on their own data and the results of several other reported studies, they concluded, "It appears that desiring or valuing health is not in itself a sufficient condition to produce a healthy lifestyle. It is also necessary for the individual to believe that he has control over his own health outcomes'' (p. 288).

Regarding a second hypothesis in their study, Abella and Heslin reported that persons exposed to a negative social environment and with an external locus of control were least likely to engage in preventive health behavior. Apparently the influence of close associates on health behavior patterns is stronger for people with an external locus of control.

Are you beginning to see the pieces of the puzzle fitting together? You have read about the numerous relationships among components of social learning theory and about the relationship of intentions to attitudes and behavior. Now it becomes apparent that there is a close relationship between values and locus of control, and between your social environment and health behavior. We now turn our attention to this latter subject.

SOCIAL SUPPORT AND SOCIAL NETWORKS

In *The Moral Order* (1983) Naroll discussed the importance of establishing a ''moralnet,'' or moral network, which he defined as ''a primary group that serves as a normative reference group'' (p. 19). He went on to say that ''the moralnet is not only the key to a happy family and personal life. It is the foundation of public morality'' (p. 20). Other writers use the terms *social network* and *social support group* to describe this same phenomenon. From a social support group, typically your family and close friends, you are likely to learn values, morals, norms, and attitudes. Beyond that, however, the group serves as a source of support for you in times of crisis and ill health, providing a ''buffering'' effect.

Benefits of a Strong Social Network

Naroll offers many health-related reasons for establishing and maintaining a strong moralnet, or social network. According to Naroll, the cause of most suicides among physically healthy people is loneliness, and people with well-established moralnets are less likely to commit suicide. Naroll theorizes that weakened moralnets are largely responsible for mental illness, pointing out that married people have low rates of mental illness compared to those who are single, widowed, divorced, or separated. He is especially assertive about the relationship between alcoholism and weakened moralnets, noting that drinking is common among social support groups but drunkenness is not. The concept behind Alcoholics Anonymous is to provide a moralnet for the person with drinking problems, a support group that shares the value of sobriety. He concludes that ''people who want to avoid trouble with alcoholism for themselves and their children would be wise to build their moralnets'' (p. 195). Rates of child abuse and juvenile delinquency are also reduced when a strong moralnet exists.

Social Networks and Health Status

Certainly Naroll is not alone in believing that social support groups serve the dual role of buffering stress and reinforcing healthy behavior (see Green's Precede Model). Dixon and Dixon (1984) wrote, ''A growing body of evidence is now documenting the role of social connections as a health factor'' (p. 5). Foremost is evidence collected from nearly 7,000 adults in Alameda County, California, in 1965, looking for connections between social networks and health status. A Social Network Index was developed, which took into consideration marital status, contacts with extended family and close friends, religious group membership, and formal and informal group memberships. Berkman and Syme (1979) did a follow-up 9 years later, again looking for connections between social networks and health status. They controlled for such factors as age, smoking behavior, alcohol consumption, obesity, physical activity, and previous health status. Independently of all these factors, the data indicated that people who lacked social and community ties were more likely to have died during the 9-year period than those with extensive social contacts. This was true for both men and women, regardless of socioeconomic status. Four primary sources of social contacts were cited: marriage, close friends and relatives, religious affiliations, and formal and informal group memberships. They concluded that "social networks and health practices are strongly associated with mortality" (p. 198).

Berkman (1984) reported that a community health study in Michigan replicated portions of the Alameda study, with similar results. She reiterated that unmarried males have higher mortality rates than married males, and that "widowed men have 7 times the homicide rate, 4 times the suicide rate, and over 6 times the mortality rate for tuberculosis and cirrhosis of the liver" (p. 425). Among the functions of social networks she describes are intimacy, a sense of belonging, nurturing, maintaining self-esteem, services, and advice.

Social Networks and Self-Esteem

Muhlenkamp and Sayles (1986) also noted the link between social support and self-esteem. They explained that social support comes from significant others, as does much of a person's self-esteem. They reported significant correlations between self-esteem and social support, self-esteem and a healthy lifestyle, and social support and a healthy lifestyle. They concluded that both high self-esteem and the social support of significant others are predictors of a healthy lifestyle.

Umberson (1987) summarized his study of the relationship between family status and health behaviors by saying, "Results indicate that marriage and the presence of children in the home have a deterrent effect on negative health behaviors" (p. 306). Among his findings: Marriage had a more positive effect on the health habits of men than on those of women; divorced men had more problems than married men with alcohol and substance abuse; widowed and divorced men and women were more likely to engage in negative health behaviors than married persons; and parents with children in the home were less likely than nonparents to drink and drive, abuse alcohol in other ways, or abuse marijuana.

Langlie (1977) offered qualified support for the social support theory. She distinguished between consistent and inconsistent practitioners of health behaviors, and between direct and indirect health risks. (For instance, drunken driving is a direct risk of health, and failing to wear a seat belt is an indirect risk). Her findings indicate that social support is more likely to influence indirect than direct health-risk behavior, and more likely to influence those whose health behavior is consistent.

Various Kinds of Social Support

Jacobsen (1986) and Wallston, Alagna, DeVellis, and DeVellis (1983) differentiated among the various types of social support that can be offered, and the appropriateness of each, in specific situations. Social support can come from one significant other or from a large network of casual contacts. Whether quantity or quality of social support is more helpful seems to depend on the person receiving the support and the situation. In times of extreme stress and grief, as when mourning the loss of a loved one, emotional support from a number of people is valuable. If you need advice, quality is more important than quantity. In certain situations, material support in the form of money, goods, or services becomes more meaningful than additional verbal support. Another factor that these researchers noted to be important is the values and attitudes of those providing the support. If members of the social support network value good health and have favorable attitudes toward healthy behavior, an individual is likely to be positively influenced, but when the social support network is composed of alcoholics or chain smokers, the effect on the individual they are "supporting" may be very unhealthy.

Jung (1984) offered yet another perspective on social support as it relates to health. According to Jung, our culture has a built-in bias in favor of social support, and we should recognize that at times the results can be negative. He used this illustration: If your friend is a diabetic, and you remind her to take insulin, we call that social support; if your friend is a drug addict, and you influence her to inject heroin, we call that peer pressure. Providing appropriate social support is a goal that is worthy but not easily achieved. Jung suggested that there are times when well-meaning friends might better leave counseling to trained professionals.

Bruhn and Phillips (1987) concurred with Jung, noting that "social ties are a two-edged sword" (p. 224). Although they are a potential source of self-esteem, social ties may also be a source of conflict and emotional stress. Bruhn and Phillips cited the work of Maslow, who believed that a healthy person is capable of both giving and receiving social support. It was Maslow's contention that a self-actualizing person is more likely to be a source, and a less self-actualizing person a recipient, of social support. "Social support that is reciprocated helps to create a positive self-image, self-acceptance, and a feeling of love-worthiness,

each of which permits a person to grow" (p. 216). This raises the question of how one becomes self-actualizing—a concept described in Maslow's hierarchy of human needs.

MASLOW'S HIERARCHY OF HUMAN NEEDS

Maslow (1970), an eminent psychologist, theorized that human beings in all cultures have the same set of needs over the course of a lifetime, which he divided into a five-level hierarchy (Figure 2.1). Needs at the lowest level are what Maslow calls our "species needs," needs that are basically the same for all of us (all members of our species). Needs at the highest level are highly individualized, varying greatly among different people.

Physiological needs are initially most important, but also most readily met. A person who is extremely hungry, thirsty, or sleepy can think of

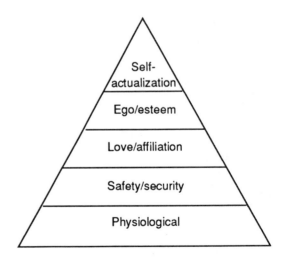

Figure 2.1. Maslow's hierarchy of human needs.

little else; after those needs are met, however, they become relatively unimportant in a person's overall hierarchy of needs. This is generally true of the needs at each level in the hierarchy. The underlying principle is that a person's needs change with changing life situations, and the dominant needs are always those lowest in the hierarchy and still unfulfilled.

Some writers contend that health is a safety or security need. Healthy people tend to feel safe and secure, unthreatened by illness or disease, and then become free to focus on their needs for affiliation, esteem, or self-actualization. Maslow, however, discussed health primarily in terms of its relationship to the self-actualizing process. You may recall from the discussion of his "being-values" in chapter 1 that the self-actualizing person is the one who comes closest to fulfilling human potential and such core values as truth, justice, and freedom.

A person who lacks love and affiliation is also likely to lack self-esteem, and a person lacking in self-esteem is unlikely to self-actualize. One who is both mentally and physically healthy is freed from other concerns and can concentrate on creative endeavors. Maslow's theory of a hierarchy of needs is consistent with the concept of social support as described earlier in this chapter, and also supports and is supported by the Rokeach System of Beliefs insofar as self-concept and ego or esteem are complementary and critical factors in human behavior.

ATTRIBUTION THEORY

A discussion of factors influencing human behavior would be incomplete without some mention of attribution theory (see Frieze & Bar-Tal, 1979). Attribution theory has been used rather extensively in treating alcoholism and drug abuse. It postulates that a person may be more likely to attribute his or her problems to bad luck or a difficult situation (external factors), but attribute success to ability or effort (internal factors). Further, that person may be prone to attribute personal good fortune to internal factors, but attribute another person's good fortune to external factors; when the outcome is negative, attributions tend to be reversed. Unhealthy behavior may also be attributed to the negative influence of peers, advertising, and the media. These are mechanisms for protecting self-esteem, and are related to locus of control. See if you can think of a recent situation in which you lacked objectivity in attributing success or failure. Can you see that this becomes a ready crutch for those who are having difficulty with health-related problems?

SUMMARY

Many factors influence your behavior in general and your health behavior in particular. You will find it easier to make wise decisions about your health behavior under the following conditions:

- Your self-esteem is high, and your self-concept is positive.
- Other needs are met, and you are self-actualizing.
- Your values and attitudes are consistent with healthy behavior.
- Your intent is to choose healthy behaviors.
- You have developed health-related skills.
- You have resources that support your healthy behavior.
- You have a strong social support system.
- Your family and friends reinforce your healthy behavior.
- You believe that healthy behavior is normal.
- You have an internal health locus of control.

- You perceive the benefits of healthy behavior to be greater than the costs.
- Your self-efficacy is high.

Your knowledge of and belief in the efficacy of these factors will enable you to promote your own health and live a wellness lifestyle, which are the topics for our next chapter.

Examining Your Values

Values are not to be confused with needs. Values need never be denied, whereas needs may or may not be denied. Animals have needs but not values; humans have both. Rokeach (1973, p. 20).

1. Consider your present needs, using Maslow's hierarchy. Given your current lifestyle, which level or levels are dominant?
2. Consider your values, as ranked in chapter 1. What do they tell you about your needs?
3. What do your needs tell you about your values?
4. Can you think of examples of when you choose not to fulfill your needs because they conflict with your values?
5. What, if anything, is preventing you from becoming a healthy, self-actualizing person?
6. What changes can you make that will allow you to become more self-actualizing?

CHAPTER 3
Health Promotion: Wellness and Prevention

We have met the enemy and he is us!

—Pogo

---------- **Self-Examination Statements** ----------

Instructions: Read each statement, then circle the x in the column at the left that most closely describes your belief about that statement. (Use a pencil. After reading this chapter you may wish to come back and change some of your responses on the basis of new information or attitudes.)

SA = strongly agree   **A** = agree   **U** = undecided   **D** = disagree   **SD** = strongly disagree

SA	A	U	D	SD	
x	x	x	x	x	I understand the concept of health promotion.
x	x	x	x	x	I understand the concept of wellness.
x	x	x	x	x	I understand the concept of prevention.
x	x	x	x	x	I understand the difference between wellness and prevention.
x	x	x	x	x	I place high value on maximizing my own wellness.
x	x	x	x	x	My self-concept is that of a person who is more well than ill.
x	x	x	x	x	I value life and want to lengthen mine if possible.
x	x	x	x	x	I believe that I will live a longer-than-normal life.
x	x	x	x	x	I am more interested in quality of life than quantity of life.
x	x	x	x	x	I believe that wellness contributes greatly to quality of life.
x	x	x	x	x	I intend to live a wellness lifestyle.
x	x	x	x	x	I believe that I am living a wellness lifestyle.
x	x	x	x	x	I believe that most of my friends are living a wellness lifestyle.
x	x	x	x	x	My best friend has a healthy, wellness-oriented lifestyle.
x	x	x	x	x	My friends respect my intent to live a wellness lifestyle.
x	x	x	x	x	Peer pressure often influences me to engage in unhealthy behavior.
x	x	x	x	x	My family is supportive of my wellness lifestyle.
x	x	x	x	x	I understand the difference between mortality and morbidity.

x	x	x	x	x	I can name seven health-related behaviors for which there is evidence that they increase life expectancy.
x	x	x	x	x	I believe I can add 10 years to my life by adopting healthy eating, drinking, smoking, and sleeping habits.
x	x	x	x	x	I almost always eat three meals a day, including breakfast.
x	x	x	x	x	I am not more than 10 percent over my ideal weight.
x	x	x	x	x	I normally get seven to eight hours sleep per night.
x	x	x	x	x	I normally exercise hard enough to perspire at least three times per week.
x	x	x	x	x	I am not a habitual smoker.
x	x	x	x	x	I rarely consume more than two alcoholic drinks a day.
x	x	x	x	x	It is my habit to brush or floss my teeth at least once daily.
x	x	x	x	x	I have the knowledge necessary to improve my level of wellness.
x	x	x	x	x	I have the skills necessary to improve my level of wellness.
x	x	x	x	x	I believe that heart disease is the leading cause of death in the United States.
x	x	x	x	x	I believe that most heart disease prior to age 70 is preventable.
x	x	x	x	x	I consciously act to reduce my risk of future heart disease.
x	x	x	x	x	I know five of the major risk factors for heart disease.
x	x	x	x	x	I don't believe I am susceptible to heart disease.
x	x	x	x	x	I believe that cancer is a leading cause of death in the United States.
x	x	x	x	x	I believe that most cases of cancer are preventable.
x	x	x	x	x	I know several major risk factors for cancer.
x	x	x	x	x	I consciously act to reduce the risk of cancer.
x	x	x	x	x	I don't believe I am susceptible to cancer.
x	x	x	x	x	I believe that my blood pressure is in the healthy range.
x	x	x	x	x	I know the difference between systolic and diastolic blood pressure.
x	x	x	x	x	I know the leading cause of death for people in my age group.
x	x	x	x	x	I act to reduce the risk of death from that cause.
x	x	x	x	x	There is more to good health than physical health.
x	x	x	x	x	Mental health is at least as important to me as physical health.
x	x	x	x	x	I believe that a positive attitude is conducive to good health.
x	x	x	x	x	I have a positive attitude toward life in general.
x	x	x	x	x	When I am happy I am also more likely to be healthy.
x	x	x	x	x	Loving and being loved are important to emotional health.
x	x	x	x	x	When my self-esteem is high, I feel healthier.
x	x	x	x	x	I am healthier when I have control over my emotions.

DEFINING TERMS AND DETERMINING PRIORITIES

Earlier we defined health as a combination of physical, mental, social, emotional, intellectual, and spiritual well-being, and we discussed health education in terms of predisposing, enabling, and reinforcing factors that lead to voluntary adoption of healthy behaviors. Now we must define some related terms: *health promotion, disease prevention*, and *wellness*.

According to Petosa (1986), "Health promotion is the organized application of educational, social and environmental resources enabling individuals to adopt and maintain behaviors that reduce risk of disease and enhance wellness" (p. 25). Petosa emphasized two important features of health promotion: allowing individuals to make their own choices among health behaviors, and conveying a positive concept of health.

Mullen (1986) described health promotion as a combination of disease prevention and wellness. She wrote, "Disease prevention is defined as efforts aimed at reducing the occurrence and severity of disease, while wellness is described as attitudes and activities which improve the quality of life and expand the potential for higher levels of functioning" (p. 34). This definition is useful because it identifies two separate motives for health behavior. Disease prevention relates to the first half of the World Health Organization (WHO) definition of health as the absence of disease; wellness speaks to the second half of the WHO definition, calling for *complete* physical, mental, and social well-being.

I would make the additional point that some activities are both preventive and wellness-oriented. For example, I exercise to reduce my risk of many diseases and also because I believe it adds to the quality of my life. When I choose not to smoke, I expect my decision to reduce my risk of disease and increase my enjoyment of clean air and tasty food. My goal with this book is to promote health, yours and mine, which requires both preventive and wellness-related activities; I will not always distinguish between the two.

Ardell (1979) has written extensively about wellness. "To begin, understand that wellness is a *positive* approach to well-being. It is something you do because the approach is more satisfying and enjoyable, not because you want to avoid disease or live a very long life" (p. 17). He identified several dimensions of high-level wellness, foremost of which is self-responsibility for one's own health. You should recall from earlier chapters in this book that two of our objectives are for you to assume more responsibility for your health (see Dennison's Activated Health Education Model on page 10) and for you to envision healthy behavior as a positive force in your life rather than as a pleasure-loss process. This approach accords with Petosa's (1986) observation that "people are more likely to adopt and maintain health-enhancing lifestyles when they are aspiring to positive levels of functioning rather than avoiding future health threats" (p. 26).

Several writers have used the automobile transmission analogy to explain the concept of health as it relates to disease prevention and wellness: Having a disease is like being in reverse, absence of disease puts you in neutral, initiating a wellness behavior puts you into forward gear, and a full range of wellness activities enables you to stay in high gear and go at top speed. Absence of disease is only the midpoint between high-level wellness and premature death. In keeping with this concept, O'Donnell (1986) defined health promotion as "the science and art of helping people change their lifestyle to move toward a state of optimal health" (p. 4).

Although many factors influence health, lifestyle seems to be the primary indicator of wellness. Ardell specifically identified four factors that influence health: heredity, environment, the medical system, and lifestyle—the key to wellness.

As Green (undated) pointed out in a recent assessment of the health behaviors of Texans, "Unhealthy lifestyles account for more than 75 percent of the mortality in this country" (p. 77). Haggarty (1977) also acknowledged the importance of lifestyle in influencing health. He reminded us that health information is probably not as persuasive in influencing health behavior as the *consequences* of behavior. He also recognized that we sometimes choose to risk health problems, or endure them, in order to continue behaviors that support values more important to us than health. For example, those who value an exciting life may choose to use alcohol or drugs in their quest for excitement and those who value accomplishment may neglect nutrition and sleep in their efforts to achieve. Such unhealthy behaviors are not likely to change independently of values and lifestyle. Best and Cameron (1986) noted that most people don't make sudden changes in lifestyle; awareness is followed by changes in attitudes and values, followed by changes in intentions and finally in behavior.

Health educators are becoming increasingly aware of the dangers of placing the entire burden for good health on the individual. Referred to in some quarters as "blaming the victim," this can produce guilt, lowered self-esteem, and poorer emotional health (Grossman, 1984). According to Faber (1980), "One danger of emphasizing individual responsibility for health is that it appears to absolve society of its responsibility . . ." (p. xiii). The North Karelia (Finland) study (Puska et al., 1985) and the Stanford (California) study (Maccoby, Farquhar, Wood, & Alexander, 1977) provided evidence that community effort can succeed in changing the health behaviors of its citizens. Individuals may control personal behaviors such as eating, drinking, smoking, and exercise, but the community is better positioned to provide mass screenings, immunizations, fluoridated water, and other such services. Further, it is difficult for an individual to adopt healthy behaviors when family or community norms are unhealthy, so these groups share responsibility for the health behaviors of their individual members.

We all want to have good health *and* an enjoyable life. The question is whether we can have both simultaneously or whether they are mutually exclusive. Ardell contended that they are mutually supportive, but others recognize that this is not always so. Levin (1981) wrote, "Health is *not* life's highest goal. Happiness is" (p. 219). People do not want risk-free lives, he continued, but want to be free to choose which risks to take and which ones to avoid. Hoyman (1975) expressed another common theme: "Health is more than wellness. Human health is a means, not an end in itself; the surest way to miss the target is to aim at health" (p. 510). Hochbaum (1979) pointed out that desiring good health doesn't mean being preoccupied with it. He insists that health should be a joyful and happy state, not burdensome and distasteful. "Health is what helps me be what I want to be, do what I want to do, and live the way I would like to live" (p. 199). I subscribe entirely to this philosophy, which I believe captures the essence of wellness. There will be choices to make and risks to take but, as Hochbaum concluded, paralleling Levin's thoughts, "We must grant people the right to choose how they want to live—and die" (p. 201).

In 1979 the U.S. Department of Health, Education, and Welfare published *Healthy People*, followed by *Promoting Health/Preventing Disease: Objectives for the Nation* (1980). The former described the state of the nation's health and identified the most critical problems. The latter recognized five major target areas for health promotion activities: smoking, fitness and exercise, nutrition and obesity, alcohol and drug abuse, and control of stress and violent behavior. One or more chapters in this book have been devoted to each of these target areas.

HEALTHY LIFESTYLES AND PREVENTIVE HEALTH BEHAVIORS

According to Kirscht (1983), "Preventive health behavior includes actions taken by people to enhance or maintain health, both within and outside the medical care system" (p. 277). There is no longer any doubt that there is a relationship between health and lifestyle (Wurtele, Britcher, & Saslawsky, 1985). Much of the evidence has come from the Human Population Laboratory in Berkeley, California, which conducted the Alameda County study (see chapter 2), the results of which have been reported by Breslow and Belloc (1972), Breslow and Enstrom (1980), and Wiley and Camacho (1980).

Health Factors and Mortality Rates

Breslow and Belloc (1972) discovered seven health practices associated with mortality (death) rates and predicted subsequent mortality rates, based on those seven practices; their predictions were confirmed. On that basis they concluded that longevity is statistically associated with the following:

- Never smoking cigarettes
- Using alcohol moderately or not at all
- Regular sleep (7 to 8 hours per night)
- Regular physical activity
- Maintaining proper weight
- Eating breakfast daily
- Eating three meals per day, with no snacks

Breslow and Enstrom (1980) updated the earlier findings, based on more recent data that continued to come in from the longitudinal study. They reported that men who followed all seven of the recommended health practices had a mortality rate only 28 percent of that for men who practiced zero to three of them. They concluded, "The data presented here indicate support for the idea that following poor health habits leads to earlier death and following good health habits leads to longer life" (p. 479).

Wiley and Camacho (1980) did their own follow-up study, with slightly different conclusions. They reported that eating between meals showed no relationship to future health for either men or women. Eating breakfast was associated only weakly with good health for men and not at all for women. Their findings did support the other five health practices originally recommended by Breslow and Belloc (1972). They also reported that moderate alcohol consumption (one to two drinks per day) was associated with better health than either complete abstention or greater consumption. Further, they noted the positive association between socioeconomic status and health; that is, more education and higher income were associated with lower mortality rates.

Two years later Wingard, Berkman, and Brand (1982) did another follow-up on the Alameda County study and reached the same conclusions as Wiley and Camacho (1980). Their review of literature cited many other studies supporting the claim that there is a high risk of mortality and morbidity (sickness) related to smoking, heavy alcohol consumption, obesity, and inactivity. Mormons and Seventh Day Adventists, who are forbidden to use alcohol or tobacco by their religious tenets, have lower than normal mortality rates, especially from heart disease and cancer.

The Demographics of Health Behaviors

Schoenborn (1986) used data from a 1985 National Health Institute Survey to study current

American habits related to the seven health practices recommended on the previous page. The survey resulted in several interesting findings.

Education, Income, and Age

Good health habits were positively associated with more education and higher income but inversely associated with age. Individuals 18 to 29 years old had the fewest good health habits. More education was positively associated with more physical activity, less smoking, more frequent but not necessarily heavier drinking, and better sleep habits. We could speculate about why this is so. Is it because education provides knowledge that eventually influences behavior? Is it because educated people have a different self-concept, which leads to different behavior? Is it because educated people have better decision-making skills? I believe that the evidence supports answering each of these questions with an unqualified "yes."

Gender

Wingard (1984) assessed differences between men and women in health behaviors and how these affect morbidity and mortality. According to her, 1980 life expectancy was 70 years for men and 77.5 years for women. She offered two possible explanations for this difference: Women are genetically and biologically superior in regard to longevity, or men take more health risks that reduce longevity. Men reportedly have higher mortality rates from each of the 12 leading causes of death in this country, including homicide, suicide, accident, coronary heart disease, lung cancer, and cirrhosis of the liver. It seems more than coincidental that each of the above is linked to behaviors that are traditionally more common among men than women— cigarette smoking, heavy use of alcohol, stress-prone behavior, and working at hazardous jobs. Gottlieb, Lloyd, and Bernstein (1987) corroborated some of Wingard's conclusions. Their data suggested that men are more likely than women to drink heavily, drink and drive, smoke, become overweight, and avoid the use of seat belts.

College Attendance

Taylor and McKillip (1980) studied the personal health habits of college students, their perceived illnesses, and their use of college medical services. They found that heavier consumption of cigarettes and coffee, and more hours of employment, were associated with more perceived illness; that getting adequate sleep and exercise correlated with less perceived illness; and that students who used the college medical services most frequently tended to be more overweight, more sexually active, and heavier consumers of cigarettes, alcohol, and coffee. Because young people typically perceive themselves as healthy and think that serious health problems are years in the future, they commonly compromise on health habits. Taylor and McKillip found that negative health behaviors result in rather immediate health consequences even for "healthy" college students.

CONSISTENT AND INCONSISTENT HEALTH BEHAVIORS

Langlie (1979) distinguished between subjects who were "consistent" or "inconsistent" in their health behavior, and between health behaviors that were "direct risks" or "indirect risks." Consistent health behavior was attributed to subjects who scored above the mean on at least 8 of the 11 preventive health behaviors (PHB) measured; all other subjects were described as "inconsistents." Each of the 11 PHBs was described as either direct risk (e.g., smoking behavior and personal hygiene) or indirect risk (e.g., eating and exercise habits), depending on whether or not those behaviors would directly lead to disease.

Although much of the literature indicates that health behavior is multidimensional and that performance of one healthy behavior is not predictive of another, Langlie's data did not support that assertion. Direct risk behaviors are those that can have an immediate effect on health. Langlie found all of these to be significantly correlated; that is, individuals who engaged in various direct risk behaviors were likely also to engage in other direct risk behaviors. Indirect risk behaviors are those that will have a long-range effect on health; over 90% of those correlated with each other. Still, the person who is a very careful driver (direct risk) may not wear a seat belt (indirect risk). Langlie concluded that for subjects described as "consistent" in their health behavior, "the direct risk and indirect risk dimensions of preventive health behavior were found to be positively related" (p. 225) in most instances, whereas the subjects described as inconsistent had much lower correlations between direct and indirect risk PHBs.

Kristiansen (1985c) used Langlie's construct of direct and indirect risk behavior and consistent and inconsistent health behavior to study the relationship between values and preventive health behaviors. She used a version of the Rokeach terminal values survey and a 15-item preventive health behavior (PHB) questionnaire. She discovered that those who reported good preventive health behavior placed higher value on health than those who reported poor preventive health behavior. She also found that a high value of health was more predictive of direct than of indirect risk behaviors, especially for subjects classified as "inconsistents." Kristiansen observed that the value one places on health is important only as it relates to competing values. More about that in a moment.

Kristiansen and Harding (1984) examined the relationship between social desirability and health behaviors. They concluded that for some people, social desirability is so important that they are willing to take certain health risks to attain it. Subjects who scored high on social desirability had a greater need for the approval of significant others and were more likely to conform to others' expectations. This may result in better or worse PHB, depending on whether the significant other is reinforcing healthy or unhealthy behavior.

Among the values that compete with health in determining behavior are the desire for an exciting life (Kristiansen, 1986), the desire for love and peer affiliation, and the desire for the self-esteem that comes with academic, professional, or personal achievement. Those who value an exciting life are more apt to engage in risky behaviors, such as drinking and driving. Those who are achievement oriented sometimes sacrifice sleep, sound nutrition, and even family relationships in their pursuit of success. Is it any wonder that even those of us who value good health do not always perform preventive health behaviors when other values are also important?

CHANGING YOUR HEALTH BEHAVIORS

How would you go about changing your health behavior, if you decided that a change was in your best interests? Milsum (1980) suggested that changing one's health-related lifestyle is a complex process, involving the following:

- Awareness
- Integration
- Action

We have discussed awareness previously in the context of Dennison's Activated Health Education model. We have also discussed action; remember that, by definition, values are action-oriented. Integration, the link between awareness and values, is the integration of self-concept with intended behavior. The notion that integration is essential for changing your health lifestyle is consistent with Rokeach's belief that a change in self-concept must precede a change in behavior. Therefore, you are advised not to attempt to change your health behavior until you are satisfied that the change is consistent with your desired self-concept; that is, will it help you be the kind of person you really want to be?

Green (1984) identified three factors that influence health behavior:

- Compliance
- Identification
- Internalization

Compliance means following rules, regulations, laws, norms, customs, and parental expectations and submitting to coercion from authority figures. *Identification* means maintaining a close emotional association with or modeling yourself after role models, peers, significant others, and similar sources of reinforcement. *Internalization* parallels Maslow's self-actualization and Rokeach's value congruence, as it involves basing your decisions on personal needs and values. Simplified, Green's theory is that your health behavior is determined by what authorities require of you, what friends expect of you, and what you choose for yourself. By now you should know that I am encouraging you to let the latter dominate your decision-making process: to take control of your life, assume responsibility for your own health behavior, be aware of the facts, and become increasingly less concerned about the expectations of others as they relate to your preferred lifestyle. You can be responsive to others and still assert yourself when your well-being is at stake.

LEADING CAUSES OF DEATH

There are four leading causes of death in the United States:

- Cardiovascular diseases
- Cancer

- Apoplexy (stroke)
- Accidents

These are sometimes referred to as "diseases of choice" because they are more affected by our lifestyles—what we eat and drink and smoke, how we exercise and sleep, how we manage stress and risks—than by communicable germs. Although we may fall short of total control, we have the power to reduce the risk of death from each of these causes simply by changing our health-related behavior. An abundance of research supports this point of view (Gottlieb et al., 1987). The three leading causes of death are addressed here. Accidents are discussed in chapter 13.

PREVENTING CARDIOVASCULAR DISEASE

Arteriosclerosis (hardening of the arteries), atherosclerosis (fatty deposits clogging the coronary arteries), and coronary thrombosis (blood clot in a coronary artery, leading to a heart attack) are examples of cardiovascular disease. Together they account for about half of all deaths in the United States. The American Heart Association has identified primary and secondary risk factors associated with cardiovascular disease. Their list, amended by the work of Leon (1987) and Dolecek et al. (1986), appears in Table 3.1.

Although some risk factors (age, sex, race, and family history) are beyond our sphere of influence, the risks from most factors can be reduced by adopting a healthy lifestyle that includes prudent habits of nutrition and exercise, control of weight and stress, and avoidance of smoking.

The Framingham Study

The famous Framingham study described by Dawber (1980), now several decades old, con-

Table 3.1 Risk Factors Associated With Cardiovascular Disease (CVD)

Modifiable risk factors	Risk increases if . . .
Cigarette smoking	. . . smoking is habitual.
High blood pressure	. . . blood pressure is greater than 140/95.
High blood cholesterol	. . . the ratio of LDL to HDL is more than 4:1.
Diet	. . . saturated fat intake increases significantly.
Sedentary lifestyle	. . . less than 2000 calories are burned per week.
Stressful lifestyle	. . . a person is a type A personality.
Obesity	. . . the body mass index is greater than 30.
Diabetes	. . . blood sugar levels increase.
Oral contraceptives	. . . the user is a smoker.

Non-modifiable risk factors	Risk increases for . . .
Age	. . . older individuals.
Sex	. . . males.
Race	. . . Caucasians.
Heredity	. . . people who have a family history of coronary heart disease.

tinues to provide much of the documentation for the relationship between health behavior and cardiovascular risk factors. Recently Hubert, Eaker, Garrison, and Castelli (1987) conducted an 8-year study of young adults who are the offspring of the original Framingham subjects. Nearly 900 people, aged 20 to 29 when the study began, contributed data. The authors concluded that the following behaviors most significantly increased the risk factor for cardiovascular disease:

• Increased body weight
• Increased alcohol consumption
• Use of oral contraceptives by women
• Interim vasectomies among men

(See chapter 12 for studies that dispute the link between vasectomies and coronary heart disease.)

The following behaviors decreased the cardiovascular risk factor:

• Weight loss
• Smoking cessation
• Discontinued use of oral contraceptives
• Increased physical activity
• Increased alcohol consumption

Hubert et al. noted that 3 times as many of their subjects stopped smoking during the 8-year period of the study as started smoking, suggesting that education and intervention are effective in altering the health behaviors of healthy young adults.

If you are an observant reader, you are probably wondering about the apparent contradiction discussed earlier, which credits increased alcohol consumption with both raising and lowering the risk-factor profile. This seeming contradiction is explained by the research of Friedman and Kimball (1986), based on 24 years of data from the original Framingham study. They noted a "U-shaped relationship between reported alcohol consumption and coronary heart disease" (p. 481). Both abstainers and heavy drinkers had more coronary heart disease than moderate drinkers (one or two drinks per day); this is consistent with the longevity findings of Wiley and Camacho (1980) reported earlier. For abstainers, increasing alcohol consumption decreased coronary disease risk; for heavy drinkers, increasing alcohol consumption increased coronary disease risk. The protective effect of moderate consumption was less evident among moderate smokers and females but reappeared among males who smoked heavily. No reason was advanced for this unexpected occurrence.

Public Awareness

The Framingham study has been given much of the credit for raising public awareness of the importance of behavior in preventing cardiovascular disease. For example, in a study reported by Harris and Guten in 1979, in which over 800 adults were asked what they did on their own to protect their health, more than half mentioned proper nutrition and over a third mentioned getting adequate sleep and exercise. Fewer than 1 in 10 mentioned alcohol, tobacco, or weight control. A decade after the Harris and Guten study, the public appears to be much better informed, and the results are encouraging.

According to McGinnis (1987b), since 1970 the heart attack death rate in the United States has declined about 30 percent and the death rate from strokes about 50 percent. Smoking rates have declined during that same time span, as has the consumption of fatty foods, known to contain cholesterol. Canadians are making similar changes, according to *Active Health Report* (Rawlings, 1987). Of the more than 11,000 Canadian citizens surveyed in 1985, over 60 percent reported that their health is good or excellent; good health is important to them; they do not smoke, use marijuana, or use alcohol excessively; they wear seat belts, and do not drink and drive; and they eat breakfast regularly. Rawlings concluded that "poor individual health habits are no longer the social norm in Canada" (p. 7). Even those whose health and health behavior were poor reported positive attitudes toward good health; if we accept Rokeach's System of Beliefs, good behavior is apt to follow.

Awareness Plus Motivation

Although we know that knowledge does not always lead to behavioral change, knowledge plus motivation may do so. Based on the Canadian survey, Stephens (1986) recommended a two-pronged approach to health promotion, based on *information* and *incentives*. Among the incentives Stephens suggested were reduced life insurance premiums for not smoking, reduced auto insurance premiums for wearing seat belts, bicycle lanes and other facilities to encourage exercise, and more smoke-free areas for non-smokers. Data clearly indicate that people are getting the message about preventive health behaviors and that public attitudes and behaviors do change when health is threatened and motivation for change is present.

This belief is supported by the results of the Stanford Heart Disease Prevention Program, as reported by Maccoby, Farquhar, Wood, and Alexander (1977), and Farquhar et al. (1977). Initiated in 1972, the Stanford program involved three California communities, two of which received experimental treatment while the third served as a control. Both experimental groups received intensive instruction through a mass media campaign, while the control group did not. In addition, high-risk individuals in one experimental group received individual instruction and counseling regarding their health behavior as it related to smoking and diet. The risk of cardiovascular disease increased in the control community during the 2 years the study was in progress, but decreased in each of the treatment communities. The combination of mass media information and individual instruction and counseling proved most effective. Screening tests were used to identify those who were at high risk; knowing that they were at high risk appeared to motivate those participants to change their behavior. Information and motivation together proved effective as change agents in this study, and both are probably prerequisites for any behavioral changes you may be planning for yourself.

PREVENTING CANCER

Many people are surprised at the parallels between preventing cardiovascular diseases and preventing cancer, the first and second leading causes of death in the United States.

Avoidable Risks

Doll and Peto (1981) did an extensive study of avoidable risks of cancer, which included the following:

- Tobacco
- Alcohol
- Diet
- Food additives
- Type of reproductive and sexual behavior
- Type of occupation
- Incidence of exposure to pollution and to ultraviolet light

They concluded that a majority, perhaps as many as 80 to 90 percent, of all cancer cases are potentially preventable. Although alcohol alone is not known to be a significant risk factor for cancer, tobacco and alcohol interact syn-

ergistically to greatly increase the risk. Carcinogens, charcoal, bacteria resulting from unrefrigerated food, and such additives as saccharin and nitrites all contribute dietary risks. Having multiple sexual partners and having no children or having children late in life are thought to increase risk of cancer of the cervix and breasts, respectively. Certain occupations place workers at greater risk, particularly those involving exposure to asbestos, soot, radiation, and pollution. Likewise, excessive exposure to sunshine or other sources of ultraviolet light increases risk of cancer.

McGinnis (1987b) substantiated many of these findings, observing diet to be the number one risk factor, accounting for 35 percent of cancer deaths, and tobacco to be the second leading risk factor (30 percent). Iacono (1987) also noted the importance of diet in the prevention of cancer. He concluded, ''There is little doubt that nutrition plays a major role in the long-term development of cardiovascular disease (CVD) and cancer'' (p. 516). According to Heimbach (1985), ''The role of diet in fostering long-term health—or, alternatively, in contributing to cardiovascular disease (CVD), cancer, and other delayed-onset diseases—has been increasingly recognized and has become a source of concern'' (p. 5). Only about one third of Heimbach's 4,000 respondents expressed any concern about dietary risk factors, so much remains to be done to inform the general public.

Warning Signs

For discussions of dietary and smoking risks for cancer, see chapters 6 and 9. Meanwhile, it is important to know that many forms of cancer can be cured if detected early enough. Lung cancer is the most common form and it is not often cured; that is why it is so important to avoid smoking. Cancer of the colon and rectum are the next most common, but their incidence can be reduced by a high-fiber diet. They are also easily detected through a variety of screening processes, and the detected cancerous polyps can be safely removed with a sigmoidoscope. Self-examination of breasts or testes is yet another simple way to detect cancer early while it can still be treated. Skin cancer can be greatly reduced by limiting overexposure to bright sunshine—by wearing a hat and a sunscreen lotion, for example. Finally, everyone should know and heed the early warning signs of cancer:

- A change in the size or color of a wart or mole
- A sore that does not heal or that heals slowly
- Unusual bleeding from the bowels or other body opening
- Thickening or lump in the breast or elsewhere
- Indigestion or loss of appetite that persists
- Obvious change in bowel or bladder habits
- Nagging cough or hoarseness; difficulty in swallowing

PREVENTING STROKE

Blood pressure is a particularly powerful predictor of stroke. Farchi, Menotti, and Conti (1987) reported that blood pressure was significantly and positively correlated with each type of mortality studied, including coronary heart disease, cancer, and stroke. Reed, MacLean, and Hayashi (1987) identified blood pressure as one of the strongest and most consistent predictors of atherosclerosis, which is the major underlying cause of many coronary and cerebral illnesses. Abernathy et al. (1986) reported that diastolic blood pressure had little effect on mortality in their study, whereas systolic blood pressure was a significant predictor of mortality from both coronary heart disease and stroke. Systole occurs when the heart contracts to force blood from the heart. Diastole occurs when the heart

relaxes between beats. Systolic pressure is always higher than diastolic. When systolic blood pressure is above 140, it is elevated and warrants medical attention. Diastolic pressure warrants medical attention when it is above 95.

SUMMARY

There is much you can do to promote your own health. You can take preventive actions designed to reduce the risk of illness, and you can pursue other initiatives that lead to a higher level of wellness. Because most deaths are the result of diseases that are caused by unhealthy lifestyle rather than germs, the quality and length of your life is largely up to you.

We have identified seven health practices associated with reduced mortality and morbidity. The extent to which you follow these practices to increase your wellness level depends partially on your self-concept and your values. Love, happiness, and self-esteem are significant elements of wellness, and these cannot be assured through physical health. They are states of mind and can be achieved best by applying the principles espoused by Rokeach, Maslow, and other social scientists and philosophers mentioned in chapters 1 and 2.

Knowles (1977) provided an excellent summary of how to *prevent* illness and disease:

If no one smoked cigarettes or consumed alcohol and everyone exercised regularly, maintained optimal weight on a low fat, low refined-carbohydrate, high fiber-content diet, reduced stress by simplifying their lives, obtained adequate rest and recreation, understood the needs of infants and children for the proper nutrition and nurturing of their intellectual and affective development, had available to them and would use genetic counseling and selected abortion, drank fluoridated water, followed the doctors' orders for medications and self-care when disease was detected, used examinations and health education-preventive medicine programs, the savings to the country would be mammoth in terms of billions of dollars, a vast reduction in human misery, and an attendant marked improvement in the quality of life. Our country would be strengthened immeasurably, and we could divert our energies—human and financial—to other pressing issues of national and international concern. (p. 1103)

To that advice I add these suggestions for achieving high-level *wellness*:

- Develop loving relationships with other people.
- Respect yourself and others, and your self-esteem will be assured.
- Be kind to and do good for others; your self-esteem will grow.
- Take control of your life and assume responsibility for it.
- Let your self-concept determine your values and attitudes; the behavior that follows will be right for you.
- Seek happiness through the self-satisfaction that comes from knowing you are the kind of person you choose to be.

Examining Your Values

Freedom is defined as a state that entitles people to do what they want up to the limit that they may not hurt other people. Shirreffs (1979, p. 38).

1. What right do I have to influence your health values?
2. What right do I have to influence your health behavior?
3. What right do you have to influence the health values of others?
4. What right do you have to influence the health behavior of others?
5. What are some examples of health-related behaviors of others that have the potential to harm you?
6. What are some examples of your health-related behavior that have potential to harm others?
7. Hochbaum wrote, "No one can be permitted to engage in actions that pose serious threats to other people's health, safety, and welfare" (1987, p. 7). Do you agree? If so, what are some of the limits on people's behavior?
8. Which of your values are more important to you than your value of freedom? How does this relate to your health behavior?

CHAPTER 4

Health Care and Health Care Ethics

The health of the people will be the foundation on which all their happiness and all their power as a state depend.

—Benjamin Disraeli

————————— **Self-Examination Statements** —————————

Instructions: Read each statement, then circle the x in the column at the left that most closely describes your belief about that statement. (Use a pencil. After reading this chapter you may wish to come back and change some of your responses on the basis of new information or attitudes.)

SA = strongly agree **A** = agree **U** = undecided **D** = disagree **SD** = strongly disagree

SA	A	U	D	SD	
x	x	x	x	x	I place high value on quality health care.
x	x	x	x	x	I believe I have made adequate provisions for health care emergencies that might arise.
x	x	x	x	x	I understand the difference between primary and secondary health care.
x	x	x	x	x	I understand the difference between secondary and tertiary health care.
x	x	x	x	x	I have a personal physician who has my medical history on file.
x	x	x	x	x	I have a personal dentist who has my dental history on file.
x	x	x	x	x	I have been immunized against polio.
x	x	x	x	x	I have had DPT shots (diphtheria, pertussis, and tetanus).
x	x	x	x	x	I am covered by personal/family health care insurance.
x	x	x	x	x	If I had a medical emergency I would know what to do.
x	x	x	x	x	I understand the concept of a health maintenance organization (HMO).
x	x	x	x	x	I believe that HMOs represent a better concept than traditional health care.
x	x	x	x	x	I belong to an HMO or would like to join one soon.
x	x	x	x	x	I understand the concept of a preferred provider organization (PPO).
x	x	x	x	x	I understand the difference between an HMO and a PPO.

X	X	X	X	X	I believe that PPOs represent a better concept than either HMOs or traditional health care.
X	X	X	X	X	I belong to a PPO or would like to join one.
X	X	X	X	X	I understand the difference between Medicare and Medicaid.
X	X	X	X	X	I understand the difference between Blue Cross and Blue Shield insurance.
X	X	X	X	X	If I had a serious medical problem I know what hospital I would prefer.
X	X	X	X	X	I understand the concept of diagnostic related groups (DRGs).
X	X	X	X	X	I know that the hospital of my choice uses DRGs.
X	X	X	X	X	I believe health care is less expensive under the DRG system.
X	X	X	X	X	I believe that the quality of health care is better under the DRG system.
X	X	X	X	X	I believe that health care is an individual responsibility.
X	X	X	X	X	I believe employers should provide comprehensive health care benefits.
X	X	X	X	X	I would vote in favor of a national health care plan.
X	X	X	X	X	If people practiced healthy preventive behavior there would be less need for a national health program.
X	X	X	X	X	I resent paying higher taxes to provide health care for those who neglect their health through irresponsible behavior.
X	X	X	X	X	Only those who can afford it deserve good health care.
X	X	X	X	X	I don't know anyone who is currently being deprived of quality health care.
X	X	X	X	X	I don't feel any obligation to provide health care for the poor or the aged.
X	X	X	X	X	I value justice and equality as they apply to national health care.
X	X	X	X	X	I understand the concept of euthanasia.
X	X	X	X	X	I understand the difference between active and passive euthanasia.
X	X	X	X	X	I believe medical science should prolong life whenever possible.
X	X	X	X	X	I am familiar with the concept of ''The Living Will.''
X	X	X	X	X	I have or would sign a Living Will.
X	X	X	X	X	I support the concept of euthanasia for others but would never want it applied to me.
X	X	X	X	X	I understand the arguments against abortion.
X	X	X	X	X	I understand the arguments in favor of abortion.
X	X	X	X	X	I would never want an embryo or fetus I helped create aborted under any circumstances.
X	X	X	X	X	I believe that a mother's right to life and health override the rights of the embryo she carries.
X	X	X	X	X	My values cause me to oppose abortion even though it is legal.
X	X	X	X	X	If I should die an accidental death, I would be pleased to know that my vital organs had been used to save the lives of others.
X	X	X	X	X	I carry a signed organ donor card.
X	X	X	X	X	I understand the concept of surrogate motherhood.

x	x	x	x	x	I would resort to surrogate motherhood if it were the only way for me to have children.
x	x	x	x	x	I understand the concept of artificial insemination.
x	x	x	x	x	I would resort to artificial insemination if it were the only way for me to have children.
x	x	x	x	x	My system of values suggests that it would be a kind act for me to be a surrogate mother (female) or an artificial inseminator (male) for someone else's child.

DEFINING TERMS AND CONCEPTS

The Knowles quotation and the values questions at the end of chapter 3 direct us to the topics for this chapter. Several questions arise that deserve your attention, and each of them is value-laden. What provisions should you make for your health care, just in case your preventive health behavior is not totally effective? Where does your responsibility for your health care end, and what is the responsibility of the nation to assure at least minimal health care for you and others? When life-and-death decisions (e.g., abortion, euthanasia) must be made, to what extent do you rely on medical authorities to make those decisions for you? Have you established a system of values that will assist you in making health-care decisions?

Health care can be divided into three categories: primary, secondary, and tertiary.

Primary Care

Primary care is self-care, anything you do to or for yourself. Some texts use the terms "primary care" and "personal hygiene" interchangeably, but most experts agree that primary care is much broader. Hygiene deals primarily with sanitation and cleanliness—bathing regularly, washing your hands before eating, brushing your teeth, and so on. Personal hygiene is an important aspect of primary care, but only a small part

of it. In many ways, primary care parallels the preventive health behaviors we discussed in chapter 3. Among the most common forms of primary care are eating nutritious foods and controlling your weight; getting the right mix of sleep and exercise; avoiding excessive use of drugs, alcohol, and tobacco; learning to cope effectively with stressful situations; and maintaining safe conditions at home, at work, and on the highway. Your self-concept, values, attitudes, beliefs, intentions, and health knowledge affect the kind of primary care you choose for yourself. Each of us is responsible for acquiring enough information to be able to distinguish between healthy and unhealthy behaviors and for acting on that knowledge.

Secondary Care

Secondary care is provided by professionals, either to prevent disease or to treat illness in its early stages. Your selection of health-care specialists serves as a bridge from your primary to your secondary care. Although the services of health-care professionals represent secondary care, your decisions about when to seek medical services and from whom fall in the category of primary care. You may need a general practitioner, a dentist, an ophthalmologist, a gynecologist or an obstetrician, an internist, a podiatrist, or any number of other specialists. It is important to select your primary caregivers when you are well, not when you are in pain and need immediate attention. This is especially true if you have moved to a new community, because you may need some time to check references and credentials. Remember that not all health-care professionals have comparable preparation and philosophies. Osteopaths and chiropractors represent two branches of medicine that differ significantly from traditional practices. Older physicians may be treatment-oriented, in accord with their training, whereas younger ones may emphasize prevention. Some physicians practice holistic medicine as a means of achieving high-level wellness, and others believe in narrow specialization. You should consider your own beliefs and preferences and seek medical care from those whose beliefs are compatible with yours.

Tertiary Care

Tertiary care is provided by hospitals and medical specialists; it typically involves treatment that sustains and saves life. Chemotherapy, open heart surgery, and organ transplants are examples of tertiary health care. Obviously, tertiary care is extremely expensive compared with primary or even secondary care. While health or medical insurance helps pay the costs of secondary care, insurance is absolutely essential for protecting yourself against the astronomical costs of tertiary care. Even so, the best protection is the preventive health behaviors described in chapter 3.

As a nation we are committed to reducing tertiary care by improving primary and secondary care. This commitment is the underlying philosophy of the medical care organizations that have emerged recently in the United States.

THE EMERGENCE OF NEW MEDICAL COVERAGE OPTIONS IN THE U.S.

The 1980s have been a decade of tremendous change in personal health care. Perhaps the greatest change has occurred in medical coverage options now available. There are at least three major options: Health Maintenance Organizations, Preferred Provider Organizations, and the more traditional Third-Party Payment Providers.

Health Maintenance Organizations

One emerging option is the Health Maintenance Organization (HMO). As of July 1986, nearly 10 percent of the United State's population was enrolled in an HMO, and the percentage was rising annually (McMillan, Lubitz, & Russell, 1987). Under the HMO concept, payment precedes illness, and the primary function of the physician is to help maintain good health and prevent disease. Comprehensive health services are provided to a voluntarily-enrolled population for a prepaid fee. Included are regular medical checkups, immunizations, nutrition education, screenings for cancer and hypertension, and other services. Anyone may join an HMO; the decision is primarily an economic and philosophic one.

Commonly an HMO is organized around the group practice of several physicians who share an office building and patients. A typical group practice might include one or more general practitioners (GPs), a cardiologist, a pediatrician, and other specialists, depending on the size and demographics of the patient clientele. Some HMOs hire physicians throughout a metropolitan area, contracting them to see members as needed. Other HMOs develop a set of regulations and a schedule of fees, then allow members to be served by any physician who agrees to provide services within those guidelines.

A November 1986 survey (Steiber, 1987a) revealed that the majority of Americans don't know what an HMO is; only 15 percent related it to medical insurance. Worse, those between the ages of 18 and 24, who are probably most likely to choose their first medical insurer, knew even less than the general public. HMOs enjoy their greatest popularity with individuals 25 to 34 years old, especially those with above-average income or education. "Persons with postgraduate degrees are three times more likely to belong to HMOs than those with less than high school educations, the survey shows" (p. 78). Also, people who knew about HMOs were generally favorably disposed toward them. There are several good reasons for their popularity among educated people.

If you belong to an HMO, you are more likely to visit your doctor when you are well, because you have paid for the service whether or not you use it. Some HMOs charge nothing for such visits. Others combine a monthly fee with a reduced rate for office visits. Still others have added fees for X-rays, emergency calls, second opinions, and other services. In theory, employers and medical insurance companies save money because HMO members seek health-care services earlier, stay well more often, and thus reduce the incidence of major medical surgery and expensive extended hospital care. The major economic benefit for the member is the ability to budget a fixed amount for monthly health care and know in advance what that cost will be; in that sense, an HMO protects against emergencies and acts as a form of health-care insurance (Califano, 1986).

A major disadvantage is the loss of control in selecting a personal physician, along with losing the special bond that might have developed in a patient-physician relationship that evolved over a period of years. A large HMO may have dozens of physicians, any one of whom might treat you on a given occasion. Another possible disadvantage, particularly for the person who is conscientious about primary care and has few medical problems, is the expense of a monthly fee even when one is perfectly healthy. Taylor and Kagay (1986) predicted that HMO membership would continue to grow rapidly into the 1990s; based on the high cost of health insurance premiums, it was seen as one way to contain medical costs. More recent reports have been less optimistic, however, as HMOs are experiencing competition from alternative health-care delivery systems, all of whom are eager for their share of the enormous market. Arnett, McKusick, Sonnefeld, and Cowell (1986) projected that health expenditures would exceed $600 billion by 1990, more than 11 percent of the gross national product or about $2,400 annually for every U.S. citizen.

Preferred Provider Organizations

One of the most popular alternatives is the Preferred Provider Organization (PPO). The growth of PPOs was spurred by federal legislation requiring employers with 25 or more employees to provide a choice between traditional group insurance and a health maintenance-type program. Lissovoy, Rice, Gabel, and Gelzer (1987) described PPOs as "an arrangement whereby hospitals, physicians, or other care givers contract to provide services to a defined group of consumers on a discounted fee-for-service basis" (p. 127). Often the contract is between an employer and the PPO, requiring all employees to seek medical services from the same group of physicians or the same hospital in return for a reduced group rate. A PPO is viewed as a middle ground between HMOs and conventional fee-for-service medicine, providing some attractive features of each. The reduced group rate provides important economic advantages to the patient; all or part of the monthly cost may be assumed by the employer, and it is often possible for patients to specify the cooperating physician by whom they wish to be treated. There will undoubtedly be spin-offs of the HMO and PPO models as health-care providers continue to refine their approaches.

Third-Party Insurance Providers

Traditional health or medical insurance is sometimes referred to as a "third-party payment" system. It is so named because a first party needs a health service, a second party provides the service, and a third party pays for it. James

Califano, former Secretary of Health, Education, and Welfare, believes that the loopholes in such a system have been largely responsible for escalating health-care costs over the years (Califano, 1986). He contends that modern medical technology has provided options that everyone wants and not everyone can afford. Good insurance brings secondary care within reach of many who would not visit a doctor for immunizations, dental care, or regular checkups if all expenses were out-of-pocket. When a third party pays, the first party tends to seek more services, and the second party tends to provide more elaborate services. This makes the costs rise.

Because the third party is usually an employer or employer's insurance representative, those who are unemployed are doubly deprived. Without group insurance coverage, very few of those who are unemployed can afford medical fees on a per-service basis. They are also most likely to need health and medical services because unemployment leads to impoverished living conditions, such as crowded and unsanitary housing, less food and less nutritious food, and higher incidence of disease. This dilemma highlights one of the most value-laden issues of our times, the extent to which the federal government should assume responsibility for personal health care.

MEDICAL CARE PHILOSOPHIES WORLDWIDE

Globally, at least three very different philosophies exist for providing personal health care: state medicine, socialized medicine, and personalized medicine.

State Medicine

State medicine is practiced in one form or another in China, Cuba, and the USSR. Under this system the government pays physicians and hospitals directly and decides when a person is sick enough to require medical attention, when hospitalization is warranted, and which physician or hospital will provide the services. Little or nothing is left to personal decision-making.

Socialized Medicine

Socialized medicine is practiced in England, Sweden, and some parts of Canada. The principle behind socialized medicine is that every citizen is entitled to the necessary medical services, regardless of their ability to pay. Socialized medicine is paid for by taxes and tends to be very expensive and subject to abuse. For example, hypochondriacs who would otherwise not seek medical attention are likely to do so when they know the total cost will be borne by the government.

Personalized Medicine

Personalized medicine as traditionally practiced in the United States allows (or requires) each individual to decide when to visit a doctor, when to resort to hospitalization, where to seek services, and how to pay for them. Unfortunately, low-income families suffer most under this system because they can least afford the insurance or the uninsured services. To counteract this, two amendments to the Social Security Act were passed in 1965, resulting in *Medicare* and *Medicaid*.

Medicare and Medicaid

Medicare and Medicaid provide medical assistance for those over age 65, the poor, and the disabled. Because Medicaid is paid for by both state and federal governments, the benefits vary from one state to another, but they are almost always insufficient to cover all medical costs. Political conservatives have argued that Medicare and Medicaid are a big step toward socialized medicine, which they fear will lead to loss of individual initiative and a dependence on government subsidy. Political liberals stress the humanitarian aspects of Medicare and Medicaid, recognizing that not everyone can afford to pay for the necessary health care. Both sides generally agree that adequate health care for all citizens is unlikely to be provided at government expense without an increase in taxes. One exception may be the referendum reported by Danielson and Mazer (1987):

> On November 4, 1986, Massachusetts voters approved by 67% to 33% a statewide ballot question urging the United States Congress to enact a national health program which provides high quality comprehensive personal health care including preventive, curative and occupational health services; is universal in coverage, community controlled, rationally organized, equitably financed, with no out-of-pocket charges, is sensitive to the particular health needs of all, and is efficient in containing its cost; and whose yearly expenditure does not exceed the proportion of the Gross National Product spent on health care in the immediately preceding fiscal year. (p. 28)

Would you vote for this legislation? The fervor with which you would either support or reject this and similar legislation undoubtedly says much about your system of personal values.

Private Coverage

Blue Cross and Blue Shield are emblematic of the private coverage available for persons who are self-employed, unemployed, or otherwise uninsured. Blue Cross covers hospital expenses, and Blue Shield covers physician expenses. In the 1950s, Blue Cross and Blue Shield covered more than half of the country's population, and they are still widely used by those who are self-employed and those whose employers do not provide a health-care plan.

Whether you have group or private coverage, it is important for you to know exactly what services are covered. Too many of us don't! For example, does your hospitalization cover outpatient surgery or only inpatient surgery? If both, does it cover lab tests, anesthetics, and medications? Does it cover mental health care? Are optical and dental coverage included in your policy? Does your insurance pay for contact lenses, eyeglasses, dentures, and bridges, or only for the professional's office fees? Does it pay for private nursing care after you leave a hospital?

Diagnostic Related Groups

This latter question is a critical one because of the recent emergence of Diagnostic Related Groups (DRGs) in response to rapidly rising health care costs. DRGs maintain predetermined fee schedules for hundreds of health care diagnoses. Once a diagnosis has been rendered by a physician, the insurance company pays the hospital a set fee regardless of the length of stay or extent of services ultimately rendered. Unlike many earlier insurance programs, DRGs offer no incentive for a hospital to extend a patient's stay; it is advantageous to the hospital to release a patient as soon as approved by an attending physician.

The intent of the DRG system was to curb costs, but it doesn't always work that way. Unless your insurance company pays for home nursing care, you may end up paying that expense while you complete your recovery at home, an expense that would have been paid by insurance if you had stayed in the hospital. When health insurance is involved, it is wise to plan carefully and stay well informed.

ETHICAL MEDICAL CARE

The trend in the United States is toward reducing the need for tertiary medical care by improving primary and secondary care. When tertiary care does become necessary, though, it often involves difficult ethical decisions for medical professionals, patients, and patients' loved ones. In this section we will discuss some of those issues.

Harris (1985) provided an overview of issues involved in medical care ethics:

> Health care is one of the clearest and most visible expressions of a society's attitude to the value of life. It is moreover one of the most important dimensions of the way in which we, as individuals and as members of society, demonstrate the value that we place on one another's lives. (p. 1)

We need to consider at least the following questions: When does life cease, and when does it cease to have value? When does life begin, and when does it begin to have value? What makes human life valuable, and what makes it more valuable than other forms of life (if it is)? Is there a limit to the expense that can be justified in saving one human life? Might money spent on prolonging the life of a terminally ill person be better spent providing for the health needs of many others? These are not rhetorical questions. They are questions that must be answered by health care professionals on a daily basis, and that each of us must answer occasionally when faced with such issues as abortion, euthanasia, and the use of medical technology to extend human life.

John Locke, the English philosopher, argued that human life is different from, and more valuable than, animal life because humans have a *conscience*—the ability to know right from wrong—and the ability to reason as opposed to relying on animal instincts. Using this premise, Harris contended that any human life that retains these distinct features—conscience and reason—has value and should not be ended, and that any person who values his or her own existence should not be deprived of life.

Euthanasia

Harron, Burnside, and Beauchamp (1983) observed that "profound technological innovation always presents moral dilemmas and shakes our certainty about established values" (p. xii). With the improvement of medical technology, it becomes increasingly possible to prolong many human lives, sometimes prolonging suffering in the process. This raises other ethical questions. A values conflict arises between saving life and avoiding unnecessary suffering. The term *euthanasia* means "good death"—death that avoids prolonged suffering. *Active euthanasia* is the taking of direct steps to end a life (e.g., administering a lethal drug); *passive euthanasia* is refusing to prolong life through medical technology (e.g., disconnecting a life-sustaining system).

In 1973 the American Medical Association approved this position statement on euthanasia: "The intentional termination of the life of one human being by another—mercy killing—is contrary to that for which the medical profession stands and is contrary to the policy of the American Medical Association" (cited in Harron et al., 1983, p. 56). Indeed, active euthanasia (mercy killing) is illegal in all 50 states. Still, there are people who believe that active euthanasia would be more humane than allowing a person to die a slow, natural, sometimes painful death, and that each person ought to have the right to decide how she or he wishes to die. (Remember Hochbaum's claim, cited in chapter 3, that we should protect each individual's right to choose how she or he wishes to live and die?)

In spite of the AMA's position and state laws against euthanasia, "Living Wills" have become increasingly common in the past decade. The Living Will is a document that authorizes and directs the withholding or withdrawing of life support systems from the individual making the will if and when there is no reasonable expectation that she or he will recover from an illness or injury. Physicians face a moral and legal dilemma when a patient has some chance for survival but no reasonable chance for recovery. The distinction between the two terms is important: survival is continuation of life in any form, however devoid of meaning; recovery implies a return to a previous or normal state of living. Some courts have upheld the right of physicians and legal guardians to substitute their own judgments when there is no Living Will; but when these parties disagree on a course of action, litigation is likely to follow. Having a Living Will often helps avoid controversy.

In 1987, a Gallup poll conducted for *Hospitals Magazine* (Steiber, 1987b) revealed that "the vast majority of Americans polled (70 percent) are willing to have their own life-support systems disconnected should they lapse into a nonreversible coma. But a significant number (46 percent) stop short of making the decision for another person" (p. 72). However, even though 70 percent agree with the principle of passive euthanasia, only 9 percent have Living Wills. This may be another example of attitudes not being translated into actions. A majority of Americans (61 percent) have a favorable attitude toward passive euthanasia as it applies to their own lives, but apparently they do not value it sufficiently to act on it. This might be due partly to the uncertain effectiveness of having such a will. Different states have different laws about Living Wills, and physicians might be legally obliged to prolong human life regardless of the wishes of the patient or relatives.

The low percentage of people having Living Wills might be for a rather different reason, though. The point was driven home by Fox (1979), who described a group exercise in values clarification. During discussion there was widespread support for "the right to die" and criticism of medical systems that keep people alive

against their will and without purpose. At the end of the discussion, however, each participant was handed a copy of a Living Will and asked to read and sign it. Although the document was not legally binding, it would formalize the intent that had been expressed verbally. Only 5 of the 20 participants signed the document. If people are unwilling to make such a commitment for their own lives, imagine how much more difficult it becomes to make this decision when another's life is at stake.

This raises the complex question of relative worth of human lives. Are all human lives of equal value, regardless of health or circumstances? If so, how can you justify ending any human life, even passively? Conversely, if you really value all human lives, how can you justify committing a million dollars in medical resources to prolong the terminally unconscious life of a loved one when that same money would save the lives of dozens of starving infants in other parts of the world? How does one make such value judgments?

The Value of Life and the Cost of Health Care

Califano (1986) described a social phenomenon he referred to as "death control." America has become the first four-generation society in the history of the world, where is it not uncommon for the two oldest generations of a family to be living in retirement while the two youngest generations provide for their health and welfare. How long this will be economically possible is hard to say. Great Britain has already responded to a similar problem by refusing to provide kidney dialysis, hip replacements, and similar services for its senior citizens. "So," says Califano, "the British National Health Service, which provides free health care, also rations what it provides, making choices about who will live and who will die'' (p. 180). Is this likely to happen in America? Would you favor it? What does your response tell you about your system of values?

The underlying problem is described by Harron et al. (1983) as the ''slippery slope'': Once you make an exception, it is difficult to draw the line further down the slope; if you don't value one person's life enough to save it, it becomes a bit easier to give up on the lives of others with lesser problems.

Where do *you* draw the line? Two schools of thought that offer quite different solutions to the problem are deontology and utilitarianism. According to Solomon (1984), a *utilitarian* would argue that the right action is the one that brings the greatest good to the greatest number of people and that actions are justified only by such consequences. In this view, ending one life to save many others can be justified. Utilitarian reasoning is sometimes used to justify war and capital punishment, and you can probably think of many familiar cases of such reasoning in daily life. A *deontologist*, in contrast, believes that the moral rightness or wrongness of an action has nothing to do with the action's consequences and that human beings have a duty to do what is morally right regardless of consequences. Most deontologists would say that it is never morally right to end a human life. In this view, ending one life to save many others would not be justified.

Whether you take one of these extreme positions or some intermediate position, euthanasia is an issue worthy of your consideration. If you tell your loved ones your views on euthanasia, you can spare them much of the mental anguish they would feel if they had to make the decision for you without knowing what you would have preferred. Just as importantly, you need to know the preferences of your parents and other loved ones regarding their own lives.

Organ Transplantation

Another ethical issue we are being forced to face by the advances of medical technology has to do with organ transplants. How do you feel about contributing your vital organs to save other lives, if your own life is beyond recovery? The Uniform Anatomical Gift Card allows a potential donor to declare that, in the event of death, his or her organs are to be transplanted to waiting recipients. One important medical and ethical issue for organ transplants is deciding when a person is really dead. Is it when the heart stops beating for 10 minutes, when respiration ceases for 20 minutes, or when irreversible loss of consciousness occurs even though the heart and respiratory systems are still functioning? Who should make that decision, relatives or medical professionals? Time is of the essence, if the organs are to be of value to anyone.

As with euthanasia, it is important that you let your wishes about organ transplants be known while you are able to make such decisions for yourself.

Abortion

Just as perplexing is the issue of abortion, a practice that has existed throughout history, both legally and illegally. In 1973 the U.S. Supreme Court (*Roe v. Wade*) made a landmark decision that legalized abortion in this country. It is now federal law that, in the United States, an abortion can legally be performed at the request of the pregnant woman at any period of pregnancy, regardless of reason, except that the states may pass laws prohibiting third-trimester abortions in pregnancies that do not threaten the life or health of the pregnant woman. However, even though abortion is now legal in the United States, the moral acceptability of abortion is still being hotly debated.

Mappes and Zembaty (1987) have provided the following list of circumstances that are sometimes said to justify abortion:

- The mother's life will be endangered by giving birth.
- The mother's subsequent physical or mental health will be impaired by having a child.
- Prenatal tests reveal that the child would be so deformed that it would be incapable of valuing its own life.
- The pregnancy has resulted from rape or incest.
- The child is illegitimate, so both mother and child would be socially stigmatized.
- Having a child will pose a financial burden for the parents.
- Having a child will interfere with the mother's career or personal happiness.

Conservatives insist that an embryo is a human being at conception, and so might claim that none of the above circumstances morally justifies abortion. Liberals might assert that an embryo does not have human qualities for at least three months, and so might condone abortion for any or all of the cited reasons. Moderates neither condemn nor condone all abortions, but consider each case on its merits. Which reasons you find acceptable and unacceptable reveals a great deal about your values. Just as with choosing a personal physician, it is a judgment that ought to be made before necessity requires a hasty and ill-considered decision.

Harris (1985) offered some insightful thoughts for our consideration. He contended that, biologically, there is nothing about a human embryo during the first trimester that would allow an observer to distinguish it from various animal embryos. Harris also rejected the notion that a human embryo ought to be considered a human life simply because it has the *potential* to become a human. He pointed out that each of us will eventually die, but we shouldn't be treated as if we were dead just because we have the *potential* to die. Therefore, he concluded, embryos ought not to be considered human simply because they have human potential. He believes that when the embryo becomes a recognizable human fetus and capable of sustaining life on its own, it is deserving of the same concern and respect accorded other human beings.

If you find yourself shocked or outraged by Harris's position, you can be assured that he has touched on a value about which you have strong feelings, the value of human life. It is in the very nature of values that we react emotionally to opposing views. I am less interested in supporting or refuting his position than I am in applauding his willingness to take a position and his ability to offer what he considers to be a rational explanation. It is the process rather than the conclusion that I commend to you. It is a process that you can apply to other ethical issues, such as surrogate motherhood, artificial insemination, predetermination of an offspring's sex, cloning, and gene-splicing. Each of these requires you to make value judgments.

SUMMARY

America has more hospitals, physicians, health educators, and advanced medical technology than any other country in the history of the world, yet we lead the world in degenerative disorders. Better primary care, over which you have direct control for yourself, would reduce your risk of heart disease, cancer, high blood pressure, stroke, emphysema, and cirrhosis of the liver. These diseases are typically caused by excesses—too much smoking, too much alcohol, too much stress, too much inactivity, and too much obesity. You can minimize your risks of these diseases by giving yourself good primary care.

Our country is in the midst of revolutionary change in the delivery of secondary and tertiary care. Health care is among the leading causes of inflation in America today. In an effort to cope with rising health care costs, we have seen the emergence or escalation of HMOs, PPOs, DRGs, outpatient surgery, walk-in emergency rooms, home nursing services, second opinions prior to major medical treatment, and incentive programs designed to reduce the need for secondary and tertiary care. It is both healthy and financially expedient for you to stay abreast of these and other changes in the health care industry.

During your lifetime you will undoubtedly be required to make difficult decisions about issues that involve value judgments and come under the general heading of medical ethics. You must consider under what circumstances you are willing to help create a human life, and under what circumstances you are willing to end a human life, whether it be your own or that of a loved one. If your system of values is well developed, your decisions are more likely to be consistent and humane. You might wish to apply Immanuel Kant's categorical imperative: Behave as you would be willing to have everyone behave in your circumstances; or treat others as they would be justified in treating you if your roles were reversed. This is the nucleus of ethical behavior, medical or otherwise.

Examining Your Values

Imagine this situation (adapted from Harron et al., 1983): A 70-year-old man has been institutionalized all his life and has a mental age of less than 2 years. He has never learned to speak, and communicates with grunts and gestures. He has now contracted a fatal form of leukemia, and his physician projects that the chemotherapy he is currently undergoing can extend his life another 3 to 6 months. However, the side effects of the chemotherapy are making him violently ill. He obviously doesn't understand why he is ill or why he is being forced to undergo this treatment. You are his lone surviving relative.

1. Would you ask the doctor to practice passive euthanasia?
2. Would you pay for his continued chemotherapy?
3. Would you expect his continued health care to be provided at the expense of taxpayers?
4. As a taxpayer, are you prepared to contribute to the continued health care of thousands of people like this?
5. Are your actions consistent with your personal system of values, as expressed earlier in this book?

Imagine this situation (adapted from Harris, 1985): Creatures from the planet Aquarius have invaded the earth. They are not humans, but they are technologically superior to us, so they have taken control.

1. Why should they treat you differently than you treat ''lesser'' creatures, like dogs, livestock, fish, or fowl, which you have probably always used to serve your own needs?
2. How would you convince them that you are ''valuable'' and thus worth saving?

CHAPTER 5
Physical Activity, Exercise, and Physical Fitness

Physical fitness is not only one of the most important keys to a healthy body, it is the basis of dynamic and creative intellectual activity.

—John F. Kennedy

A human being is the kind of machine that wears out from lack *of use.*

—George Leonard

Self-Examination Statements

Instructions: Read each statement, then circle the x in the column at the left that most closely describes your belief about that statement. (Use a pencil. After reading this chapter you may wish to come back and change some of your responses on the basis of new information or attitudes.)

SA = strongly agree   **A** = agree   **U** = undecided   **D** = disagree   **SD** = strongly disagree

SA	A	U	D	SD	
x	x	x	x	x	I understand the concept of exercise.
x	x	x	x	x	I understand the difference between physical activity and exercise.
x	x	x	x	x	I understand the difference between physical activity and physical fitness.
x	x	x	x	x	I think of myself as a physically fit person.
x	x	x	x	x	My self-concept improves as I become more physically fit.
x	x	x	x	x	I value being physically fit for health reasons.
x	x	x	x	x	I value being physically fit for reasons other than health.
x	x	x	x	x	My family places high value on physical fitness.
x	x	x	x	x	My best friend is more physically fit than I am.
x	x	x	x	x	I am more physically fit than the average person my age.
x	x	x	x	x	I know how to measure my physical fitness.
x	x	x	x	x	I don't exercise regularly because I don't see the value in it.

X	X	X	X	X	I don't exercise regularly because I don't have time.
X	X	X	X	X	I don't exercise regularly because it is too inconvenient.
X	X	X	X	X	I don't exercise regularly because it requires expending too much energy.
X	X	X	X	X	I intend to get/stay physically fit.
X	X	X	X	X	I know exactly what to do to get/stay physically fit.
X	X	X	X	X	I currently have a physical fitness program.
X	X	X	X	X	I have an internal locus of control when it comes to physical fitness.
X	X	X	X	X	I get a great deal of physical activity in a normal day.
X	X	X	X	X	I look for ways to be more physically active.
X	X	X	X	X	I think of myself as more physically active than physically fit.
X	X	X	X	X	I stay physically fit by participating in sports.
X	X	X	X	X	My favorite sports cause me to perspire.
X	X	X	X	X	I know the major health benefits of exercise.
X	X	X	X	X	I know five health-related attributes of physical fitness.
X	X	X	X	X	I understand the concept of aerobic exercise.
X	X	X	X	X	I understand the difference between aerobic and anaerobic exercise.
X	X	X	X	X	I can name at least five kinds of aerobic exercise.
X	X	X	X	X	I believe that regular and vigorous exercise helps prevent heart disease.
X	X	X	X	X	I am more interested in the wellness aspect of physical fitness than in the preventive aspect.
X	X	X	X	X	I feel better mentally when I am physically fit.
X	X	X	X	X	Keeping fit gives me more energy for routine daily activities.
X	X	X	X	X	I like the appearance of muscles that are well toned and/or well defined.
X	X	X	X	X	I know how to efficiently develop muscular strength.
X	X	X	X	X	I know how to efficiently develop muscular endurance.
X	X	X	X	X	I can distinguish between isometric, isotonic, and isokinetic exercise.
X	X	X	X	X	It is my perception that many people who used to exercise have quit because of injuries.
X	X	X	X	X	I know how to protect myself from injury when I exercise or participate in sports.
X	X	X	X	X	I believe that stretching prior to exercise reduces the risk of injury.
X	X	X	X	X	I understand the difference between active and passive stretching.
X	X	X	X	X	I understand the difference between stretching and warming up.
X	X	X	X	X	Being safe from injury and illness is a major factor in my choice of physical activities.
X	X	X	X	X	I purposely choose activities that involve some risk-taking; that's what makes them rewarding.
X	X	X	X	X	What I enjoy most about fitness activities is the affiliation with other people.
X	X	X	X	X	I enjoy sports because of the competition, with myself and others.

| x | x | x | x | x | I like activities that provide opportunities for achievement and recognition. |
| x | x | x | x | x | Physical activities are a great way to self-actualize—become the best I am capable of becoming. |

DEFINING TERMS AND CONCEPTS

According to Slater, Green, Vernon, and Keith (1987), "The first U.S. Surgeon General's Report on Health Promotion and Disease Prevention gave fitness its first prominence in health policy, singling it out as one of 15 priorities for health promotion" (p. 107). In 1980 the publication *Promoting Health/Preventing Disease: Objectives for the Nation* called for participation in *regular* and *vigorous* physical activity by 90 percent of youths and 60 percent of adults by 1990. "Although increased physical activity is thought to be beneficial to health, different researchers have reached opposite conclusions, perhaps because they used such widely varying definitions of 'physical activity' " (Washburn, Adams, & Haile, 1987, p. 636).

Various studies have estimated that as few as 15 percent and as many as 78 percent of Americans are "physically active," depending on their definition of that term. It seems that a person can be "physically active" without being "physically fit" and without "exercising." Casperson, Powell, and Christianson (1985) recognized the problems created by using those three terms inconsistently or interchangeably. They proposed the following definitions, which clearly distinguish the three:

- *Physical activity* is defined as any bodily movement produced by skeletal muscles that results in energy expenditure. The energy expenditure can be measured in kilocalories. Physical activity in daily life can be categorized into occupational, sports, conditioning, household, or other activities.

- *Exercise* is a subset of physical activity that is planned, structured, and repetitive and has as a final or an intermediate objective the improvement or maintenance of physical fitness.

- *Physical fitness* is a set of attributes that are either health- or skill-related. The degree to which people have these attributes can be measured with specific tests. (p. 126)

Health-related fitness attributes include cardiorespiratory and cardiovascular endurance, muscular endurance, muscular strength, body composition, and flexibility. Skill-related fitness attributes include agility, balance, coordination, speed, power, and reaction time.

Virtually everything we do each day requires physical activity, but most of it does not qualify as exercise because it is not planned, structured, repetitive, or done with the intent of acquiring physical fitness. Walking is a good example of a physical activity that may or may not qualify as a form of exercise; whether it is depends on its *frequency, intensity*, and *duration*, factors that determine whether or not an activity leads to any of the health-related fitness attributes mentioned. There are well-established guidelines for exercising to meet physical fitness objectives, as we will see later.

FITNESS AS A FORM OF PREVENTION

Much of the literature on physical fitness emphasizes its role in preventing coronary heart disease (CHD). CHD is the leading cause of death in the United States, killing more than 750,000 people each year. Researchers at the Centers for Disease Control in Atlanta now believe that the link between heart disease and physical inactivity may be as predictive of CHD as the links between heart disease and smoking or high blood pressure; a 2-year analysis by Powell, Thompson, Casperson, and Kendrick (1987) of the best studies on CHD concluded that the least active people are almost twice as likely to have heart disease as those who are most active. Further, ''The observations reported in the literature support the inference that physical activity is inversely and *causally* [emphasis added] related to the incidence of CHD'' (p. 283). This is a very powerful statement! Only 10 to 20 percent of Americans engage in regular aerobic exercise, which is the best kind for developing and maintaining a healthy heart, so the vast majority of Americans are placing themselves unnecessarily at risk with their sedentary lifestyle. The authors urged a public policy that provides citizens with incentives for engaging in regular physical activity. Among them might be released time from work for exercise (a practice that has been common in the armed services for years), availability of free public biking and hiking trails throughout the country, or a federal income tax break for those whose activity patterns result in a healthy level of physical fitness.

Benefits of Regular, Vigorous Exercise

Paffenbarger and his associates (1978, 1984, 1986) have provided some of the most persuasive evidence of the protective effects of regular and vigorous exercise. They began gathering data on Harvard alumni in 1962. By 1978 they had information about nearly 17,000 individuals, of whom 572 had experienced heart attacks. The authors compared the physical activity patterns of heart attack victims with those who had not had

an attack. Their measures of physical activity included flights of stairs climbed, city blocks walked, time spent engaged in light sports (e.g., golf, bowling, boating), and time spent engaged in strenuous sports (e.g., running, swimming, skiing). They discovered that any combination of these activities that burned 2,000 kilocalories or more per week reduced the risk of CHD by one quarter to one third. ''Death rates declined steadily as energy expended on such activity increased from less than 500 to 3500 kcal per week, beyond which rates increased slightly'' (Paffenbarger, Hyde, Wing, & Hsich, 1986, p. 605).

Is It Possible to Overdo?

If this suggests to you that there is also a risk of getting too much physical activity, consider the following. Climbing one flight of stairs burns approximately 4 kilocalories; unless you are climbing more than 1,000 flights of stairs per week, you probably don't have to worry about overexertion. Walking one city block expends about 8 kilocalories, so you can walk over 400 blocks per week without worry. Strenuous sports burn about 10 kilocalories per minute, or 600 per hour, and light sports about half that amount. (Table 7.2 on page 99 provides a list of additional activities and an approximate number of kilocalories burned by each.) Therefore, 3 hours per week of strenuous sports activity, plus some lighter activity interspersed throughout the week, would be sufficient to move you into the recommended 2,000 kilocalories-per-week range. More than 6 hours of vigorous activity per week might lead to diminishing returns in terms of protection from CHD, but there may be offsetting benefits in other areas. According to the Harvard data, alumni who reported no sports activity during their normal week were at 38 percent greater risk of CHD than those who reported weekly strenuous sports activity. It is on the basis of this and similar research that *regular* and *vigorous* physical activity is advocated as a preventive behavior.

Is Moderate Activity Beneficial?

For those not interested in sports, or those not willing or not able to exert themselves at that level, lighter forms of activity (like walking) may be just as healthy; it simply takes longer to burn the desired number of calories. Many health professionals believe that this is the wiser course of action as one gets older, considering the injuries possible from many strenuous forms of exercise. It is important to understand, though, that physical activity is not an all-or-none proposition; the difference between no activity and moderate activity may be even more critical than going from moderate to strenuous activity.

The Effects of Lifelong Activity and Smoking

Two other points of interest should be noted from the 1986 Harvard study. First, alumni who had been varsity athletes in college fared no better than their nonvarsity classmates unless they continued to maintain a high level of physical activity after graduation. Second, the study confirmed the commonly-held notion that cigarette smoking and exercise have strong opposite influences on health. "At each level of exercise, a reduction in smoking from one or more packs down to none cut the risk of death in half" (Paffenbarger et al., 1986, p. 608). Can you afford to pass up that kind of benefit?

Aerobic Exercise and Heart Disease

Similar results have been reported by most other researchers, so there can be little doubt about the benefits of physical activity and physical fitness. Dr. Kenneth Cooper, founder of the Aerobic Institute in Dallas, Texas, has written extensively about the benefits of aerobic ("with oxygen") exercise (Cooper, 1982). He believes that aerobic exercise produces a training effect vastly superior to that of anaerobic exercise; details on this topic will appear later in this chapter. Blair, Goodyear, Gibbons, and Cooper (1984) used treadmills to measure the physical fitness of over 6,000 men and women aged 20 to 65. Based on their review of the literature and their own data, they concluded that low levels of physical fitness are associated with increased CHD and contribute to increased risk of hypertension and that regular aerobic exercise increases physical fitness and improves CHD risk profiles for both men and women.

Results of Studies in Great Britain and Belgium

Morris, Pollard, Everitt, and Shane (1980) studied nearly 18,000 middle-aged men in Great Britain. They reported that over the 8-1/2 years of the study, the incidence of CHD for men who engaged in vigorous sports or otherwise kept fit was less than half that of subjects who reported no vigorous exercise. The authors defined vigorous exercise as exercise "above the intensity required for a training effect" (p. 1210). The training effect is any combination of changes that make the body function more efficiently, particularly in its transport and use of oxygen. As in the Harvard alumni study, they controlled for other risk factors such as age, family history of CHD, obesity, cigarette smoking, and hypertension.

Sobolski et al. (1987) tested healthy male factory workers in Belgium for 5 years. Their initial measure of physical fitness was ability to sustain exercise at a heart rate of 150 beats per minute. They measured physical activity as the combined total of calories burned daily on the job and during leisure activities. Comparing the incidence of coronary heart disease at each level of physical fitness and physical activity, the authors concluded that fitness, but not activity, protects against heart disease.

Aerobic Activity in the U.S.

Stephens, Jacobs, and White (1985) reviewed eight U.S. and Canadian national surveys of leisure-time physical activity patterns. The authors concluded that "the proportion of the population that is physically active during its leisure time has increased substantially in recent years" (p. 155). Still, only about 20 percent met the level recommended for cardiovascular benefits, another 40 percent were moderately active, perhaps enough to receive some health benefits, and the final 40 percent were completely sedentary. Using income, education, and occupation as criteria for socioeconomic status, the authors noted a positive relationship between higher levels of physical activity and higher socioeconomic status. It is also interesting to note that the most popular activities—walking, swimming, calisthenics, bicycling, and jogging—are inexpensive and convenient and allow for varying intensities and flexible scheduling. The absence of these characteristics is often perceived as a barrier to continuing an activity (see Hochbaum's Health Belief Model).

Physical Activity and Cancer

There are other benefits of physical activity besides reducing the risk of coronary heart disease. Malesky (1988) reported that there may be a link with cancer prevention as well. One Harvard study found that, of college women, those who were active in sports had fewer than half as many cases of cancer of the breasts, uterus, ovaries, cervix, and vagina as those who were not active in sports. Many studies have concluded that physically active men are much less likely to develop colon cancer than inactive men (Friend, 1988). Although these studies do not prove that exercise prevents cancer, Malesky

(1988) points out that the evidence "has been enough to convince the American Cancer Society to recommend exercise as one possible way to reduce the risk of this killer disease" (pp. 28, 30). There are already many good reasons to exercise, but preventing cancer could be one more!

As we have already seen, many factors besides health influence human behavior, and knowledge that a behavior is healthy is not sufficient to induce the behavior if there are significant barriers or costs. However, even though regular and vigorous physical activity clearly is healthy, our earlier premise was that our choices of behavior should be based primarily on quality of life and not prevention of illness. Many of us would probably continue to seek vigorous activity even if it were not healthy. Let us consider why this is so.

FITNESS AS A FORM OF WELLNESS

In chapters 1 and 2 we mentioned Maslow's hierarchy of human needs. We return to it now as a useful model for explaining why people behave as they do.

Using physical activity to prevent heart disease and other illnesses is an excellent way to satisfy your needs for safety and security. You may recall, however, that safety and security represent only the second level (after physiological needs) of Maslow's hierarchy, there being three higher levels of needs. It is my belief that, when one begins to use physical activity to fulfill higher level needs for affiliation, esteem, and self-actualization, physical activity is serving wellness rather than prevention purposes.

The Role of Fitness in Developing a Social Support Group

In chapter 2 we learned about the importance of developing what Naroll called a moral network, a group of friends and family members to whom we give and from whom we receive social support. These are the people we turn to in troubled times; but they are also the people who add quality to our lives during good times, which is what wellness is all about.

Remembering that physical fitness can be achieved not only through formal exercise but also through less formal physical activity, think of the rich variety of physical activities that enable us to combine affiliation and physical fitness needs: team sport membership; regular participation in a golf foursome; doubles competition in bowling or tennis; a jog in the park, a swim at the lake, or a bike ride through the country with a friend; a walk on the beach or dancing with a loved one. You can add your own examples, from skiing to scuba diving, from aerobic dance to yachting, but the bottom line is that physical activity should be fun! It is usually more fun when done with other people, especially with people we know and care about, than when done alone. The fact that it is also good for our health should be viewed as a bonus, not as our primary motivation for being active.

Developing Self-Esteem Through Fitness

The fourth level on Maslow's hierarchy is the need for ego/self-esteem, which has to do with achievement and recognition. Sports are a part of our culture that provides endless opportunities for achievement and recognition, as a glimpse at any newspaper will attest. Check television programming and you will again discover the prominent place of sports in our society. You may surmise, as I do, that American obsession with sports has become excessive, yet the potential of sports for fulfilling human needs makes them appealing for all age groups. In addition to high school, college, and professional athletes, we increasingly recognize the achievements of youth participants and senior citizens. Where else in life can one get similar recognition

by doing something that is healthy, enjoyable, and filled with innumerable opportunities for affiliation with others of like interests?

Aside from sports, there is evidence that simply being physically fit improves self-concept, thus improving self-esteem. Recall that, in the Rokeach system of beliefs, changing self-concept is central to initiating changes in behavior. Pauly, Palmer, Wright, and Pfeiffer (1982) reported on a study of male and female employees of the Xerox Corporation who participated in a 14-week aerobic exercise program. The authors found that "significant improvements overall were found in self-concept (physical, personal and social)" (p. 457). This is not an unusual finding for such studies. Fitness programs produce health benefits, lower medical and insurance costs, and lower sick-leave rates. But employers are discovering that productivity also rises because employees with positive self-concepts and high self-esteem are more dedicated to their work and miss fewer days for nonhealth reasons.

Fitness's Contribution to Self-Actualization

This brings us to Maslow's fifth and highest level of needs, the need to self-actualize, or the satisfaction you feel from doing your best. I recommend that you read *The Joy of Sports* (1976) by Michael Novak because it beautifully describes how we can self-actualize through physical activity and, specifically, competitive sports.

The Joy of Competition

Novak believes that the joy of sport is in the competition, but he is quick to add that the ultimate satisfaction is competing with oneself rather than against opponents, constantly striving to achieve higher levels of skill and performance. This explains why records are kept and cherished. The stopwatch and the tape measure provide evidence of excellence even when there is no opponent in sight. The 300 game in bowling, the par round in golf, and the 4-minute mile are measures of excellence understood worldwide. The real challengers in competitive sports are often these standards of excellence and not the particular opponents. Millions of Americans who started jogging for health reasons have entered competition, ranging from 5-kilometer runs to ultramarathons and triathlons. Almost without exception, these individuals are more pleased by a new personal-best performance than by winning a particular race against other competitors. Anyone who has experienced this joy of sport can appreciate the fact that competition can enhance quality of life and help us approach high-level wellness.

The Benefits of Noncompetitive Exercise

For those who are less competitive by nature, there is adequate evidence that noncompetitive exercise also has its benefits. Hayes and Ross (1986) have concluded, consistent with the findings of many other researchers, that "persons who exercise more and persons with good physical health have higher levels of psychological well-being than those who exercise less and have poor physical health" (p. 394). One of the reasons is that exercise changes the chemical balance of the body, stimulating the production of endorphins, which are natural opiates that tend to increase feelings of well-being and euphoria commonly referred to as "runner's high." Another reason offered by Hayes and Ross is that physical health and fitness are highly valued in our society; thus, there is a social incentive beyond the physical and emotional dimensions. Further verification of the important role of physical activity comes from Dishman, Ickes, and Morgan (1980), who concluded that "there is substantial evidence to support the prevalent belief within the health sciences that

habitual physical activity enhances both physiological and psychological well-being" (p. 116).

Despite the evidence, you may choose to avoid physical activity and to risk possible coronary heart disease and other illnesses. Or you may choose to participate in physical activity or exercise because you think it is healthy and will keep you safe from illness in general. You might also choose to be physically active because it propels you toward a higher level of wellness, meeting personal needs for affiliation, esteem, and self-satisfaction. Applying the values clarification process should help you make this choice. I believe that an active lifestyle will add years and quality to my life, and that it will do the same for you. If you highly value a long life with the benefits exercise provides, your choice should be an easy one.

FITNESS THROUGH EXERCISE

One approach to physical fitness is to develop a lifestyle filled with a variety of spontaneous physical activities. Another, as defined by Casperson et al. (1985), is to develop a planned, structured, and repetitive program of activity, which we call *exercise*. The latter is the more methodical approach and normally involves giving attention to the 5 health-related attributes identified earlier:

- Cardiovascular and cardiorespiratory endurance
- Muscular strength
- Muscular endurance
- Flexibility
- Body composition

There are certain principles of exercise that will enable you to achieve health-related fitness more efficiently. The remainder of this chapter is devoted to those principles.

Cardiovascular and Cardiorespiratory Endurance

A healthy body requires a healthy heart, healthy blood vessels, and healthy lungs. *Cardio* refers to heart, *vascular* to vessels, and *respiratory* to lungs. Together, cardiovascular and cardiorespiratory endurance are generally conceded to be the most important health factors. The following are some of the health hazards associated with poor cardiovascular and cardiorespiratory endurance:

- Coronary thrombosis
- Atherosclerosis
- Arteriosclerosis
- Hypertension
- Apoplexy
- Emphysema

A thrombus is a blood clot, and a coronary thrombosis is a heart attack caused by a thrombus that blocks a coronary artery of the heart. This is the number one cause of death in the United States today. Atherosclerosis is a clogging of the blood vessels, in particular the coronary arteries, shutting off the supply of blood to the heart muscle. Substances that clog the arteries are commonly referred to as fats, lipids, cholesterol, or plaque. Coronaries and heart attacks typically result from clogged arteries.

Arteriosclerosis is hardening of the arteries. Hypertension is high blood pressure, and is often caused by arteriosclerosis. Apoplexy, or stroke, is a result of a ruptured blood vessel in the brain, the product of extreme hypertension, which in turn was probably precipitated by arteriosclerosis. Apoplexy is the third leading cause of death.

Emphysema destroys the alveoli, tiny air sacs in the lungs that process oxygen to the bloodstream. Exercise enhances the efficiency of the alveoli, whereas smoking diminishes that efficiency and causes emphysema.

Anything that causes blood vessels to harden, clog, or break is detrimental to your health, as is anything that reduces the efficiency of the respiratory system. Similarly, behaviors that keep the blood vessels soft, pliable, and open, so that blood may flow through them freely, are conducive to good health. This is the role of *aerobic* exercise.

Effects of Aerobic Exercise

Aerobic exercise is the only type of exercise that significantly develops cardiovascular and cardiorespiratory endurance, and it is therefore the most important from the standpoint of health maintenance. The concept of aerobic exercise became popular in the early 1970s, and many authorities believe that Dr. Kenneth Cooper (1968, 1972, 1982) provided the primary impetus for the fitness movement that has swept the United States since that time. *Aerobic* means "with oxygen." To be aerobic, a form of exercise must be rhythmic, continuous, and vigorous enough in nature to increase aerobic efficiency (often called *the training effect*—which will be described later in this chapter). Activities widely used to create the training effect follow.

- Jogging
- Swimming
- Cycling
- Cross-country skiing
- Rowing
- Aerobic dance

Walking may also qualify, depending on the pulse rate attained.

Effects of Anaerobic Exercise

By contrast, anaerobic means "without oxygen." Anaerobic exercise lacks the rhythmic and vigorous movement necessary to qualify as aerobic activity (e.g., golf or bowling), or it may be too vigorous (e.g., running or swimming sprints) and thus lack the continuity that produces the training effect. Physical activity of sudden, brief intensity produces oxygen debt, a feeling of breathlessness that causes the participant to stop activity long enough to recover, and the activity is therefore too brief to move the body into an aerobic state. When oxygen debt occurs, the heart and lungs cannot meet the body's demands for oxygen. Aerobic exercise is of moderate intensity, fast enough to increase the body's demand for oxygen, but slow enough to allow continuation without reaching a state of extreme oxygen debt.

Establishing Aerobic Training Effect

The training effect is a combination of the following systematic changes that occur primarily in the circulatory and respiratory systems as a result of regular and vigorous aerobic exercise:

- Lower resting pulse rate
- Lower working (post-exercise) pulse rate
- Faster recovery of the pulse to normal
- Increase in the body's blood volume
- Higher red blood cell and hemoglobin count
- Larger stroke volume of the heart
- Greater elasticity of the blood vessels
- Increase in collateral circulation in the coronary arteries
- Lower systolic and diastolic blood pressure
- Increase of high density lipids (HDL) in the blood
- Decrease of low density lipids (LDL) and triglycerides
- Increase in the vital capacity of the lungs
- Decrease in the residual volume of the lungs
- Higher resting metabolic rate (RMR)
- Activation of beta endorphins ("runner's high")
- Decrease in anxiety and depression
- Harder bones, reducing the risk of osteoporosis

Part of the training effect is that the heart becomes larger, heavier, and stronger, increasing its *stroke volume*—the amount of blood pumped by the heart with each beat. The body's blood volume also increases with training. A trained individual may have 6 quarts of blood, as opposed to the 5 quarts or so that are normal for an untrained person of the same size. In the trained body, each unit of blood has a greater number of red blood cells and a higher hemoglobin count. Because oxygen is carried to the muscles by the hemoglobin in the red blood cells, this increase has great significance for the overall training effect.

Aerobic exercise also increases the *vital capacity* and reduces the *residual volume* of the lungs. Vital capacity is the amount of air exhaled in one breath, and residual volume is the air that remains in the lungs after a complete exhalation. One way to get more oxygen to the working muscles is to exhale more completely, thereby allowing more space in the lungs for freshly oxygenated air. For example, a person with emphysema might only be able to exhale about 25 percent of the air in the lungs, whereas a trained athlete can exhale approximately 75 percent of the air in the lungs.

Although complete exhalation is never desirable because the lungs would collapse, a healthy person who is physically fit has a higher percentage of air exchange per respiration than an unfit person. The common measure of physical fitness is *maximum oxygen uptake ($\dot{V}O_2max$)*, the amount of air that can be exchanged by the lungs in a specified period of time. A physically fit person is able to inhale more deeply, exhale more completely, and do so more often per minute, thereby maximizing the oxygen exchange rate.

Three other important aspects of the training effect are elasticity of blood vessels, lowered blood pressure, and collateral circulation. As the heart becomes stronger and stroke volume increases, the force with which the blood passes through the vessels also increases. This results in a flushing effect, preventing plaque and cholesterol from collecting in the coronary arteries. Elasticity negates arteriosclerosis, and the flushing effect negates atherosclerosis. That combination also helps keep blood pressure down, because open and elastic blood vessels ease circulation. Blood pressure, the force of blood pushing against arterial walls, is greater when the heart contracts (*systolic* pressure) than when it is at rest between beats (*diastolic* pressure). Remember, systolic pressure is always greater than diastolic, but an elevation in either one may indicate hypertension. Although there is some disagreement about how high these measures can be before you enter the danger range, if your diastolic pressure is 90 or above or your systolic pressure is 140 or above, you ought to seek medical attention (Rodale, 1987b).

Collateral circulation involves those arteries, veins, and capillaries that come into use on a supply-and-demand basis. Just as a telephone switchboard has a network of lines, most of which go unused at any given time but all of which can be used during peak periods of demand, many of the body's blood vessels go unused except in periods of peak demand (Cooper, 1968). Aerobic exercise causes more of the vessels to be used. As a result, the body's circulatory system becomes more efficient at carrying oxygen to the muscles.

Another important aspect of the training effect is the increase in the high density lipids (HDL) in the blood and the decrease in the low density lipids (LDL) and triglycerides. You may recall from chapter 3 that HDL seems to have a protective effect against coronary heart disease, whereas higher levels of LDL and triglycerides are associated with higher incidences of coronary heart disease. One explanation is that HDL lubricates the interior of the coronary arteries, reducing the amount of LDL or plaque that

might otherwise collect and block blood flow through the vessels. However it works, the increase in HDL that accompanies aerobic training is a major health bonus.

Finally, as the human body becomes more efficient at processing oxygen during aerobic exercise, it also becomes more efficient at rest. The resting pulse rate decreases because, for example, the trained heart can pump as much blood in 50 contractions per minute as the untrained heart might require 75 contractions to transport. Thus, resting heart rate is often used as one indication of fitness. The lower the resting heart rate, the more physically fit the individual. A fit individual also recovers more quickly from vigorous exercise, and the pulse rate returns to near normal more readily. This becomes significant over a long period of time because the heart of the unfit individual, compared to that of the fit individual, works much harder even during very mild activity and continues working harder long after activity ceases.

The Three Factors of Aerobic Efficiency

The efficiency with which aerobic exercise produces cardiorespiratory fitness is based on three factors (FIT):

- **F**requency
- **I**ntensity
- **T**ime or duration

The American College of Sports Medicine established effective guidelines for each of these variables, based on years of accumulated research (Howley & Franks, 1986).

Exercising on alternate days is generally regarded as more efficient than exercising on consecutive days, and a frequency of 3 days per week is sufficient to produce significant gains in cardiovascular and cardiorespiratory endurance.

Intensity is easily measured in terms of maximal heart rate, the recommended range being

65 to 90 percent of maximum capacity. Because age decreases maximal heart rate, a widely adopted formula is 220 minus age, times desired percentage of work rate. Thus a 20-year-old athlete preparing for competition might exercise at an intensity of 180 heartbeats per minute

$$(220 - 20 \text{ yrs} = 200 \times 90\% = 180),$$

whereas a middle-aged adult who is primarily interested in maintaining a healthy heart might choose to work at 135 beats per minute

$$(220 - 40 \text{ yrs} = 180 \times 75\% = 135).$$

Can you calculate your desired level of intensity based on your age and your purpose for exercising?

The duration or time of the aerobic workout is also important. Significant benefits are not likely in less than 30 minutes, 20 of which should be devoted to the aerobic activity, preceded by 5 minutes of warming up and followed by 5 minutes of warming down (cooling off).

Pulse rate is a useful gauge of both exercise intensity and level of fitness. It can be determined by applying light pressure with the index and middle fingers either on the carotid artery along either side of the neck or on the radial artery at the base of the thumb. Resting pulse rates vary widely among individuals, but most are in the range of 50 to 80 beats per minute. The lower resting pulse rates usually correlate positively with cardiorespiratory fitness, although hereditary influences and certain medications make this an imperfect measure. Still, if your resting pulse rate is gradually declining, you can be fairly certain that your fitness level is rising.

Muscular Strength and Muscular Endurance

Muscular strength and muscular endurance are actually two separate health-related attributes of physical fitness, but for our purposes it will suffice to discuss them in the same category. To be truly healthy, you need sufficient muscular strength and endurance to be able to perform routine daily tasks and to meet unusual or emergency situations as they arise. Even nonathletes need a reasonable level of strength and stamina if they are to avoid injury and meet the demands of a busy day. The strength and endurance of skeletal muscles can be improved by using one or more of the following types of exercise:

- Isotonic
- Isometric
- Isokinetic

By definition, *isotonic* exercise is muscular tension with muscular movement, while *isometric* exercise involves muscular tension without range of motion. Lifting 50 pounds would be isotonic; trying and failing to lift 500 pounds would be isometric. Although isometrics have less potential for improving muscular strength and endurance, they are a convenient and inexpensive supplement to isotonic and isokinetic exercise. Most exercise is isotonic; weight training, calisthenics, chopping wood, and spading a garden are examples. *Isokinetic* exercise has become increasingly popular in the past two decades and differs from isotonic exercise in that there is constant resistance throughout the range of motion. Nautilus is one of several lines of weight training equipment that utilizes isokinetic principles.

To appreciate why weight training and calisthenics are used to develop muscular strength and endurance, you need to understand the principles of *overload, specificity*, and *progressive resistance*.

Overload

Unused muscles atrophy (get smaller), and muscles used extensively hypertrophy (grow larger). The overload principle is based on the fact that placing a greater burden on a particular muscle makes it work harder and thus causes it to become stronger. A muscle needs to be worked at approximately 75 percent of its maximum capacity if it is to develop both strength and endurance (Table 5.1) Working a muscle at less than about 60 percent of its maximum capacity will not yield significant results; this is referred to as the *lower threshold* of training. Working a muscle at more than about 90 percent of its maximum capacity is too intense and does not allow the exercise to continue long enough (duration) to yield the best results; hence, it is referred to as the *upper threshold* of training.

Specificity

The principle of specificity is that the best results are obtained when a specific muscle is isolated

Table 5.1 The Overload Principle

Percent of muscular capacity	Threshold descriptors
100	Exercise beyond what is necessary to improve fitness
90	Upper threshold of training
75	Optimal threshold of improvement
60	Lower threshold of training
50	Exercise insufficient to improve fitness

Table 5.2 Major Muscle Groups and Exercises for Strengthening Them

Muscle	Weight training exercise(s)	Calisthenic(s)
Forearms	Wrist curls, reverse curls	Wrist rollers
Biceps	Curls (barbell and dumbbell)	Pull-ups (supinated)
Triceps	Bench and military presses	Chins and push-ups
Deltoids	Upright rowing and military press	Dips
Pectorals	Bench, bent-arm pullover	Push-ups
Abdominals	Pullovers, slant-board	Curlups and sit-ups
Trapezius	Upright rowing, shrugs	Chins (front and back)
Latissimus	Pulldowns, T-bar row	Chins (front and back)
Obliques	Dumbbell lifts and twists	Trunk twists, sit-ups
Gluteals	Squats, dead lift	Back extensions, jumps
Quadriceps	Half squats, leg press	Running, jumps
Hamstrings	Squats, leg press and curl	Sprints, running
Calves	Toe raises, leg extensions	Jump rope, hill runs
Neck	Flexions and extensions	Wrestler's bridges

from surrounding muscles and required to do work. Again, Nautilus is one example of weight training equipment designed with the principle of specificity in mind. Body builders use a variety of barbell and dumbbell exercises (Table 5.2) because they are interested in muscle definition, which is achieved primarily through specificity training.

Progressive Resistance

The third principle related to muscular strength and endurance training is progressive resistance. The *resistance* is the amount of weight being lifted; *progressive* refers to increasing the amount of weight according to a schedule or formula. Progress is measured by the number of pounds lifted, the number of repetitions performed, or the number of sets done. Lifting a weight 5 times is referred to as 5 *repetitions*. When successive repetitions cease, a *set* has been completed. A set may contain any number of repetitions. More repetitions of the same exercise, following a rest period, constitute a second set.

Strength Versus Endurance Training

Exercising to develop muscular strength requires a somewhat different training regimen than exercising to develop muscular endurance (Berger, 1984). Strength training requires lifting heavier weights. Because the weights are heavier, one is likely to do fewer repetitions and, because there are fewer repetitions per set, a strength trainer may have to do more sets. Conversely, if you are more interested in muscular endurance you will need to do more repetitions in each set and, as a result, will likely use lighter weights and do fewer sets. Research reported by Berger and others suggests that strength trainers ought to do multiple sets of up to 7 repetitions each, whereas the person who is more interested in muscle toning and muscular endurance is advised to do at least 15 repetitions before adding weight. Those interested in increasing muscle

mass ought to concentrate on strength training, and those who prefer to limit muscle mass ought to use endurance training techniques.

Flexibility Training

Flexibility is the ability to maintain complete range of motion in a joint, and it is important primarily because it prevents injuries. Flexibility is associated with youth because people typically become less flexible as they get older, but as you age you can maintain most of your flexibility through a daily routine of stretching exercises. If you have poor flexibility, you will have shorter muscles, immobile joints, and a risk of sprains and strains when you must perform unusual or unexpected movements.

Most joint injuries occur at the knees, ankles, hips, shoulders, or elbows. Any good flexibility program includes exercises devised to use those five joints, stretching the muscles and tendons that attach at those sites. The stretching may be active (ballistic) or passive (static). Ballistic stretching involves bouncing movements that result in the stretch reflex; if this is the only kind of stretching you do, it may be counterproductive, making muscles contract rather than lengthen. Static stretching is generally considered to be more desirable because it involves slow, steady lengthening of the involved muscles. At the very least, static stretching should precede and dominate any ballistic stretching, and some experts advocate no ballistic stretching at all.

There is a distinction between warming up and stretching. To warm up is to elevate the pulse and respiratory rates and increase blood flow to the muscles that will be used most heavily in the activity to follow. Calisthenics are a good warm-up activity and should precede static stretching to reduce the risk of injury. A good exercise routine will take the form of a bell-shaped curve: mild exercise as a warm-up activity, increasingly intense exercise, then milder exercise again, followed by static stretching at the end of the workout period. The purpose of the warm-up is to allow the body to gradually prepare for cardiorespiratory and musculoskeletal activity.

Body Composition

The fifth and final health-related attribute of physical fitness is body composition, sometimes discussed in terms of weight control. Body composition is the percentage of body weight that is fat, bone, muscle, or organ weight. The next two chapters are devoted to nutrition and weight control, respectively, including body composition.

SUMMARY

Physical activity is any muscular movement that expends energy. Physical fitness is the measurable result of regular and vigorous physical activity. The health-related components of physical fitness include cardiorespiratory and cardiovascular endurance, muscular strength and endurance, flexibility, and body composi-

tion. Exercise is programmed physical activity designed to enhance one's level of physical fitness.

There is a strong positive correlation between physical fitness and general health and wellness. Higher levels of cardiorespiratory fitness are related to lower levels of coronary heart disease, the number one killer in America. Aerobic exercise is highly recommended for physical fitness because it improves the efficiency of the cardiovascular and respiratory systems, a process called *the training effect*. Any rhythmic activity can produce the training effect, but aerobic dancing, jogging, biking, swimming, and cross-country skiing are among the most popular forms of aerobic exercise.

Three principles central to the development of muscular strength and endurance are the overload principle, the principle of specificity, and the principle of progressive resistance. (The overload principle also applies to aerobic exercise.) The frequency, intensity, and duration of exercise affect cardiorespiratory endurance, muscular strength, and muscular endurance. Maintaining body flexibility is desirable because it reduces the risk of injury and delays the effects of the aging process.

Examining Your Values

According to Bandura's social learning theory (see chapter 2), whether or not you choose to exercise and whether or not you choose a generally active lifestyle depends on the outcome you expect and how effectively you believe you can pursue that outcome. If you accept the Health Belief Model of Hochbaum and Rosenstock, as outlined in chapter 2, you will weigh the perceived costs or barriers versus the perceived benefits before deciding on a course of action or inaction. With these two models in mind, ask yourself these questions:

1. Where does health rank among my values at this moment?
2. What is my attitude toward exercise?
3. What is my current pattern of physical activity?
4. Is there consistency among my values, attitudes, and behavior?
5. Would a more active lifestyle benefit me? If so, how?
6. What are the barriers to a more active lifestyle for me?
7. Based on my knowledge of health and physical fitness and my self-concept, can I justify making a change in my behavior as it relates to fitness? (Can I justify *not* making a change?)

CHAPTER 6
Nutrition and Healthy Eating

The foods you eat need not be health hazards to taste good!

—John Farquhar

——————— **Self-Examination Statements** ———————

Instructions: Read each statement, then circle the x in the column at the left that most closely describes your belief about that statement. (Use a pencil. After reading this chapter you may wish to come back and change some of your responses on the basis of new information or attitudes.)

SA = strongly agree   **A** = agree   **U** = undecided   **D** = disagree   **SD** = strongly disagree

SA	A	U	D	SD	
x	x	x	x	x	I believe that good nutrition is a major factor in maintaining good health.
x	x	x	x	x	I have a good working knowledge of nutrition.
x	x	x	x	x	I grew up in a family that valued good nutrition.
x	x	x	x	x	I established good eating habits during childhood.
x	x	x	x	x	I value eating healthy, nutritious foods.
x	x	x	x	x	When I fix my own meals, I tend to eat nutritiously.
x	x	x	x	x	When I am with my friends it is more difficult for me to eat nutritiously.
x	x	x	x	x	I have an internal locus of control when it comes to eating.
x	x	x	x	x	I believe that my diet will be healthy without my taking any particular action to control it.
x	x	x	x	x	I believe that eating an unhealthy diet makes me more susceptible to morbidity and mortality.
x	x	x	x	x	Taste influences my choice of foods more often than does nutrition.
x	x	x	x	x	Food that is ''good for you'' usually tastes bad.
x	x	x	x	x	Food that is ''bad for you'' usually tastes good.
x	x	x	x	x	When I eat ''fast foods'' it is due more to their convenience than their taste.
x	x	x	x	x	I routinely salt food before tasting it.
x	x	x	x	x	I like the taste of foods that have been deep-fat-fried.

x	x	x	x	x	I have a "sweet tooth"—I like the taste of sweet foods.
x	x	x	x	x	I can name two or three excellent sources of Vitamins A, B, C, and D.
x	x	x	x	x	I can name four minerals the body needs for proper nutrition, and several good food sources for each.
x	x	x	x	x	I know the primary function of protein and several good food sources of protein.
x	x	x	x	x	I know the primary function of fat and several good sources of fat.
x	x	x	x	x	I know the primary function of carbohydrates and several good food sources of carbohydrates.
x	x	x	x	x	I understand the difference between simple and complex carbohydrates.
x	x	x	x	x	I eat more simple than complex carbohydrates.
x	x	x	x	x	I understand the difference between saturated and unsaturated fats.
x	x	x	x	x	I believe that saturated fats are a major risk factor for coronary heart disease (CHD).
x	x	x	x	x	I know that I am hereditarily predisposed to CHD.
x	x	x	x	x	I am willing to risk CHD in order to eat foods that I enjoy.
x	x	x	x	x	I know at least five foods that are high in saturated fats.
x	x	x	x	x	I understand the difference between high density lipids (HDL) and low density lipids (LDL).
x	x	x	x	x	I prefer red meat to fish or poultry.
x	x	x	x	x	I eat eggs at least once a day when they are available.
x	x	x	x	x	I prefer whole milk to low-fat or skim milk.
x	x	x	x	x	I believe that certain foods increase the risk of apoplexy.
x	x	x	x	x	I believe that a proper diet can reduce the risk of hypertension.
x	x	x	x	x	I believe that there is a correlation between salt intake and hypertension.
x	x	x	x	x	I believe that a proper diet can reduce the risk of cancer.
x	x	x	x	x	I can name at least three foods that increase the risk of cancer.
x	x	x	x	x	I can name at least three foods that decrease the risk of cancer.
x	x	x	x	x	I understand the value of water to good nutrition.
x	x	x	x	x	I drink at least six glasses of water daily.
x	x	x	x	x	I drink more water than coffee and soft drinks combined.
x	x	x	x	x	I drink more water than beer and soft drinks combined.

DEFINING TERMS AND CONCEPTS

It is not an accident that this chapter on nutrition follows a chapter on physical fitness, nor that the next chapter is about weight control. The relationships among physical fitness, nutrition, and weight control are many. As Cooper (1982) observed, "Good nutrition is the first key to the high level of physical conditioning that is necessary for total well-being" (p. 38). This thought was echoed by Barrett-Connor (1987), who wrote, "Nutrition is the single most important potential component of health maintenance programs" (p. 2).

Nutrition is the science of food, its use by the body, and its relationship to good health (Williams, 1983). Nutrition is vital to the good health of all people at all ages. Food is comprised primarily of six nutrients: proteins, fats, carbohydrates, vitamins, minerals, and water. These six nutrients are subdivided into saturated and unsaturated fats; simple and complex carbohydrates; vitamins A, B, C, D, E, and K; and such critical minerals as calcium, sodium, potassium, magnesium, and iron. This section describes the role of these essential dietary ingredients. Later sections describe how good nutrition helps prevent disease, and how it contributes to high-level wellness.

Food is fuel, and it is used by the body as a source of energy as well as to build tissue. Energy from food is measured in calories (technically, kilocalories). Barrett-Connor, perhaps only half in jest, defined calories as "little units that measure how good a food tastes" (p. 5). The primary source of energy is carbohydrates, followed by fats and, to a much lesser extent, protein. The primary role of protein is not to provide energy but to build tissue. Because carbohydrates are the primary source of energy, they should constitute at least 50 percent of your daily caloric intake.

Carbohydrates

There are two kinds of carbohydrates, simple and complex. Complex carbohydrates include the following:

- Fruits and vegetables
- Whole grain products (breads and cereals)
- Potatoes
- Starchy pastas—spaghetti, noodles, macaroni

These carbohydrates are converted into glucose, then stored as glycogen in the muscles and liver, stored as fat deposits, or used as a source of energy during physical activity.

Simple carbohydrates, on the other hand, include natural sugars (e.g., honey, molasses, sorghum) and refined flour and sugar products (e.g., cakes, cookies, candy, soda pop). The latter are often referred to as "empty calories" and "junk foods" because they are high in fats, sugars, and calories, but low in vitamins and minerals. Simple carbohydrates break down and enter the bloodstream much more quickly than complex carbohydrates and are therefore not available as a source of energy when needed.

Fats

Fats are also an excellent source of energy and should be consumed for nutritional balance. They should constitute up to 30 percent of your daily caloric intake, depending on your weight and body composition. However, because fats contain twice as many calories per gram as carbohydrates and proteins, excessive consumption of fat leads to obesity (see chapter 7).

There are saturated and unsaturated fats, the latter subdividing into polyunsaturated and monounsaturated fats. Saturated fats are typically animal fats. They are solid at room temperature (e.g., butter, cheese, and lard) and are high in cholesterol. Polyunsaturated fats, on the other hand, tend to be liquid at room temperature and are less likely to raise blood cholesterol levels. Monounsaturated fats may take a liquid (olive oil or cottonseed oil) or solid form (fish and nuts), and have an intermediate and nonthreatening effect on blood cholesterol levels. Saturated fats appear in animal products—meat, milk, cheese, eggs—while unsaturated fats come from vegetables and plants. Avocados, peanuts, peanut butter, olives, haddock, and flounder are primary sources of monounsaturated fats. As will be seen in the section on prevention, there is significantly higher risk of coronary heart disease associated with animal fats than with most plant fats.

Protein

Protein is the third nutrient that serves as a source of calories and energy. Protein consists of 22 amino acids, 8 of which are considered essential to life. Foods that contain all 8 amino acids are described as *complete* proteins. Many animal products (e.g., meat, milk, eggs) provide complete protein, as do various combinations of vegetables (e.g., rice combined with beans). The ease of attaining complete proteins by eating animals and animal products is one reason why these foods are such a prominent part of the diet despite their high cholesterol content. Plant foods individually are sources of incomplete proteins. It is possible for vegetarians to get sufficient complete protein by eating appropriate combinations of a variety of beans, grain products, fruits, and vegetables.

Proteins are most important during the rapid growth periods of childhood and adolescence. Adults often allow protein to make up 25 to 30 percent of their daily caloric intake, when 10 to 20 percent would adequately meet their nutritional needs.

Vitamins, Minerals, and Water

The other three primary nutrients—vitamins, minerals and water—assume a lesser role in nutritional planning than fats, carbohydrates, and proteins, for several reasons. First, they are not a source of calories or energy. Second, although each serves an important function, the needed quantity is much smaller than for the energy nutrients. Third, it is often assumed that a well-balanced diet of carbohydrates, fats and proteins will inherently contain sufficient quantities of vitamins and minerals; this assumption is controversial among nutritional experts.

Vitamins

Vitamins can be divided into two major groups, water soluble and fat soluble. Vitamin C and all the B-complex vitamins are water soluble and can be consumed in almost unlimited quantities because the body will excrete unused portions in the urine. Vitamins A, D, E, and K, however, are fat-soluble vitamins, which means that they are stored in the fatty tissues of the body. Megadoses of these vitamins can cause serious illnesses in the same way that almost any drug or substance in excess can harm the body.

Minerals

Minerals also serve important functions, and care must be taken to assure that they appear regularly in the diet. Each of us needs to consume calcium, potassium, phosphorus, iron, zinc, and lesser amounts of other minerals on a regular basis. Recommended dietary allowances (RDAs), published by the national Food and Nutrition Board, are often printed on food containers to help us estimate our needs and consumption of each vitamin and mineral. Table 6.1 lists some vitamins and minerals and some common food sources in which they are found. Vitamins and minerals tend to work in combinations in a relatively complex manner, so it is not advisable for you to prescribe supplements for yourself without medical advice.

The consensus is that it should not be necessary to take supplements because sufficient quantities of vitamins and minerals are contained in a balanced diet. Unfortunately, not everyone consumes a balanced diet. Some of us avoid certain foods because we dislike their taste. Others avoid certain foods for religious or philosophic reasons. Weight-loss programs restrict the diet of still others. Convenience, cost, and social lifestyle are other factors that affect our food choices. Haas (1983) believes that athletes, especially females, may need supplements to improve performance. Any of these factors may be adequate justification for considering vitamin or mineral supplements under the guidance of a physician or nutritionist.

Table 6.1 Food Sources of Vitamins and Minerals

Vitamin	Food source
A	Milk, eggs, butter, liver, vegetables
B₁ (Thiamine)	Meat, eggs, potatoes, grains
B₂ (Riboflavin)	Milk, cheese, meat, eggs
B complex (Niacin)	Nuts, yeast, liver, wheat germ
C	Citrus fruits, potatoes, tomatoes
D	Milk, butter, eggs, fish
E	Cereals, lettuce, eggs, vegetable oils
K	Liver, tomatoes, eggs, green vegetables

Mineral	Food source
Calcium	Dairy products, citrus fruits, leafy vegetables
Iron	Meat, eggs, liver, legumes, shellfish, dried fruits
Potassium	Bananas, orange juice, beans, nuts, dried fruit
Phosphorus	Grain cereals, dairy products, beans, broccoli
Zinc	Poultry, seafood, red meat
Iodine	Iodized salt
Fluorine	Fluoridated water

Water

We consider water to be a nutrient because, although it has no nutritional value in itself, it is essential for transporting other nutrients. The majority of your body is water, and many foods consist primarily of water. Drinking six to eight glasses of water daily is a healthy habit and plays a key role in weight control because water is calorie free; fruit juices and fresh fruits also replace fluids, but are not devoid of calories. Replacing fluids is especially important for people who are physically active or tend to perspire freely.

Food Groups and Moderation

Virtually all nutritional experts agree that balance and moderation in diet are prerequisites for good health. Food groups have been established with that in mind, and we are urged to consume at least one or two foods from each group each day. There are four traditional food groups:

- Meat and meat substitutes
- Dairy products
- Fruits and vegetables
- Whole grain products (breads and cereals)

Some nutritionists prefer to separate meat from meat substitutes; others put fruits and vegetables in separate categories, or put green leafy vegetables in a separate category, and so on. Certain foods do not fit easily into a single category (for instance, beef and vegetable soup, or chop suey). Pennington (1981) placed foods into four levels according to recommended rates of consumption, as follows:

- Liberal consumption—vegetables, fruits, grain products, and legumes
- Moderate consumption—lean meats, fish, poultry, lowfat milk, cheese, and yogurt
- Very moderate consumption—fatty meats, eggs, whole milk, nuts, and seeds
- Sparse consumption—sweets, desserts, fats, and alcohol

Pennington's recommendations outline a diet that is very likely to adhere to the following guidelines for healthy eating provided by the American Heart Association ("New Guidelines for the Prudent," 1987):

- Carbohydrates should make up over 50 percent of your caloric intake, most of them coming from complex carbohydrates.
- Fat intake should constitute less than 30 percent of your caloric intake; saturated fats should make up no more than 10 percent of your diet, with polyunsaturated and monounsaturated fats making up the balance.
- Protein intake should be about 15 percent of your total daily caloric intake.
- You should eat a variety of foods to get all of the essential vitamins and minerals.
- Your total caloric intake should be based on maintaining your ideal weight.

Ratto (1987a) summarized several sets of similar dietary guidelines stressing balance and variety of foods consumed; less fat, sugar, and sodium; and more complex carbohydrates and fiber.

Glanz and Damberg (1987) concluded that "today, Americans are healthier than ever before" (p. 211). This opinion was echoed by a nutrition committee of the National Center for Health Statistics (NCHS) (1986): "The American diet has supported a reasonably healthy population for decades. In general, our health and life expectancy has never been better" (p. 35). Mortality and morbidity rates have been dropping, and one of the reasons is greater public awareness of proper diet. Still, there is room for improvement as long as unhealthy eating is responsible for disease.

Preventing Disease Through Healthy Eating

Glanz and Damberg (1987) claimed, "A relationship has been clearly established between certain dietary habits and at least five of the ten leading causes of death. Nutrition plays a key role in heart disease, some cancers, stroke, arteriosclerosis, and diabetes" (p. 211). According to the NCHS's Joint Nutrition Monitoring Evaluation Committee (1986), "The principal nutrition-related health problems experienced by Americans arise from overconsumption of certain food components: fat, saturated fatty acids, cholesterol, and sodium. Excessive intakes of these food components are associated with an increased risk of developing cardiovascular diseases" (p. 2). Let us consider some of the evidence that supports these conclusions.

Keys et al. (1986) spent 15 years studying over 11,000 men from seven countries. During that time span, more than 2,000 of their subjects died; the study examined the causes of those deaths. There were four critical factors:

- Age
- Serum cholesterol
- Blood pressure
- Smoking habits

Combined, these factors accounted for 80 percent of coronary heart disease deaths, 46 percent of deaths from all causes, 45 percent of deaths from strokes, and 35 percent of deaths from cancer. Of the four factors, the latter three are subject to behavioral modification, and at least cholesterol is subject to dietary modification. For example, these researchers discovered that the death rate from CHD was highest among men whose diets were highest in saturated fats, and lowest among men whose diets were highest in monounsaturated fats—olive oil in particular.

DIETARY FAT AND CORONARY HEALTH

Cooper (1982) was among the first writers to make the public aware of the distinction between high density lipoproteins (HDL) and low density lipoproteins (LDL). Combined, these constitute the total blood serum cholesterol count. The consensus of opinion had been that the lower the total cholesterol count, the lower the risk of CHD. According to Cooper, however, the *ratio* of total cholesterol to HDL is the best single indicator of future coronary heart disease. He emphasized that it is healthy for the HDL to be high and the LDL to be low. It is his belief that HDL should be at least one fifth of the total cholesterol count, and that a relatively high total can be offset by a high HDL count. His recommendations included participating in vigorous aerobic exercise to increase the HDL count, and eating fewer saturated fats to decrease LDL.

Exercise and Cholesterol

When a physician does a complete medical examination of a patient, she or he usually routinely takes a blood sample. Such a sample should produce two separate cholesterol counts. By adding the two, and comparing the HDL to the LDL, you can determine for yourself whether or not you have a cholesterol problem. For example, if your HDL count is 50, a total cholesterol count of 240 includes only 190 of LDL, which is below the 4:1 ratio and may not put you at risk. However, if your HDL count is only 40, a total of 240 represents a 5:1 ratio of LDL to HDL, and becomes a more significant risk factor. Remember that aerobic exercise is the surest way to increase your HDL; this is one of the relationships between diet and exercise alluded to earlier.

Diet and Cholesterol

The 8-Week Cholesterol Cure (Kowalski, 1987) takes quite a different approach to solving the cholesterol dilemma. According to Kowalski, a person may have elevated cholesterol levels because of the following:

- The diet contains too many animal fats.
- The liver is manufacturing too much cholesterol.
- The body is inefficient at excreting cholesterol.

Kowalski's solution is a low-fat diet that includes oat bran and niacin supplements. It was his contention that modest reductions in the use of animal fats is a good beginning, but not sufficient in itself. Taking niacin reduces the liver's production of cholesterol. Oat bran (in the form of muffins, cereals, or products made from recipes in his book) absorbs cholesterol as it passes through the digestive tract, so that a larger percentage of cholesterol is excreted. He cited numerous studies that have demonstrated that "oat bran significantly lowers total cholesterol and LDL cholesterol while not at all lowering the protective HDL levels" (p. 48).

Niacin Supplementation and Cholesterol

Regarding niacin, Kowalski cited a 1986 *Journal of the American Medical Association* "Special Communication" that recommended niacin as the first choice in treating high cholesterol because it costs so much less than medication.

He admitted that there may be some irritating, although completely harmless, side effects from taking niacin, including a reddening of the skin similar to sunburn and perhaps an itching rash. Despite these temporary conditions, "Many physicians have been using niacin to treat patients with elevated cholesterol and triglyceride levels for years" (p. 65). He concluded that niacin can be used indefinitely, safely, and effectively.

DIETARY RECOMMENDATIONS

The most obvious preventive measure, though, is to reduce the intake of saturated fats. Table 6.2 identifies some foods that are high in fat per serving and foods that are high in cholesterol per serving. Although these lists are not all-inclusive, they should serve as a useful guide for anyone who wishes to avoid high LDL.

Food Choices and Cancer

Patterson and Block (1988) reported two sets of dietary recommendations for reducing risk of cancer, one by the National Research Council in 1982 and one by the American Cancer Society in 1984. Both recommended reduced fat intake (below 30 percent of daily caloric intake); daily consumption of fruits, vegetables, and whole grain breads and cereals; moderate or less use of alcohol; and minimal consumption of smoked, salted, and pickled foods. In addition, the American Cancer Society urged that obesity be avoided, and specifically recommended cruciferous vegetables such as cabbage, cauliflower, and broccoli.

Regarding the relationship between food choices and cancer, Maleskey (1987a) wrote, "Researchers now know that the most common cancers in the United States also have the strongest links with diet, smoking, and drinking"

(p. 88). She offered suggestions for reducing the risk of various forms of cancer by selecting certain foods, as follows:

- Colon cancer—Eat more high-fiber foods (bran, whole-grain products, vegetables and fruits), increase calcium consumption (dairy products), and take vitamin C and E supplements.
- Breast cancer—Reduce intake of animal fats, and increase intake of omega-3 fish oil (tuna, salmon).
- Lung cancer—Avoid smoking cigarettes, and increase intake of vitamins A, C, E, B_{12}, and folate.
- Mouth and throat cancer—Eat more beta-carotene (carrots, fruits, green leafy vegetables), and avoid the smoking/alcohol combination.
- Cervical cancer—Follow the same advice as for mouth and throat cancer.

Behme (1987) reported on a series of presentations made at a Canadian symposium on diet, nutrition, and health. Many of the presentations supported and embellished recommendations made above—for instance, that 75 percent of colon and breast cancer could be prevented by a diet low in saturated fats; that charbroiled meats are an especially potent source of carcinogens; and that the risk of cancer could be reduced by reducing total food intake, fat intake, and the intake of burnt meats. Exercise was advocated as a means of reducing body fat and thus reducing risk of cancer—another link between diet and exercise! Behme concluded, "That diet is all important for the maintenance of health and prevention of disease cannot be disputed" (p. 30).

The Effects of Fiber on Colon Cancers

Maleskey's suggestions appear to be based more on empirical evidence than on scientific studies, and not all researchers agree with her. McKeown

Table 6.2 High-Risk Foods for LDL

Foods high in fat	Fat (%)
Butter/margarine	100
Vegetable oils	100
Shortening/lard	100
Avocados	90
Almonds	82
Roast beef	81
Bacon	80
Bologna	79
Cheese, American	77
Peanuts	77
Beefsteak	74
Cashews	73
Ham	70
Roast pork	70
Cheese, cheddar	70
Cheese, Swiss	69
Hamburger	63
Milk, whole	50
Ice cream	49
Yogurt, whole	49

Foods high in cholesterol	Serving size	Cholesterol (mg)
Liver	3 oz	372
Eggs	1 ea	252
Pastries	4 ea	157
Shrimp	3 oz	130
French toast	1 pc	130
Sardines	3 oz	120
Apple pie	1 pc	120
Waffles	1 ea	112
Ice cream	1 cup	100

(Cont.)

Table 6.2 (Continued)

Foods high in cholesterol	Serving size	Cholesterol (mg)
Lemon meringue pie	1 pc	98
Veal and lamb	3 oz	86
Turkey and chicken w/o skin	3 oz	80
Beef and pork	3 oz	80
Spaghetti and meatballs	1 cup	75
Cheese (American, Swiss, etc.)	3 oz	75
Lobster	3 oz	72

Note. A maximum daily cholesterol consumption of 300 mg is recommended.

(1987), for example, examined the protective effects of a high-fiber diet for colon cancer, and concluded that the data are not sufficient "to establish beyond doubt a protective effect of fiber" (p. 532). Despite the lack of certainty, however, McKeown recommended a diet low in fat and high in fiber, which seems to side with Maleskey and with the conclusion of Barrett-Connor (1987) that "we can't wait for scientific studies to prove every single dietary consideration. We have already made some positive dietary changes, based largely on epidemiological observations, and we should continue to do so" (p. 10).

Insel and Roth (1985) offered yet another variation on the relationship between cancer and fiber:

Some populations, particularly vegetarians, have little or no colon cancer. The vegetarian diet typically is high in fiber, which suggests, according to some scientists, that colon cancer is related to a lack of fiber in the diet. Fiber does not supply nutrition; it provides bulk needed to move other foods through the digestive tract. The shorter transit time afforded by a high-fiber diet is believed by some to be an important factor in the low colon cancer rates of vegetarians. (p. 414)

Calcium's Contributions to Good Health

Calcium is increasingly being recommended as a preventer of osteoporosis and high blood pressure. Many of us who have reduced our consumption of dairy products because of their high cholesterol content are faced with the possibility of getting less than the recommended daily allowance (RDA) of calcium, which is 1,000 mg. Osteoporosis is a progressive deterioration of bone that especially affects postmenopausal women. The time to take preventive action is well before menopause. One preventive measure is to consume more calcium; skim milk is a good source that is also low in cholesterol. Another preventive measure is a lifetime of physical activity (see Table 5.1 on the training effect).

Prevention Magazine (Malesky, 1987b) reported on several studies that confirm the preventive role of calcium in combating high blood pressure. It has long been known that sodium (salt) elevates blood pressure, and that some individuals are more susceptible than others to this influence. It has been discovered more recently that, for those individuals, ''the more salt elevates blood pressure, the more calcium lowers it'' (p. 26). Among the other foods recommended for lowering blood pressure were the following:

- Fruits
- Vegetables
- Fish
- Whole grains
- Beans
- Olive oil

Pectin is reportedly one of the best substances for reducing both high blood pressure and high cholesterol. It acts as a sponge, soaking up LDL in the same manner as the oat bran advocated by Kowalski. Foods high in pectin include the following:

- Oranges
- Apples
- Bananas
- Pears
- Potatoes
- Broccoli

Caffeine's Controversial Role in Heart Disease

Caffeine is a controversial component of the American diet. Most of us consume caffeine daily in the form of coffee, tea, colas, chocolate, or other sources. A typical cup of coffee contains about 100 mg of caffeine, about twice as much as a 12-ounce can of soft drink or a cup of tea, and several times as much as chocolate or cocoa beverages. Weight-control tablets, cold tablets, and other nonprescription drugs commonly contain even more, often as much as 200 mg each.

Caffeine is usually thought of as a relatively mild and harmless stimulant, the primary effect of which is to keep us awake (whether or not we wish to be). However, caffeine in excess of 300 to 400 mg per day, depending on individual tolerance, often results in nervousness and irritability. More importantly, there is increasing evidence that excessive consumption of caffeinated coffee contributes to the risk of coronary heart disease.

LaCroix, Mead, Liang, Thomas, and Pearson (1986) defined heavy coffee consumption as five or more cups per day. They followed the mortality and morbidity of over 1,100 males for periods ranging from 19 to 35 years, and discovered that the risk of CHD was 2.8 times as high among the heavy coffee drinkers as among the nondrinkers. After adjusting for age, smoking habits, hypertension, and serum cholesterol levels, the risk factor was still about 2.5 times greater among the heavy coffee drinkers.

Rosenberg, Werler, Kaufman, and Shapiro (1987) found a more modest association between coffee consumption and myocardial infarction (heart attack). When they eliminated decaffeinated coffee drinkers, however, and compared caffeinated coffee drinkers to nondrinkers of coffee, they found that heavy coffee drinkers (10 cups or more per day) had twice the risk of myocardial infarction as nondrinkers. A study by LeGrady et al. (1987) examined mortality from coronary heart disease among more than 1,900 males over a period of 19 years, and discovered that CHD mortality was highest among those who drank more than 6 cups of coffee per day.

Pincomb, Lovallo, and Passey (1987) studied the effects of caffeine on the blood pressure of medical students. They reported that final exams increased systolic blood pressure, as did caffeine. This combination pushed some subjects into the borderline hypertensive range. They concluded that using caffeine to deal with stressful situations may only exacerbate the stress response.

To be fair, not all studies have found a strong relationship between use of caffeine and CHD or high blood pressure. One can only act on the best evidence available, and the most recent evidence seems to suggest that heavy coffee consumption involves health risks.

Diabetes and Diet

Among all the diseases that affect mankind, diabetes is among those most closely associated with diet. Most diabetics take insulin to stabilize blood glucose levels; the primary risk is wildly fluctuating levels of blood sugar, caused by too many or too few simple carbohydrates (sugars). Research reported by Nuttall (1987) encourages a significant change from the traditional diabetic diet. Some of the complex carbohydrates—cooked potatoes, cold and cooked cereals, and bread—cause an even greater fluctuation of glucose concentration than simple carbohydrates like table sugar and honey, and should be avoided by diabetics.

Fruits and vegetables appear most likely to facilitate stable glucose levels. A diet low in fat is also recommended because diabetes is easier to control when one maintains ideal weight—another of the links between exercise, diet, and weight control. The changing theories about diabetic diets are typical of the changes that are constantly occurring throughout the field of nutrition. Staying informed of changes as they occur is not easy, but it is important.

PROMOTING WELLNESS THROUGH GOOD NUTRITION

Certainly there is more to good nutrition than preventing disease. Rodale (1987b) wrote, "When you are eating right, staying fit, not smoking, and controlling drinking, you enjoy life more. You're more productive, have more job security, and resist stress much more easily"

(p. 30). These thoughts may represent a mixture of fact and opinion, but they are reflective of a wellness lifestyle and consistent with my own experience.

The Pritikin Diet

Many of you have undoubtedly heard of the Pritikin Diet (Schapell, Bell, & Blackburn, 1987). Its originator always referred to it as the "Pritikin Program" (Pritikin, 1979) because it is much more than just a diet, and weight loss is not its primary goal. Nathan Pritikin originally devised the plan in the 1950s when he was first troubled by heart disease, and he lived by it until his death in 1985. In addition to weight control, the plan advocated cessation of smoking, avoidance of caffeinated drinks, regular exercise, and learning to cope with stress. Pritikin, like Rodale, understood that wellness is dependent on far more than merely eating nutritiously.

The diet that Pritikin recommends is too extreme for all but the most highly motivated individuals, so few people stay with it. It allows only 10 percent of caloric intake to be made up of fats. This presents difficulties in a society where fatty foods are standard fare and the norm for consumption is closer to 40 percent. His plan forbids all fatty meats, all sugars and egg yolks, and most cheeses and dairy products. It allows fresh fruits and vegetables in unlimited quantities and whole grain products that are high in fiber. For highly disciplined individuals, the Pritikin Plan is an effective method of attaining high-level wellness, but there are less extreme methods for moving toward that goal.

Eating Well Can Mean Delicious Eating

Having a positive attitude is the first prerequisite for good nutrition. Eating only nutritious foods is the equivalent of drinking water from a half-

Table 6.3   Low-Risk Foods for LDL

Foods	Fat (%)	Cholesterol (mg)	Foods	Fat (%)	Cholesterol (mg)
Apples	< 1	0	Cauliflower	< 1	0
Applesauce	< 1	0	Celery	< 1	0
Apricots	< 1	0	Corn on the cob	< 1	0
Bananas	< 1	0	Green beans	< 1	0
Blueberries	< 1	0	Lettuce	< 1	0
Cantaloupe	< 1	0	Peas	< 1	0
Grapefruit	< 1	0	Pickles	< 1	0
Grapes	< 1	0	Potatoes, baked	< 1	0
Honeydew melon	< 1	0	Spinach	< 1	0
Oranges	< 1	0	Tomatoes	< 1	0
Peaches	< 1	0	Bran flakes	< 1	0
Pears	< 1	0	Corn flakes	< 1	0
Pineapples	< 1	0	Oatmeal	1	0
Plums	< 1	0	Rice puffs	< 1	0
Raisins	< 1	0	Shredded wheat	1	0
Raspberries	< 1	0	Apple juice	< 1	0
Sweet cherries	< 1	0	Orange juice	< 1	0
Strawberries	< 1	0	Tomato juice	< 1	0
Watermelons	< 1	0	Carbonated beverages	0	0
Asparagus	< 1	0	Coffee/tea	0	0
Beets	< 1	0	Jello	0	0
Broccoli	< 1	0	Popcorn	2	0
Carrots	< 1	0			

filled glass; one can be pleased with having so much or lament not having more. When you saw the list of high-risk foods in Table 6.2, what was your reaction? Some of you probably said, "Wow, this is a list of my favorite foods, and I'd starve without them" (the half-empty syndrome), whereas others of you probably thought, "I'm glad there are lots of great-tasting foods that aren't on this list" (the half-full outlook).

Table 6.3 contains a partial list of foods that are low in fat and cholesterol. Here is an opportunity for you to clarify your values.

If you had to subsist entirely on foods from either Table 6.2 or Table 6.3, which would you choose? It is probable that neither table lists all of your favorite foods and that each contains many foods you enjoy. Would it detract from your enjoyment of life to plan each meal around several items from the latter list and limit yourself to one item per meal from the former? Remember, the key is moderation.

Taste Is Acquired

The traditional approach to dividing foods into basic food groups, usually four or more as described earlier in this chapter, has been criticized by Ratto (1987a) on the grounds that an increasing number of foods do not fit neatly into one group. Into which food group do you put a four-topping pizza; a Big Mac; a bacon, lettuce, and tomato sandwich; or vegetable lasagna? Further, arbitrary groups fail to recognize nutritional differences among foods in the same group; for instance, a hot dog does not have the same nutritional value as broiled fish, nor is an ice cream sundae the equivalent of skimmed milk. Ratto aptly makes the point that lack of nutrients is not the problem of the '80s, because most Americans have access to the recommended daily allowances (RDAs) for vitamins and minerals.

Taste rather than nutrition often determines what we eat, and taste is largely acquired. Americans have become accustomed to foods that are sweet, salty, and fatty, both in restaurants and grocery stores. Most snack foods are simple carbohydrates, whose taste appeal is based on salt, sugar, or fat (e.g., potato chips, pretzels, doughnuts, cupcakes, candy bars, and cookies). The primary alternative is complex carbohydrates, which are also good snack foods if you like fruit, fruit juices, and raw vegetables. There is no question which is more nutritious, simple or complex carbohydrates, so the choice comes down to health beliefs, attitudes, and values.

How to Make Dietary Choices

One way to make dietary choices is to use the Health Belief Model (HBM) described in chapter

2. You know that there are benefits from certain kinds of foods and that there are costs connected to eating certain other kinds of foods, including weight gain and the possibility of various diseases. The HBM suggests that you consider your perceived susceptibility to each of the related diseases and the relative seriousness of each. For example, if there is no history of heart disease in your family and your latest blood test indicates that your total cholesterol count is below 200, your risk in eating high-cholesterol foods is greatly reduced. If you do have a family history of heart disease, however, and your cholesterol count is over 200, your food choices should be quite different.

Feldman and Mayhew (1984) integrated elements of the HBM and the Ajzen-Fishbein and Wallston and Wallston models in an effort to predict nutritional behavior. According to their model, what one intends to eat will be determined by attitudes, perceived consequences, social norms, and personal norms (habits). They found that the best predictor of behavioral intent, as it relates to diet, is attitude, but that three factors predict actual eating behavior:

- Intent
- Habits
- Conditions

They reassured their readers that old habits can be broken if there is intent to change. Other studies, notably the Stanford and North Karelia studies reported in chapter 3, reached the same conclusion.

Hayes and Ross (1987) applied locus of control theories to eating habits. They concluded that people with a greater concern for their health and an internal locus of control have better eating habits than externals and those who lack concern for health. It is that combination that improves eating habits. Knowledge of good nutrition is not sufficient to produce behavioral change, but it is a prerequisite. You will undoubtedly make wise choices if you know which foods are most nutritious and which foods place you at greater risk of coronary heart disease, cancer, and other killers; if you have an internal locus of control; if you intend to eat foods that are good for you; if you value good health and a high level of wellness; and if you have weighed the costs and benefits of your choices. The choices are yours, as is the responsibility.

SUMMARY

Good health depends on eating sufficient quantities of the six nutrients—proteins, fats, carbohydrates, vitamins, minerals, and water. It is important to understand their functions.

Proteins, fats, and carbohydrates are sources of energy that contain varying calories per gram. Complex carbohydrates, such as fresh fruits and vegetables and whole-grain products, are the healthiest sources of energy and the richest sources of vitamins and minerals. However, they cannot duplicate the tissue-building functions of proteins or the body-process functions of fats. Complex carbohydrates should contribute up to one half of daily caloric intake. One can maintain nutritive balance by knowing which foods are the best sources for the various vitamins and minerals and including them in the daily diet. Water is designated a nutrient because it is essential to the digestive process.

Foods high in certain types of cholesterol increase the risk of developing coronary heart disease. HDL is a healthy form of cholesterol; the LDL form clogs coronary arteries. An unhealthy diet also contributes to the development of cancer and diabetes. We need to understand these relationships to help safeguard our health.

Examining Your Values

Newman (1986) wrote that the bottom line of nutrition is this:

> There are no simple solutions, only intelligent choices. . . . You want to make slow and steady change in the right direction. It's what you do 80% of the time that is really important. You can blow it 20% of the time, but try to blow it on quality stuff. (p. 24)

It is a philosophy to which I wholly subscribe. You can "have your cake and eat it too," but you can't have two pieces with every meal!

Examine your eating preferences and values by applying the above philosophy to this hypothetical situation:

You have no access to food except what is brought to you. You may have unlimited quantities of whatever foods you choose, and they will be prepared according to your taste. However, you must choose only seven primary foods that will account for 80 percent of your caloric intake. If you choose potatoes, you can have them baked, boiled, mashed, home-fried, au gratin, and so on. If you choose pizza, you can have it with your preferred toppings, and it will still count as only one primary food. Oranges can be juiced or eaten whole, apples can be made into sauce, and so forth. As a bonus, you can also have all the water you want. Remember that you must choose foods that will satisfy your needs for breakfast, lunch, dinner, and snacks, and you will be eating them every day for the rest of your life, so variety is important. List your choices below:

1.   2.
3.   4.
5.   6.
7.

Were your choices motivated primarily by taste or nutrition? My hunch is that you chose seven basic foods that are both tasty and nutritious, knowing that you have 20 percent of your calories remaining to "blow" on less-nutritious foods that appeal to your taste buds. Are all the basic food groups represented in your choices? What do your choices tell you about your value of healthy eating?

CHAPTER 7
Weight Control

A man is rich in proportion to the number of things which he can afford to let alone.

—Henry David Thoreau

Self-Examination Statements

Instructions: Read each statement, then circle the x in the column at the left that most closely describes your belief about that statement. (Use a pencil. After reading this chapter you may wish to come back and change some of your responses on the basis of new information or attitudes.)

SA = strongly agree   **A** = agree   **U** = undecided   **D** = disagree   **SD** = strongly disagree

SA	A	U	D	SD	
x	x	x	x	x	I believe that I am within 10 percent of my ideal weight.
x	x	x	x	x	Maintaining normal body weight is important to me.
x	x	x	x	x	My weight does not influence my self-concept.
x	x	x	x	x	Weight is not a factor in how I judge others.
x	x	x	x	x	Weight was (will be) a factor in my choice of a "significant other."
x	x	x	x	x	I have at least one close friend who is obese.
x	x	x	x	x	At least one member of my immediate family is obese.
x	x	x	x	x	Our society discriminates against obese people.
x	x	x	x	x	Obesity is more common in the U.S. than in most countries.
x	x	x	x	x	I believe that most people could keep their weight in a normal range if they had the willpower.
x	x	x	x	x	I can control my weight because I have an internal locus of control.
x	x	x	x	x	I believe that obesity is a serious health problem.
x	x	x	x	x	Being emaciated is as great a health problem as being obese.
x	x	x	x	x	If I am obese, that increases my risk of coronary heart disease.
x	x	x	x	x	If I am obese, that increases my risk of cancer.
x	x	x	x	x	If I am obese, that increases my risk of hypertension.
x	x	x	x	x	If I am obese, that increases my risk of diabetes.
x	x	x	x	x	I understand the concept of anorexia nervosa.
x	x	x	x	x	I understand the concept of bulimia.
x	x	x	x	x	Being obese is healthier than being anorexic or bulimic.

x	x	x	x	x	I am familiar with the concept of body mass index.
x	x	x	x	x	I know what my current body mass index (BMI) is.
x	x	x	x	x	My present BMI is in a healthy range.
x	x	x	x	x	Percent of body fat is more important to good health than total body weight.
x	x	x	x	x	I know my current percent of body fat, plus or minus 3 percent.
x	x	x	x	x	My present percent of body fat is within healthy limits.
x	x	x	x	x	I understand the concept of basal metabolic rate (BMR).
x	x	x	x	x	Most obesity is hereditary, caused by a slow BMR.
x	x	x	x	x	I understand the concept of set point theory.
x	x	x	x	x	Set point theory encourages me to go on a diet.
x	x	x	x	x	The key to weight control is caloric intake and expenditure.
x	x	x	x	x	I know about how many calories I consume each day.
x	x	x	x	x	I believe that reducing caloric intake is the healthiest way to lose weight.
x	x	x	x	x	Limiting caloric intake to 1,000 calories per day is the surest way to lose weight.
x	x	x	x	x	Vigorous exercise is an effective way for me to control my weight.
x	x	x	x	x	I know about how many calories I expend in 30 minutes of vigorous aerobic activity.
x	x	x	x	x	I know what causes fat loss, fluid loss, and muscle tissue loss.
x	x	x	x	x	Some kinds of activity burn fat more readily than others.
x	x	x	x	x	I expend as many calories walking a mile as jogging a mile.
x	x	x	x	x	It is unhealthy to lose more than about 2 pounds per week.
x	x	x	x	x	It is unwise to attempt weight loss without first consulting a physician.
x	x	x	x	x	I know at least two popular diets that are healthy.
x	x	x	x	x	A high protein diet is an effective and healthy way to lose weight.
x	x	x	x	x	High carbohydrate intake almost always leads to weight gains.
x	x	x	x	x	Eliminating all fat from my diet is an effective way for me to lose weight.
x	x	x	x	x	I know what percentages of my caloric intake ought to be protein, fat, simple carbohydrates, and complex carbohydrates in order to lose fat weight.
x	x	x	x	x	The Pritikin Plan is an effective and healthy way to lose weight.
x	x	x	x	x	Weight Watchers is an effective and healthy weight-loss program.
x	x	x	x	x	TOPS (Take Off Pounds Sensibly) is a healthy and effective way to lose weight.
x	x	x	x	x	I see no advantage to group weight-loss programs like TOPS.
x	x	x	x	x	Having a strong social support group makes it easier to lose weight.
x	x	x	x	x	Group weight-loss programs are best for people who have an external locus of control.

| x | x | x | x | x | I believe that I am susceptible to serious disease if I don't control my weight. |
| x | x | x | x | x | The benefits of weight control far outweigh the costs/barriers. |

DEFINING TERMS AND CONCEPTS

To control your weight means to avoid being either extremely underweight or overweight. Because obesity is a much greater problem than being underweight for most people in the United States, we tend to lose sight of the fact that, on a worldwide basis, there are far more people underweight than overweight. Even in this country, medical authorities believe that more elderly people are unhealthy due to being underweight than to being overweight. Some of them can't afford to eat nutritious food; others are too feeble to shop and cook as they did in earlier years, so they gradually stop eating three balanced meals a day. For most Americans, however, obesity is of far greater concern than being underweight. According to McDonough (1987), "Obesity has been classified as the most serious nutrition disturbance in the American society" (p. 5).

Overweight and Overfat

Some authorities distinguish between being overweight and being overfat, so we need to define those terms. Almost every health textbook includes a chart that estimates ideal weight for any given height. Gradually, however, researchers have recognized serious shortcomings in this simplified approach. These tables fail to consider two important factors, body type and percent body fat.

Defining Body Types
Human beings come in many shapes and sizes, influenced by heredity. People who remain very thin regardless of what they eat are called *ectomorphs*. Those who remain obese in spite of eating very little are called *endomorphs*. Others seem to be naturally muscular, and they are referred to as *mesomorphs*. It is quite possible for a mesomorph to be overweight on the basis of height and weight charts, yet have a relatively low and healthy percent body fat. For example, two people of the same sex might each be 5 feet, 6 inches tall and weigh 140 pounds, but one may be a mesomorph with only 15 percent body fat while the other may be an endomorph with 30 percent body fat. Fat skinfold testing has come into prominence in recent years as a means of distinguishing between those who are overweight and those who are overfat.

Measuring Percent Body Fat
There are several methods of measuring percent body fat. One is hydrostatic (underwater) weighing, which is the most accurate but involves expensive equipment. A more common measure involves the use of fat skinfold calipers to estimate subcutaneous fat at three or four body sites (Howley & Franks, 1986). There are several formulas for measuring body fat using skinfolds, and the accuracy of the measurement is somewhat dependent on the person using the calipers. Any competent nutritionist or exercise physiologist can perform the measurement in less than 5 minutes.

My professional colleagues and I have measured the body fat of hundreds of college students and older adults since 1980. Norms for college students appear in Table 7.1; the numbers reflect the percent body fat that causes a person to be described as anorexic, normal, obese, and so on. National norms for the adult population tend to be slightly higher. There is a difference between what is desired and what is normal, however, as the average American tends to have more body fat than is generally considered healthy and desirable. Ratto (1987b) estimated that the average American woman is about 25 to 28 percent fat; the desired range for women is 22 to 25 percent. For men, the comparable figures are an average of 15 to 18 percent fat, with 12 to 15 percent desired. According to Baumgartner, Roche, Chumlea, Siervogel, and Gluech (1987), 30 percent body fat for women and 25 percent body fat for men constitute obesity. Rosen and Gross (1987) used the criterion of ± 15 percent from ideal weight as a definition of overweight and underweight, respectively.

Table 7.1 Range of Body Fat Among College Students

Description	% Fat, female	% Fat, male
Anorexic	12	4
Below-average fat	15	7
Healthy low normal	18	10
Healthy average	21	13
Healthy high normal	24	16
Above-average fat	27	19
Borderline obesity	30	22
Obese	33	25

Calculating Healthy Weight Range

For those who lack access to a measure of body fat, Body Mass Index (BMI) is being used extensively to calculate a healthy weight range. The formula is: BMI = weight (kilograms) ÷ height (meters^2). One kilogram equals 2.2 pounds, and 1 meter equals 39.37 inches. To illustrate the formula in a way that simplifies the mathe-

matics, suppose that you were 6 feet, 7 inches tall and weighed 220 pounds. You would be 2 meters tall and weigh exactly 100 kilograms. Thus, the formula would read:

$$BMI = 100 \div 2^2 = 100 \div 4 = 25.$$

Ratto (1987b) suggested the following desired ranges and obesity levels for each sex:

Women: desirable BMI = 21 to 23; obesity is > 27.5

Men: desirable BMI = 22 to 24; obesity is > 28.5

On this basis, the person described above is slightly overweight, but not obese. Now use the formula to calculate your BMI. Are you in the desired range?

Eating Disorders

The word *anorexic* was used in Table 7.1 to describe those individuals who have the least body fat. Anorexia nervosa and bulimia are diseases that have become common in recent years. They are associated primarily with young females who become obsessed with weight control, perceive themselves as heavier than others see them, and resort to extreme measures to keep their weight down. Autrey, Stover, Reatig, and Casper (1986) described anorexia nervosa as self-starvation accompanied by a loss of over 25 percent of previous body weight; they defined bulimia as "rapid consumption of large amounts of food in a short period of time, frequently followed by self-induced vomiting or the use of cathartics or diuretics" (p. 536). They acknowledged that the prevalence of anorexia and bulimia is increasing and is becoming an issue of importance for public health.

Dieting

A less extreme measure is to resort to dieting to prevent obesity. Dieting is reducing caloric intake without increasing physical activity. There are two primary reasons why dieting alone is an ineffective way to counteract obesity. One has to do with the relationship between *basal metabolic rate* and *set point theory*; the other has to do with the causes of fluid, muscle, and fat loss.

Basal Metabolic Rate

Metabolism is the rate at which the human body uses energy. Basal metabolic rate (BMR) is the minimum expenditure of energy necessary for basic functions such as respiration and circulation. BMR varies considerably from one individual to another. Just as we tend to inherit a body type that is endomorphic, mesomorphic, or ectomorphic, we also tend to inherit a metabolic rate, which may be well above or below average. If you have a high BMR, you will burn more calories at rest than someone with a low metabolic rate. Unjust as it may seem, people with high BMRs can eat more and be less physically active without getting fat. However, a person born with a body type that tends toward obesity can modify his or her body type to a certain extent over a long period of time by increasing or decreasing caloric intake, eating more or fewer fatty foods, and using a progressive resistance weight training program. Likewise, it is widely believed that BMR changes slightly according to the level of activity. This view is known as set point theory (Brownell, 1986).

Set Point Theory

According to set point theory, most of us have a weight range and a range of body fat that are normal for our body type. It is believed that the hypothalamus in the brain works with the fat cells to control weight and body fat at a "set point," much as a thermostat works to control room temperature. When a person who is used to consuming 2,000 calories per day reduces that to 1,500 calories, the body's set point rises and the basal metabolic rate (BMR) declines in order

to burn fewer calories and thereby maintain the same weight as before. If the dieter decides to cut caloric intake to 1,000 calories per day, the body again responds by raising its set point and lowering its BMR. This explains why dieting without exercise is ineffective.

Metabolic Acceleration

Exercise has a tendency to accelerate the metabolic process, during *and* following exercise, thus burning more calories during the exercise period and for several hours thereafter. There is evidence that moderate-speed aerobic exercise tends to burn stored body fats, whereas more vigorous aerobic exercise burns mostly carbohydrates. For this reason, aerobic exercise is the key to permanent weight loss.

It is more efficient to lose weight by maintaining caloric intake and increasing activity than it is to maintain activity and decrease caloric intake. Not all researchers are convinced that there is sufficient evidence in support of set point theory to validate it beyond doubt, but there is a growing body of circumstantial evidence to support it and little to refute it.

Fat Versus Fluid and Muscle Loss

Dieting may result in quick weight loss, but that initial loss of a few pounds is unlikely to be permanent because most of it will be fluid loss. A person who reduces caloric intake by 50 percent but is very inactive is also as likely to lose muscle tissue as fat tissue. However, when exercise is central to the weight-control plan, muscle tissue is being developed rather than lost. Losing weight by exercising is slower and harder—that's why more people don't do it—but it is also more permanent and results in greater fat loss (Zuti & Golding, 1976). There is another incentive for using exercise as a weight-control device. According to Rosato (1986), muscle tissue uses more energy than fat does during rest and during physical activity. So, if you are muscular you can consume more calories than a friend whose weight is equal to yours but who has more body fat than you do. Can you see how important the link is between physical activity and weight control?

CONTROLLING WEIGHT TO PREVENT DISEASE

Ratto (1987b) put the issue squarely in perspective by stating, "Obesity is deadly. Those who are obese, defined as 20 percent or more overweight, are at significantly increased risk for hypertension, cancer, stroke, heart disease, and adult-onset diabetes, which together account for 70 percent of U.S. deaths" (p. 28). She further pointed out that obesity in the abdominal area places a person at greater risk of diabetes, hypertension, and heart disease than obesity in the lower limbs. This claim has been corroborated by many researchers in recent years and represents a major shift in thinking about obesity.

Body Fat Location

Ducimetiere, Richard, and Cambien (1986) acknowledged that until recently the study of obesity as it relates to heart disease was one-dimensional. During the past 10 years, however, many studies have demonstrated that coronary heart disease (CHD) is associated not with obesity in general but with fat deposits on the body trunk as opposed to the lower extremities.

Ducimetiere and colleagues measured fat skinfold at 13 body sites on over 6,000 males. They compared the fat deposits of subjects who developed CHD during the 6 years of their study to those of subjects who avoided CHD. They concluded that trunk fat, mainly abdominal fat, was associated with CHD, and is a significant predictor of CHD.

Baumgartner et al. (1987) hypothesized that, in keeping with the literature on the subject, having a greater percent body fat on the trunk than on the extremities would correlate with higher blood pressure, cholesterol, and blood lipids. They reported that, although men had more fat-free body mass (bone and muscle) than women and comparable overall body fat after controlling for height, their male subjects had more trunk fat than women. Males also had higher levels of LDL and triglycerides, higher blood pressure, and lower levels of HDL. They concluded that overall percent body fat was significantly correlated with these factors for men but not for women.

Body Fat, Cholesterol, and Blood Pressure

Haines, Imeson, and Meade (1987) wrote, "It has been known for many years that obesity predisposes to raised levels of serum cholesterol and blood pressure. Fat laid down in adult life tends to be deposited on the trunk rather than the limbs" (p. 86). They proceeded to study the relationship of fat skinfold measurements at four body sites (two on the limbs and two on the trunk) to known coronary risk factors. In their study, all four skinfolds were separately and significantly associated with each risk factor for males; for females, only the trunk skinfolds were predictive of coronary risk factors.

Modifying Obesity Risk Factors

Krotkiewski and Bjorntorp (1986) reported that abdominal obesity is a male trait and is frequently found to be associated with diabetes and higher levels of blood lipids and blood pressure, culminating in higher rates of cardiovascular disease, stroke, and total mortality. They were particularly interested in the effects of physical training on obesity. They concluded that physical training is more likely to result in decreased body fat and increased metabolism when the fat is primarily on the trunk; although this pertains mostly to men, it also applies to women who have similar fat distribution. The practical application is that women with fatty thighs and buttocks may find exercise less helpful in losing weight than women whose fat is primarily abdominal.

Borkan, Sparrow, Wisniewski, and Vokonas (1986) conducted a 15-year longitudinal study that involved nearly 1,400 men. They looked for an association between long-term weight change and coronary disease risks, and reported that "long-term weight change was significantly associated with change in all eight coronary disease risk factors studied" (p. 416). They found increased weight to be associated with the following:

- Increased systolic blood pressure
- Higher cholesterol and triglyceride levels
- Decreased vital capacity of the lungs

They concluded that the fact that excess body weight seems to contribute to the risk of various diseases "emphasizes the necessity of weight reduction as a critical intervention in modifying risk" (p. 416).

Blood Lipids and Disease

Foster et al. (1987) also noted that upper body fat is more closely associated with disease than) lower body fat. In particular, they observed that upper body fat is associated with higher triglyceride levels, which in turn are associated with larger but not necessarily more fat cells. For many years it was thought that the primary cause of increased body mass was an increase in size rather than number of cells; although researchers now believe that the number of cells increases in advanced cases of obesity, such was not the case in this study. Instead, upper body fat was associated with LDL; HDL and triglycerides were associated with body build, body composition, and fat distribution patterns. The study also identified the following factors

other than obesity that influenced blood lipid levels:

- Heredity
- Alcohol
- Coffee
- Smoking
- Dietary fat and cholesterol
- Recent weight loss
- Physical activity
- Oral contraceptives
- Steroids
- Blood pressure medications

We have already discussed several of these factors as risks or contributors to good health, and the others will be addressed in appropriate subsequent chapters.

Eating Habits and Disease

Berry, Hirsch, Most, and Thornton (1986) did a chemical analysis of adipose tissue to determine whether or not obese and normal-weight people differ in the foods they eat and the way their bodies store those foods. They also looked for correlations between Body Mass Index (BMI) and cardiovascular risk factors. They reported that BMI is correlated with total cholesterol, LDL, HDL (negatively), triglycerides, blood pressure, and the combination of these factors. Regarding eating habits, they offered these generalizations: Obese people consume more animal fats; normal-weight people consume more vegetable oils; normal-weight people consume more carbohydrates and less total fat; and obesity is not primarily a function of how people's bodies store or use fat. The underlying conclusion is that obesity is more a function of eating habits than of body chemistry.

Obesity, Hypertension, and High-Fiber Diets

Garrison, Kannel, Stokes, and Castelli (1987) did an 8-year follow-up to the original Framingham study which helped identify the primary risk factors associated with coronary heart disease, using over 4,000 offspring as subjects. They were looking for factors associated with hypertension, and obesity was identified as one of those factors for both men and women. They concluded that excessive body fat contributes to high blood pressure, that the amount of body fat can be controlled, and that the general population ought to use weight control to curb high blood pressure. The following were their three criteria for hypertension:

- Systolic pressure over 160
- Diastolic pressure over 95
- Current use of hypertension medication

Would you qualify as a hypertensive by any of those criteria? If so, weight control deserves your special attention.

Solum, Ryttig, Solum, and Larsen (1987) conducted a well-controlled study designed to measure the influence of a high-fiber diet on weight control. Half of their female subjects were given dietary fiber tablets, and the other half were given placebo tablets. Both groups lost a significant amount of weight, but the high-fiber group lost significantly more. The high-fiber group also experienced a significant reduction in both systolic and diastolic blood pressure, and the placebo group did not. Neither group had a significant drop in level of blood cholesterol or triglycerides. The authors concluded that "supplementation with dietary fiber of the form used in this study is useful in the treatment of overweight women" (p. 67).

The opposite conclusion was reached by Baron, Schori, Crow, Carter, and Mann (1986), who studied overweight British women. They reported that a low-carbohydrate/low-fiber diet was more conducive to weight loss than a high-carbohydrate/high-fiber regimen, when calories were limited to 1,000 per day. They concluded, "In view of these results, we believe previous claims of the benefits of fiber for weight loss

may have been overstated" (p. 1293). In fairness, different experimental designs quite often produce different results. In this case we don't know whether the carbohydrates were simple or complex, and that alone could have influenced the findings.

ANOREXIA AND BULIMIA

We must not lose sight of the fact that obesity is only one side, albeit the most obvious one, of the weight control coin. The extreme weight loss in some people caused by anorexia nervosa and bulimia is of grave concern. There are indications that these diseases are as much psychological as physical. According to Autrey et al. (1986):

> Anorexia nervosa patients often come from upper middle-class families with high achievement orientation. One of the parents, usually the mother, tends to be dominant and over-protective, while the other parent is weak, submissive, and often absent from the home for long periods of time (p. 537).

Strober and Humphrey (1987) also acknowledged that family relationships can play an important role in the development of anorexic or bulimic tendencies. A lack of parental affection and an overly negative or hostile environment may lead to negative effects on self-esteem and self-efficacy, which can result in extreme eating habits. According to Shisslak, Crago, Neal, and Swain (1987), a combination of personality, family, and social factors may create a bulimic or anorexic. About 90 percent of the victims are females, undoubtedly due to the cultural bias toward female thinness. Especially at risk are actresses, models, dancers, and athletes in sports like gymnastics, for whom a weight gain may mean the end of a career.

There are risks at either extreme of the body weight continuum. The net result is the American public's obsession with weight control. Zuti (1984) observed that "weight management is obviously the most popular of all the health and wellness activities" (p. 110). You can confirm this statement by browsing through any standard bookstore. The number of books and magazines on diet and weight-control exercise programs is astounding. Unfortunately, most of the programs being advocated do not work! People who go on diets usually go off diets, and therein lies the problem. Have you ever been on a diet that you read about in a magazine? If so, are you still on it? If you are a typical American, your answers were "yes" and "no," respectively. The only way to control weight is to develop healthy lifelong habits of eating and exercise. It is to that process that we now turn our attention.

PROMOTING WELLNESS THROUGH WEIGHT CONTROL

Having considered some of the consequences of being severely overweight or underweight, and in keeping with the theme of this text, let's emphasize the importance of remembering the positive aspects of maintaining normal weight. Among the most obvious and often-mentioned benefits of weight control are desirable physical appearance and the heightened self-esteem that accompanies it.

You may recall that self-esteem occupies a prominent place in Maslow's hierarchy of human needs, and that it is also one of Rokeach's terminal values. For most of us, self-esteem is at least somewhat dependent on affiliation, defined as a close, meaningful association with another person. Anyone who has experienced the ostracism that so often accompanies obesity knows how important and elusive affiliation can

be. Friendships and romantic relationships are more accessible to those who are physically attractive, and in our society attractiveness is associated with desirable weight.

We've all known someone whose social life suffered because he or she was overweight. The psychological impact of being overweight can be at least as damaging as the physical aspect. Aside from disease prevention, there is no lack of incentive for maintaining ideal weight. Whether one is looking for a date, a mate, or a profession, the choices are greater for a person whose weight does not detract from his or her appearance.

Attitudes, Behaviors, and Motivations

Saltzer (1978) applied the principles of locus of control and behavioral intent to weight loss. Remember that the Ajzen-Fishbein model postulated that behavior is a function of attitudes and social norms (i.e., one's perceptions of what significant others are doing and thinking). Based on this model, Saltzer expected that

only individuals having either a high value on health and/or a high value on physical appearance would consider losing weight to be an important behavior since, for them, a certain standard of health or physical appearance is an important reward. (p. 121)

As with exercise, weight control may be motivated by factors that have little or nothing to do with health, in which case attendant health benefits may be a peripheral bonus.

Internal Locus of Control

Saltzer hypothesized that people with an internal locus of control would more likely be motivated by the personal health value of weight control, and that those with an external locus of control would be more influenced by social factors such as appearance. Her data, generated from a Weight Locus of Control (WLOC) scale she developed, supported that hypothesis. Approximately half of her subjects, who were mostly young adults, rated health as one of their top three values, which is consistent with studies reported in chapter 3 and substantiates Rokeach's belief that values influence attitudes and behavior.

Self-Concept

The Rokeach system of beliefs is applicable to weight control in other ways, as is Bandura's social learning theory and Hochbaum's Health Belief Model. It was Rokeach's contention that self-concept is central to behavioral change and influences values. Think of your own self-concept as it relates to weight control. Do you think of yourself as being physically attractive? Do you believe your physical attractiveness is based at least in part on your ability to maintain a desirable weight? Do you believe that you have the ability to control your weight? Do you believe that the benefits of weight control exceed the costs and barriers? Do you have a positive attitude toward weight-control activities? Do you intend to maintain a desirable weight? If the answer to each of these questions is "yes," you are almost certain to maintain an attractive weight, which will coincide with a higher level of wellness and the self-satisfaction that Maslow credited to the self-actualizing process.

Behavioral Contracts

Ureda (1980) reported on other applications of general learning theory for weight-loss programs. Motivation is always a critical factor in behavior, and Ureda hypothesized that the motivation to lose weight would be stronger if subjects signed a behavior contract committing them to losing weight, especially if the contract were signed in the presence of a witness. Both hypotheses were confirmed by the results of the study. It was concluded that a behavior contract is effective because it makes objectives more explicit, strengthens expectations, enhances commitment to action, and increases acceptance of responsibility for one's actions. This is consistent with Dennison's Activated Health Education Model, which advocates involvement, awareness, and responsibility. The behavioral contract is a procedure you can use whether your goal is weight loss or some other behavioral change, and whether your motivation is health-related or totally independent of health.

Self-Efficacy

Other researchers have effectively applied behavioral theories to weight-control problems. Nash (1987) used Bandura's social learning theory, notably self-efficacy, to explain stimulus/response eating patterns. Nash believed that all of us are more likely to eat as a result of external cues (sight or smell of food, associations with TV or drinking) than as a result of internal cues (hunger). Therefore we must develop confidence in our ability to control caloric intake when faced with external cues. Nash discovered that obese individuals often have low self-esteem that undermines their ability to resist external cues (self-efficacy). Once again we see that feeling good about oneself is a prerequisite to taking action that leads toward wellness.

Becker, Maiman, Kirscht, Haefner, and Drachman (1977) applied the Health Belief Model (HBM) to eating behavior. Key components of that model are efficacy, perception of susceptibility to a health program, and the balance between the benefits and the costs of or barriers to taking action. The reported findings supported the usefulness of the HBM in explaining adherence to a diet. That is, we tend to act when it is obvious to us that the benefits outweigh the costs and when we are confident that we will be successful in achieving the desired outcome.

Dieting Advice

Each year millions of people make a decision to diet, after consciously or unconsciously considering efficacy and costs versus benefits. Certain diets are much more likely to lead to the desired outcome than others, but are passed over in favor of a diet that offers quick weight loss with very little effort (cost). Fad diets typically promote fluid weight loss rather than a more permanent fat loss, often at the expense of nutritional balance.

Schapell, Bell, and Blackburn (1987), Haggerty and Blackburn (1987), and Kowalski (1987) provide excellent reviews of which diets are safe and effective and which ones are dangerous or ineffective. Their findings on various popular diets are synthesized here for your consideration:

- **Weight Watchers International**—Highly recommended because it promotes healthy, lifelong change in eating behavior. It is a classic model of a balanced, common-sense approach to weight reduction. It includes exercise and behavior modification components, allows for individual tastes, limits intake of fats and alcohol, and encourages a gradual weight loss of 1 to 2 pounds per week.
- **Bloomingdale's Eat Healthy Diet**—A balanced and sensible plan that incorporates behavior modification, exercise, and other lifestyle changes. It emphasizes a high intake of complex carbohydrates, especially fresh vegetables, fresh fruits, and grain products, and low-fat cooking, all intended to reduce blood cholesterol levels.
- **TOPS** (Take Off Pounds Sensibly)— Comparable to the preceding two in terms of being healthy and effective.
- **The Pritikin Program**—It definitely produces weight loss and general wellness, but it is unrealistically restrictive for most people. Its best features include daily exercise, replacing unneeded fats and protein with complex carbohydrates, and daily helpings of raw vegetables. It also emphasizes avoiding cigarettes, caffeine, and alcohol, and eating one serving each per day of grain, fruit, and meat. A modified version may be a healthy alternative.
- **Scarsdale Medical Diet**—This diet should not be followed for more than 2 weeks at a time because of its limited variety and nutritional deficiencies. It emphasizes high protein intake to promote ketosis, a process for metabolizing stored fats.
- **Cambridge Diet**—This diet is likely to produce quick weight loss without nutritional danger, but it is not a realistic lifetime plan. Its users get bored with drinking the same liquid every meal, miss the taste of real food, and eventually begin to cheat on the diet.

The researchers agreed that the following diets are not recommended under any circumstances: the Beverly Hills Diet, which involves eating lots of fruit and little else, resulting in weight loss due to diarrhea (hardly a lifelong plan); Fit for Life, which also advocates the "cleansing property" (i.e., diarrhea) of large quantities of fruits and vegetables, and is a gimmick diet that is unsafe and scientifically unsound; Dr. Atkins's Diet Revolution (also known as the "Drinking Man's Diet," the "Air Force Diet," and the "Mayo Clinic Diet")—described as "dangerous" by the American Medical Association, it produces only temporary fluid weight loss; and Dr. Stillman's Diet (also known as the "Rice Diet"), which also produces temporary fluid loss and is nutritionally deficient.

Many of the diets just described are based on limiting caloric intake, usually to about 1,000 to 1,500 calories per day. Such diets may be obsolete according to a scientific breakthrough reported by Ratto (1987b). She informs us that researchers have discovered that fat calories are more responsible for weight gains than complex carbohydrate calories, so it no longer suffices to control weight by counting calories. The good news is that the body does not manufacture fat as readily from complex carbohydrates as from fats. Further, eating complex carbohydrates accelerates the body's metabolism, causing it to burn even more calories. She concluded, "The new message for dieters is: Don't focus on calories. Don't deprive yourself of carbohydrate, in fact, eat *more* carbohydrate. Just cut down on fat, and get regular exercise" (p. 27).

A POSITIVE EATING PLAN

Cooper (1982) advocated what he referred to as a "positive eating plan." It is an essential part of his overall protocol for total wellness, and I heartily endorse it. Here are some of his best tips:

- Eat meals that are more than 50 percent carbohydrates, less than 20 percent protein, and less than 30 percent fat.
- Eat most of your calories before 1 p.m. The metabolic rate slows down as the day progresses, and a large evening meal is more likely to be stored as fat and less likely to be expended for energy during sleep.
- Eat breakfast each day to reduce the need for a large evening meal.
- Substitute daily two glasses of water for two glasses of any high-calorie fluid (e.g., whole milk or beer), which will result in a swing of about 3,500 calories per week, for a weight loss of 1 pound per week and 52 pounds per year!
- Eat slowly. You are likely to feel full about 20 minutes after you have begun eating, regardless of how many calories you have consumed. Eating chewy or crunchy food will slow you down and facilitate this process.

- Eat as many fresh foods as possible. Canned and packaged foods contain high amounts of sodium and also increase your beverage intake.
- Read labels on cans and packages so you will know how many calories you are consuming.
- Use exercise rather than eating and drinking to cope with excessive stress.
- Have a plan and follow it. Keep a written record of daily exercise and food intake, so that you can balance that intake with caloric expenditure. This is an excellent technique for taking control of your weight and your lifestyle.

Two other kinds of information may prove helpful to you as you work toward weight control. One is a list of physical activities and the number of calories expended per hour in each (see Table 7.2). The other is a list of foods and calories per serving (see "Caloric Content of Selected Foods and Beverages," Appendix A); despite Ratto's advice to stop counting calories, it is still useful to know how many "fat calories" you are consuming.

Finally, Snow and Harris (1985) compared the exercise habits of former dieters, some of whom had maintained weight loss and some of whom regained lost weight. Those who maintained reported exercising more both during and following their diets. Snow and Harris's advice provides a fitting summary to this section:

Ultimately, for someone who has experienced a lifetime battle with weight (losing and gaining weight over and over again), advice to gradually increase exercise, to limit food intake only very mildly, and to try to be less concerned about weight and more concerned about a healthy lifestyle may be the best we currently have to offer. (p. 253)

Table 7.2 Caloric Expenditures by Occupation and Activity

Occupation	Kcal/day[a]
Middle-aged housewife	2,090
Female university student	2,290
Female factory worker	2,320
Male office worker	2,520
Male university student	2,930
Male steel worker	3,280
Male coal miner	3,660

Athletic activity	Kcal/150 lbs body wt/hr[b]
Cross-country ski racing	960
Running, 6-minute miles	900
Bicycle racing	900
Judo/karate	780
Canoe racing	780
Mountain climbing	780
Cross-country skiing	720
Ice hockey	720
Jogging, 10-minute miles	720
Swimming, 50 yards/minute	660
Bicycling, 13 miles/hour	660
Skating, vigorous	600
Handball/raquetball, competitive	600
Soccer	600
Dancing, fast/aerobic	600
Walking, 5 miles/hour	600
Downhill skiing	540
Squash/tennis/badminton, competitive	540
Basketball, full court	540
Bicycling, 10 miles/hour	480

(Cont.)

Table 7.2   (Continued)

Occupation	Kcal/day[a]
Water skiing	480
Calisthenics	420
Canoeing, 4 miles/hr	420
Badminton/tennis/volleyball, recreational	360
Weight lifting	360
Softball/baseball	300
Swimming, 20 yards/minute	300
Golf, walking	240
Sailing	240
Bowling	240
Table tennis	240
Walking, 2 miles/hour	180

Note. [a]These figures reflect the fact that the typical male is larger than the typical female, increasing caloric consumption. [b]These are estimates. Caloric expenditures vary considerably according to the intensity with which the activities are performed. *Sources:* Howley & Franks (1986) and McCardle, Katch, & Katch (1986).

SUMMARY

It is unhealthy to be extremely overweight or underweight. Worldwide, being underweight is more common, but obesity is a greater concern for Americans, who tend to consume more calories than their bodies need. Obesity is defined as being more than 20 percent over one's ideal weight, having a Body Mass Index higher than 28 percent, or having a percent body fat higher than 30 for women or 25 for men.

Obesity is a high-risk factor for developing coronary heart disease and also contributes to cancer, diabetes, and other diseases. Underweight can be caused by anorexia nervosa or bulimia, eating disorders that are most prevalent among adolescent females. A basal metabolic rate that is abnormally fast or slow may make weight control more difficult for some, but poor eating and exercise habits are more common causes of unhealthy weight.

The most effective long-range plan for losing weight is to exercise a bit more and eat a bit less. For those who are obese, losing 1 pound per week is a reasonable and healthy goal. Low-calorie diets not accompanied by exercise are not recommended because they tend to cause early fluid loss followed by muscle tissue loss; fat loss is minimal. The set point theory holds that low-calorie diets slow the basal metabolic rate so the body can conserve energy, which defeats the purpose of restricting calories. Exercise is a doubly effective weight-loss strategy: It burns calories immediately and also raises the basal metabolic rate both during and following exercise. Cooper's "positive eating plan" is a healthy alternative to crash dieting because it emphasizes behavior modification.

Examining Your Values

Return to chapter 1 and the list of terminal values. How many relate to your appearance and, specifically, to maintaining normal weight? I count at least six on mine and perhaps as many as nine, depending on the extent to which self-concept is dependent on appearance.

1. Is your self-esteem enhanced by your being at normal weight?
2. Is your health enhanced by your being at normal weight?
3. Is your social recognition enhanced by your being at normal weight?
4. Is your likelihood of close companionship, including sexual intimacy, enhanced by your being at normal weight?
5. Is your likelihood of a stimulating, active life enhanced by your being at normal weight?
6. Are your happiness and inner harmony promoted by your being at normal weight?
7. If these are the benefits of weight control, can you identify costs or barriers sufficient to override all of them? What are they?

CHAPTER 8

Alcohol Use and Abuse

It is better to debate a question without settling it than to settle a question without debating it.

—Joseph Joubert

Self-Examination Statements

Instructions: Read each statement, then circle the x in the column at the left that most closely describes your belief about that statement. (Use a pencil. After reading this chapter you may wish to come back and change some of your responses on the basis of new information or attitudes.)

SA = strongly agree   **A** = agree   **U** = undecided   **D** = disagree   **SD** = strongly disagree

SA	A	U	D	SD	
x	x	x	x	x	Alcohol doesn't affect me because I don't drink.
x	x	x	x	x	I think of myself as a social drinker.
x	x	x	x	x	I believe there is some value in moderate use of alcohol.
x	x	x	x	x	I have never lost self-respect because I drank too much.
x	x	x	x	x	I never drink unless I am with other people.
x	x	x	x	x	I first began drinking at home with my family.
x	x	x	x	x	No one in my family (that I know of) is an alcoholic.
x	x	x	x	x	I am more apt to drink in a home than in a bar.
x	x	x	x	x	I always feel that I am in complete control of my drinking.
x	x	x	x	x	I could stop drinking any time I wanted to.
x	x	x	x	x	Drinking is the social norm for American adults.
x	x	x	x	x	Drinking is the social norm among my friends.
x	x	x	x	x	If I didn't drink I would lose valued friendships.
x	x	x	x	x	I have never lost a friend because I drank too much.
x	x	x	x	x	I believe that most of my friends drink more than I do.
x	x	x	x	x	If my friends were all nondrinkers, I probably wouldn't drink.
x	x	x	x	x	I value alcohol because it makes me less inhibited and more sociable.
x	x	x	x	x	I value alcohol because it helps me cope with stress and tension.
x	x	x	x	x	I believe that alcohol causes more problems than it solves.
x	x	x	x	x	Alcohol is only a problem if one becomes an alcoholic.
x	x	x	x	x	The tendency to become an alcoholic is hereditary.
x	x	x	x	x	I don't believe that I am susceptible to becoming an alcoholic.

x	x	x	x	x	I believe a person who drinks only beer will never become an alcoholic.
x	x	x	x	x	I can drink more than most people without getting drunk.
x	x	x	x	x	My parents/spouse have never expressed concern about my drinking habits.
x	x	x	x	x	My closest friends have never expressed concern about my drinking habits.
x	x	x	x	x	I have never experienced health problems because I drank too much.
x	x	x	x	x	A little alcohol (one or two drinks) each day is good for my health.
x	x	x	x	x	Total abstainers have more health problems than social drinkers.
x	x	x	x	x	One problem associated with heavy drinking is weight control.
x	x	x	x	x	I don't believe that cirrhosis of the liver is a serious problem for social drinkers.
x	x	x	x	x	I understand the distinction between social drinking and problem drinking.
x	x	x	x	x	Anyone who regularly drinks six or more drinks per occasion is a problem drinker.
x	x	x	x	x	When I drink I often intend to get drunk.
x	x	x	x	x	Intoxication is not a problem unless one tries to drive.
x	x	x	x	x	I have never been intoxicated.
x	x	x	x	x	I have never been in trouble with the law because of alcohol.
x	x	x	x	x	I have never tried to drive while under the influence of alcohol.
x	x	x	x	x	I favor strict laws against drunken driving.
x	x	x	x	x	I have been in an accident caused by a drunk driver.
x	x	x	x	x	I personally knew someone who was killed by a drunk driver.
x	x	x	x	x	When I drive at night, I worry about being hit by someone who has been drinking.
x	x	x	x	x	I understand the concept of blood alcohol content (BAC).
x	x	x	x	x	I favor a national minimun drinking age of 21.
x	x	x	x	x	Countries with no minimum drinking age have fewer alcohol-related problems.
x	x	x	x	x	If all American youngsters learned to drink at home, as they do in France, we would have fewer alcohol problems.
x	x	x	x	x	Cultural values play a prominent role in acceptable drinking behavior.
x	x	x	x	x	The drinking habits of American men and women are becoming increasingly similar.
x	x	x	x	x	Advertisements have a significant effect on the drinking habits of the American people.
x	x	x	x	x	Advertisements have a significant effect on my drinking behavior.
x	x	x	x	x	Using alcohol is not a problem, but bad judgment in when and how to use it is.

DEFINING TERMS AND CONCEPTS

It is important to distinguish between *use* and *abuse* of alcohol. Alcohol has been used by people since the beginning of recorded history. Kinney and Leaton (1982) remind us that alcohol is perceived as "one of God's great gifts" by those who enjoy it without problems, and as "an invitation of the devil" by those who suffer from its ills. People in both camps have been prejudiced by their own experiences with alcohol, and both are probably right. Alcohol was widely used as a medicine for hundreds of years before better medications became available. In some societies alcohol is served as a part of the main meal. Many cultures use alcohol to celebrate births, deaths, marriages, and other commemorative occasions. Although drunkenness is not unheard of in these contexts, it is usually neither common nor accepted.

From Use to Abuse

Christiansen and Goldman (1983) identified three drinking styles that seem to lead from alcohol use to abuse. "Family drinking style" involves drinking in a home with close friends or family members, and generally entails few problems. "Frequent social drinking style" is typified by drinking outside the home, more often and in greater quantities, sometimes ending in inebriation. "Problem drinking style" is typified by fighting, passing out, committing illegal acts, and encountering problems with police.

A change from widespread use of alcohol to widespread abuse of alcohol seems to have begun around the sixteenth century, when the process of distilling liquor was developed. Prior to that time, the strongest liquors that could be obtained through the process of fermentation were about 14 percent alcohol. Distillation produced a much more concentrated beverage. The percentage of alcohol in a beverage is about half of its proof, as indicated on the label. For example, a bourbon that is 100 proof is about 50 percent alcohol. Obviously, a distilled liquor that contains 50 percent alcohol is much more potent to the user than a fermented beverage that contains only 14 percent alcohol (Table 8.1).

Table 8.1   Alcoholic Drinks and Alcohol Content

Type of drink	Volume (oz)	Percent alcohol
Bourbon/whiskey	1.5	40-50
Gin	1.5	40-50
Rum	1.5	35-45
Vodka	1.5	35-40
Liqueur	1.5	30-60
Schnapps	1.5	20-25
Wine	4-5	10-20
Wine coolers	12	4-6
Beer and ale	12-16	3.5-7
Light beer	12	3.5-7

Prohibition

The 18th Amendment to the United States Constitution was passed in 1919, ushering in Prohibition. For the next 14 years it was illegal to manufacture, sell, or consume alcoholic beverages. In 1933 the 21st Amendment repealed Prohibition due to the problems it caused (e.g., bootlegging and speakeasies). It had become obvious that people who chose to use alcohol would do so whether it was legal or illegal, and much the same is true today. During the Prohibition years alcohol became an emotional issue that divided our nation. Citizens developed love or hate relationships with alcohol, there seemingly being little middle ground.

Although estimates vary, there is general agreement that about two thirds of adult Americans use or abuse alcohol and about one third consider themselves to be abstainers. The drinking rate is higher among men than women, and greater among younger than older adults. Although the latter is often attributed to peer pressure, it more likely represents a period of experimentation. Roughly 90 percent of college students reportedly do some drinking, and only two thirds of older adults described themselves as drinkers; evidently some young drinkers ultimately decide against continued usage—or die in alcohol-related accidents before reaching adulthood.

Defining Levels of Use

Levels of use and abuse can be defined as light, moderate, heavy, social, problem, alcoholic, and so on. Gordon and Doyle (1987) totaled monthly consumption of alcohol, then categorized drinking according to average daily consumption:

- None
- 0-1 drinks per day
- 1-2 drinks per day
- 2-3 drinks per day
- Over 3 drinks per day

These categories parallel the descriptive phrases "abstainer," "infrequent drinker," "light," "moderate," and "heavy drinker," respectively, although Gordon and Doyle did not use those terms. Nearly half of the 1,910 adult male subjects reported drinking 0-1 drinks per day, and another third reported no drinking. Only 9 percent were in the upper two categories, averaging 2 or more drinks per day. Clearly, the majority were users, not abusers, of alcohol.

Wiggins and Wiggins (1987) also identified five levels of drinking, but unlike the previous study they included binge drinking as a criterion. A binge drinker might abstain for six days, then consume 7 drinks in one day, while a moderate drinker might consume a drink each day for seven days; the total amount consumed by each would be the same, but the former would be described as a heavy or problem drinker while the latter would not. Their subjects were college students, and the drinking rates were slightly higher than those reported by the adults in the Gordon and Doyle study. Still, 20 percent of their sample reported abstaining, and another 25 percent classified themselves as moderate drinkers, meaning no more than 5 drinks on one occasion. Their three categories of "heavy" drinkers were these:

- Infrequent heavy drinkers, 6 or more drinks on one occasion less than once a month (20 percent)
- Frequent heavy drinkers, 6 or more drinks on one occasion 1 to 3 times per month (20 percent)
- Most frequent heavy drinkers, 6 or more drinks on one occasion at least weekly (15 percent)

Which description best fits your drinking behavior? Which is most descriptive of the social norms for your circle of friends?

An even more elaborate classification of drinking habits was reported by Hickenbottom, Bissonette, and O'Shea (1987). Eighty-seven percent of their college student subjects reported some drinking, ranging from occasional to heavy (Table 8.2).

Over two thirds of their subjects were in Categories 2, 3, and 4, denoting lighter drinking, but the standards for moderate drinking in this study were significantly more liberal than those of previous researchers cited. As you can see, how terms are defined is pivotal to one's determining alcohol use and abuse.

Table 8.2 Continuum of Drinking Quantity/Frequency of College Students

Percent	Category	Description
13	1	Nondrinkers
23	2	Occasional drinkers (1-2 drinks, less than once a week)
25	3	Light drinkers (1-2 drinks once or twice a week and 3-4 drinks less than once a week)
21	4	Light-to-moderate drinkers (1-2 drinks more than twice a week, 3-4 drinks once or twice a week, and 5-6 drinks less than once a week)
11	5	Moderate drinkers (3-4 drinks more than twice a week, 5-6 drinks once or twice a week, and 7 or more drinks less than once a week)
05	6	Moderately heavy drinkers (5-6 drinks more than twice a week and 7 or more drinks once or twice a week)
02	7	Heavy drinkers (7 or more drinks more than twice a week)

EXPLORING THE LIMITS OF SOCIAL AND PROBLEM DRINKING

Alles, Lambert, and Bibeau (1984) defined problem drinking as "characterized by consuming a large quantity on a given occasion, high BAC (blood alcohol content), and loss of control" (p. 5). Seventy percent of their college student population described themselves as light drinkers, 19 percent as heavy drinkers, and 11 percent as nondrinkers. However, 27 percent indicated that they usually drink to get drunk, which seems to represent a contradiction in terms because 8 percent of the "light" drinkers apparently drank to intoxication.

Intoxication and Metabolism

Intoxication is a legal concept as well as a physical state. Drinking alcoholic beverages produces a change in the BAC. The exact amount of that change depends on the size of the drinker, the concentration of alcohol in the beverage being consumed, and the speed with which drinking occurs. The term "drink" usually refers to one 12-ounce beer, one glass of wine (4 to 5 ounces), or one shot of hard liquor (1.5 ounces). Any one of these will raise the BAC approximately

.02 percent, although a smaller person may be affected more than a larger one.

Just as metabolic rate is an important factor in weight control, it is also important to those who use alcohol. The human body metabolizes approximately one drink per hour, depending on body size, use of medications or other drugs, and whether the stomach is empty or filled with food. A social drinker could consume one drink per hour for an indefinite period of time without ever reaching a state of intoxication. Further, consuming five drinks, spread evenly over a 3-hour period, produces a BAC of approximately .04 percent because three of the drinks would have been metabolized; after such drinking, a person could reasonably expect to retain the judgment and reaction time necessary for safe driving. Those who imbibe more rapidly or more extensively may accurately conclude that they are drinking for other than social reasons and that they should not drive after drinking.

Social Drinking and the Law

Social drinking is characterized by a moderate intake of alcohol that keeps the BAC under .05 percent, an important limit for legal reasons. In Pennsylvania and many other states, a person is legally intoxicated when the BAC reaches .10 percent. It would take five drinks consumed within 1 hour for an average-sized person to reach .10 percent BAC. However, a person whose BAC is more than .05 but less than .10 percent may be arrested for DUI, even though not legally intoxicated. DUI is "driving under the influence" of alcohol and is the leading cause of death for persons aged 16 to 24 (Wallack & Corbett, 1987). With this in mind, the federal government passed legislation mandating a common legal drinking age of 21. Any state that failed to comply would lose federal financial support for highway construction. As of 1989, every state had 21 as its legal drinking age.

A DISEASE CALLED ALCOHOLISM

Another distinction that needs to be made is between *problem drinking* and *alcoholism*. A problem drinker is one who loses ability to control his actions; devotes undue time, money, or importance to alcohol; drinks to cope with life's problems; frequently drinks to intoxication; attempts to drive while intoxicated; or otherwise engages in activities that would not be attempted if drinking had not occurred. Problem drinkers are more likely than social drinkers or non-drinkers to get in trouble with the law, attempt suicide, or be the victim of a homicide.

In contrast, alcoholism is a chronic disease with a genetic basis ("Out in the Open," 1987). According to Claydon (1987), alcoholism tends to run in families, whether for genetic or environmental reasons. An alcoholic lacks the ability to stop after one or two drinks, is more likely than the problem drinker to drink daily, and is more likely to suffer loss of job, spouse, or health. Nathan (1987) describes the history of alcoholism in the U.S. from the founding of Alcoholics Anonymous in 1935 to 1985. Fifty years ago alcoholism was thought to be a problem that affected only adult males and that resulted from improper upbringing and lack of moral character; now we know that those assumptions are false. Nathan contended that by 1985 medical specialists generally agreed that alcoholism is more the result of a genetically determined predisposition than a psychological disorder.

Douglas (1986) does not accept the theory that alcoholism is a disease, preferring to believe that alcoholism *causes* disease. According to him, the alcoholic must understand that there is no treatment for alcoholism that will allow a return to "normal drinking" and that the only cure for the condition caused by alcoholism is total abstinence.

THE CAUSES OF DRINKING

Many theories have been forwarded about the causes and effects of alcoholism and problem drinking in addition to the theory of genetic predisposition. According to Forsyth and Hundleby (1987), research literature suggests that younger people are more apt to drink for reasons of extroversion and sensation seeking, whereas older people are more likely to drink as a result of anxiety and depression. The authors described five basic kinds of drinking:

- Convivial
- Ceremonial
- Bored
- Stressful
- Neutral

They associated convivial drinking with happiness and ceremonial drinking with contentment; neither of these usually creates problems. Drinking out of boredom is less desirable, and drinking to reduce anxiety or depression is even more problematic. Neutral drinking is done for no reason except habit. Each of these last three types of drinking is more apt to lead to problem drinking than the first two.

According to Berkowitz and Perkins (1987), three primary reasons for drinking were given by college students:

- To enhance sociability and social interaction
- To reduce stress and encourage relaxation
- To alter consciousness (get drunk)

Although college men traditionally have used alcohol more often, in greater quantities, and with more negative consequences than college women, those differences between the sexes are narrowing. Controlling for body weight, the drinking rates for women are now about as high as for men, but women drink with different attitudes and intentions than men (for instance, women have less desire to become intoxicated). The authors also noted that underclassmen have more alcohol-related problems, whereas upperclassmen apparently learn to control their drinking. Peers continue to be a strong influence on drinking behavior at the college level.

Alcohol and Depression

Anesheusel and Huba (1983) questioned the wisdom of using alcohol to cope with depression, although "studies of alcoholics and nonalcoholic drinkers suggest that a major motivation for drinking is to alleviate depressed mood" (p. 134). Their data, collected from over 700 adult subjects, indicated that, in the short term, use of alcohol may lead to decreased levels of depression, but the long-term causal effect is *increased* depression. The usual sequence seems to be to drink alcohol when feeling depressed; then the excessive drinking leads to social impairment, and the social impairment causes failure and further depression.

Alcohol and Poor Self-Concept

Brown and Munson (1987) studied the relationship between personality and alcohol consumption among college students. Their review of previous research indicated that poor self-concept has been consistently associated with excessive alcohol use and alcohol-related problems. (Think about the Rokeach system of beliefs, and you will know why.) They compared the drinking habits of introverted and extroverted students and discovered that extroverted students were more likely to drink to be sociable and to relax. Introverted students more often expected drinking to reduce social anxieties and improve sexual performance.

Predicting Drinking Behavior

Downs (1987) identified three factors as being predictive of drinking behavior:

- Previous drinking habits
- Drinking habits of closest friend
- Attitudes about the perceived harm due to use of alcohol

In this particular study, peers other than the closest friend had little or no impact on either attitudes toward drinking or drinking behavior. Downs agreed with Berkowitz and Perkins that gender differences in drinking behavior are disappearing.

Self-Consciousness

Hull, Young, and Jouriles (1986) studied the relationship between self-consciousness and alcohol consumption. Their hypothesis, which was confirmed, was that highly self-conscious individuals would drink more following personal failure in order to reduce self-awareness, and would drink less following personal success. In contrast, individuals with a low level of self-consciousness had drinking habits that were relatively independent of success or failure.

Steele and Southwick (1985) acknowledged that alcohol has an effect on social behavior, increasing aggression, self-disclosure, and sexual adventurousness. It also tends to decrease inhibition and the ability to foresee negative consequences. Their data revealed that, when faced with a conflict between inhibiting and initiating cues, a person under the influence of alcohol is more likely to ignore inhibitions and

act on the initiating cues. For example, one might ignore feelings of dizziness and an unsteady gait—cues that should inhibit further drinking—but act on such initiating cues as the invitation of a friend to "have one more for the road" or a television commercial that makes another drink sound appealing. This was not true for low-conflict situations, but the greater the conflict, the more likely the subject was to ignore inhibitions and initiate action.

Personal Failure

Hull (1981) offered additional insights into the causes of alcohol consumption. His contention was that alcohol reduces one's state of self-awareness and the tendency to be critical of one's level of performance or standards of conduct. Thus, following personal failure, alcohol makes self-evaluation and self-criticism less likely. It was Hull's opinion that drinking is a strategic attempt to limit unfavorable information about self and becomes, to that extent, a source of psychological relief. He reported two studies that supported his belief that persons with a high level of self-awareness, who also experience continued personal failure, are most likely to sustain high levels of alcohol consumption.

THE EFFECTS OF HEAVY DRINKING

We have looked at some of the causes of heavy alcohol consumption, but we have not yet examined the effects. Hull, in the 1981 study just cited, wrote, "In addition to being involved in the majority of traffic deaths, alcohol has been cited as a major factor in drownings, fires, assaults, murders, robberies, and sex-related crimes" (p. 586). Substantiation for these and similar effects came from a 1985 National Health Interview Survey as reported by Williams, Dufour, and Bertolucci (1986). They wrote:

It has been estimated that up to 150,000 Americans die each year from alcohol-related causes. Chronic liver disease, motor vehicle accidents, suicides, and homicides account for much of this mortality, but there are also many deaths from alcohol-related falls, drownings, and fires. (p. 593)

Sex crimes, child abuse, domestic violence, and a host of other problems are also alcohol-related in excess numbers and there is a high rate of alcohol-related problems among the rising number of homeless people.

In a special report to the U.S. Congress, the Secretary of Health and Human Services (1985) observed that 10 percent of the nation's population consumes 50 percent of the alcohol! One effect is more crime and violence among those persons; more than half of all those convicted of violent crimes had been drinking at the time of the offense.

Domestic Strife

Estep (1987) observed that women with alcohol problems were more likely to be single, separated, divorced, or cohabiting than happily married. Whether alcohol causes marital problems, or marital problems lead to increased use of alcohol, is still debatable. In this study, however, 50 women who had a history of having used alcohol and prescription drugs were compared to 50 women who had not. The alcohol group was associated with a stronger preference for hard liquor, more binge drinking, more conflicts with family members and friends, more instances of impaired judgment due to alcohol abuse, and more arrests for driving under the influence.

Motor Vehicle Accidents

According to Bradstock et al. (1987), alcohol is involved in approximately 58 percent of all fatal motor vehicle accidents, accounting for about 25,000 deaths annually. Because young people have the highest rates of alcohol-involved fatal accidents, most lost-years-of-life come from that group; that is, a 20-year-old who dies in an auto accident loses more years of life than a 50-year-old victim. Younger people are also more likely to drink and drive, a practice 3 times more prevalent among males than females. The authors also reported that (as you would expect) individuals who drink in response to stress are more likely to drink and drive than those who exercise in response to stress.

Teen Drinking

Temple and Fillmore (1986) studied the drinking habits of 18-year-old males and followed them to age 31. They concluded that adolescent problem drinkers, compared to adolescents who were not problem drinkers, were more likely to experience conflicts between parental and peer expectations, be more influenced by peers than by parents, have friends with drinking and other behavioral problems, have parents who drink heavily themselves, have parents who are relatively uninvolved with them and their lives, place higher value on autonomy from parents, place lower value on academic achievement, hold lower expectations of academic success, attach less importance to religion, and tolerate more deviant behavior. The authors discovered, however, that drinking behavior at age 18 was not a good predictor of drinking behavior at age 31. Some of the key factors that affect adolescent drinking behavior (e.g., negative influence of peers and conflicts with parents) exert diminishing influence during adulthood.

Many of the causes and effects of alcohol use and abuse that have been mentioned in this section are related to mental, social, and emotional health. Alcohol also has a major impact on risks related to several prominent diseases.

ALCOHOL CONSUMPTION AND DISEASE

Alcohol has various effects on the human body. In recent years alcohol use has been thought to have a limited positive effect on coronary heart disease. Let's explore the true picture of the positives and negatives of alcohol consumption for our health.

Alcohol and Coronary Heart Disease

Earlier discussion of low density lipids (LDL) and high density lipids (HDL) included mention of the possible protective effects of alcohol against coronary heart disease (CHD). This has been the subject of a continuing controversy among researchers. According to Criqui et al. (1987):

> Moderate alcohol consumption has been reported to offer some protection against coronary heart disease, but overall alcohol consumption appears to have a U-shaped relation to total mortality, and some reports indicate a U-shaped relation to coronary heart disease and cardiovascular disease. (p. 630)

The authors studied over 7,000 American men and women for 8-1/2 years before concluding that moderate alcohol consumption is only weakly protective against cardiovascular disease. Ferrence, Truscott, and Whitehead (1986) fear that the protective effects of alcohol consumption on heart disease have been exaggerated and overpublicized. They remind us that moderate alcohol intake does not lead to lower overall mortality rates, just to weak protection from some forms of heart disease. They strongly discourage nondrinkers from using alcohol to reduce heart disease mortality because this may create more problems than it solves.

A study of New Zealanders by Scragg, Stewart, Jackson, and Beaglehole (1987) reported that "alcohol drinkers had decreased relative risks of both myocardial infarction and sudden coronary death compared with nondrinkers" (p. 77). However, Croft et al. (1987) reached a more conservative conclusion. They studied risk factors for cardiovascular disease among 990 young American adults. Although other studies have reported that alcohol raises HDL and thus protects against CHD, they reported, "A statistically significant association between alcohol intake and HDL cholesterol levels ($r = 0.24$) was observed only in white females who did not smoke" (p. 202). Despite these conflicting reports, the preponderance of evidence suggests that one or two drinks per day are not likely to be detrimental to your health and wellness, but more than that will be!

Conditions That Restrict Alcohol Use

There are instances when even limited use of alcohol may be hazardous to health. For pregnant women, for example, Anokute (1986) reported that the relative risk of a stillbirth more than doubled for women who had even one drink per day, and more than tripled for those who had more than two drinks per day. For women who smoked a pack of cigarettes along with their two drinks per day, the risk of a stillbirth was more than 5 times as high as for a nonsmoking, nondrinking mother. Mintz, Boyd, Rose, Charwastra, and Jarvik (1985) studied the relationship between drinking and smoking and found numerous studies claiming that "people who drink alcohol are more likely to smoke than those who do not" (p. 203). Further, problem drinkers are particularly heavy smokers. Their own study concluded that "drinking alcohol significantly increased the amount and rate of smoking" (p. 203). It would seem then that one way to reduce the risk of smoking-related diseases (e.g., cancers, emphysema) would be to use alcohol sparingly.

Alcohol Use and Liver Disease

Cirrhosis of the liver is one of the 10 leading causes of death in the United States and has long been associated with alcohol abuse. It has shown a declining rate in recent years, however, according to the previously cited 1985 special report to Congress on Alcohol and Health. Per capita consumption of alcohol has been declining since 1981, with about one third of the U.S. population abstaining altogether. Circumstantial evidence suggests that cirrhosis of the liver is largely preventable if alcohol intake is controlled.

Alcohol and Body Weight

Williamson et al. (1987) reported that "alcohol contributes more than 10 percent of the total caloric intake of adult drinkers in the United States" (p. 1324). Because there is no nutritive value in alcohol, it has generally been assumed that the "empty calories" from alcohol make weight control more difficult. These authors, however, reported that alcohol was related to only a slight increase in the weight of their male subjects and was associated with a substantial reduction in the weight of female subjects who averaged up to two drinks per day.

Similar results were reported by Camargo, Vranizan, Dreon, Frey-Hewitt, and Wood (1987). They found that one drink per day was positively associated with an increase in basal metabolic rate (BMR) of about 13 percent, which was enough to offset the additional calories. BMR did *not* continue to rise as drinking increased. They also reported no significant difference in the percent body fat between drinkers and abstainers, and noted that, because about two thirds of American adults use alcohol and only about one quarter are overweight,

the relationship between the two is apparently quite limited.

ALCOHOL AND WELLNESS

Let's return to social learning theory and look at its implications for alcohol use and wellness. Hays (1985) noted that the internal-external locus of control construct, the Health Belief Model, and Ajzen-Fishbein's theory of reasoned action all stem from value-expectancy theory. Hays proceeded to develop an Integrated Value-Expectancy Model designed to explain alcohol and drug use. According to this model, our use of alcohol is determined by perceived norms (what we think others are doing), our locus of control, and our behavioral intentions. The latter, in turn, are influenced by our attitudes toward the behavior and by our value-expectancy system.

Huckstadt (1987) hypothesized that use of alcohol would be related to locus of control. As he predicted, the alcoholics in his study had the lowest scores on internal locus of control (ILC), recovering alcoholics had higher scores, and the highest scores on ILC were for nonalcoholics. One of the foremost goals of treatment for alcoholics is to help the individual regain greater control over life events. Research related to the concept of locus of control has repeatedly supported a relationship between one's ability and willingness to assume control over health behaviors and higher levels of wellness.

Value Perceptions

Several studies have been done on the relationship between values and the use and abuse of alcohol. Teahan (1987) used the Rokeach survey of values to study the drinking motivations of American college students. He found that male college students placed higher value on independence and achievement than on affiliation or affection, and that their approach to drinking was macho and pleasure-seeking. Female college students placed higher value on self-respect and a comfortable life and were more likely than males to use alcohol as a tranquilizer or to release inhibitions.

Women

Morgan (1987) charged that the double standard that exists for men and women related to sexual behavior also exists for use of alcohol. He asserted that self-control has been an important American middle-class value. When women drink in public and become uninhibited, males attach a negative connotation to that lack of self-control but do not apply the same standard to themselves or other males.

The more self-control is valued by a society, or any subset of it, the more alcohol is shunned. In some social circles, however, moderate use of alcohol is associated with higher status and genteel behavior, in which case controlled use of alcohol is favored. Thus, alcohol can enhance or diminish quality of life, depending on how it is perceived and used.

Native Americans

Flores (1986) also used the Rokeach Values Survey to compare the values of Native Americans (Indians) and Anglos and, within each of those groups, alcoholics and nonalcoholics. He presented evidence "which suggests that Native Americans' values are measurably and significantly different from Anglo values" (p. 1708). The values of alcoholics and nonalcoholics from the same culture were more similar than the values of alcoholics from the two cultures. For example, Native Americans seemed to prefer personal values (happiness, a comfortable life) to the societal goals of the Anglo population (a world at peace, national security). Among national norms provided by Rokeach, the two leading

instrumental values were *honesty* and *responsibility*. Native American alcoholics ranked those values seventh and eleventh, respectively; they also ranked self-respect lower than any of the other groups. Flores reasoned that these differences in values may help explain the ineffectiveness of alcohol and drug treatment provided by Anglos to Native Americans. It also gives insight as to why our efforts to "help" others may be ineffective if we do not share their values.

Collegians

Beck (1981) applied the Ajzen-Fishbein model of reasoned action and the Health Belief Model to the drinking and driving behavior of American college students. Thirty percent of the 800 college students polled admitted to driving after drinking excessively. Their belief that they could drive while under the influence, without getting caught by the police or causing an accident, was an important factor in their decision to drive after drinking. The Fishbein model proved effective in predicting drinking and driving behavior based on stated intentions to drink and drive. The Health Belief Model was ineffective in predicting drinking and driving behavior based on perceived susceptibility to accidents.

Influence of Media and Advertising

Some Americans believe that the health and wellness of the nation is being undermined by television programming and by advertising. SMART (Stop Marketing Alcohol on Radio and Television) is a private organization dedicated to eliminating all advertising of alcohol on radio and TV in the same way that cigarette advertising has already been banned. Support for such a goal requires balancing conflicting values such as freedom of choice versus national welfare.

Minkler, Wallack, and Madden (1987) pointed out the inconsistency in the editorial and advertising policies of *Ms.*, a leading national magazine for women. The magazine's editorial policy stresses health and fitness practices, but their advertising policy is to promote alcohol and tobacco products for financial gain. The authors believe that this sends mixed signals and concluded that the magazine misleads it readers by glamorizing the use of alcohol and tobacco in its ads and downplaying the health risks of these two products. Califano (1986) presents similar analyses of *Time, Newsweek*, and other magazines.

Wallack, Breed, and Cruz (1987) described television as a de facto health educator and as an alcohol educator in particular. From a content analysis of 116 prime-time TV programs, they found that 80 percent of the programs contained at least one appearance of alcohol and that alcohol was actually consumed in 60 percent of those programs. A typical hour's viewing contained over 10 drinking acts, although heavy drinking and intoxication were rarely shown. They concluded:

> Alcohol is ubiquitous in television life. The strong suggestion conveyed to viewers is that alcohol is taken for granted, routine and even necessary, that most people drink and that drinking is a part of everyday life. The drinkers are frequently glamorous; for many viewers they are setting an example regarding lifestyle. These images are at variance with the problematic nature of alcohol in society. (p. 37)

Perceptions of Abuse

This raises the thorny question of how best to educate the public about use and abuse of alcohol. People commonly believe that alcohol is a serious problem for others but not for themselves (Williams & Knox, 1987). This was confirmed by a poll of 1,000 college students who were asked the question, "How serious is alcohol abuse?" On a scale of 1 to 5, 5 being most serious, the average responses were as follows:

- In the United States: 3.3
- At this University: 2.9
- In my dormitory: 2.2
- On my floor: 1.9

These perceptions reflect the curious belief that an alcohol problem exists in society at large but that it is not a serious problem for oneself and one's close associates. This phenomenon is common to virtually all health-related behaviors having to do with risk. Do you have these beliefs?

Initiative Against Abuse

Many groups have reduced alcohol abuse by taking the initiative without federal or state support.

Mothers Against Drunk Driving

Perhaps the best known of these is MADD (Mothers Against Drunk Driving), which became a national force about 1981. At about that same time, in response to an outcry against drunk drivers, legal drinking ages were being raised in many states, harsher penalties were being enacted for DUI, and greater efforts were being made to enforce existing laws. The Associated Press (1988) reported that arrests for DUI peaked in 1983 and have dropped 14 percent among 18- to 20-year-olds since that time as a result of our states making 21 the minimum drinking age. According to Brown and Skiffington (1987), in New Jersey, between 1981 and 1984, drunk driving fatalities were reduced 74 percent in the 18 to 20 age group after the legal drinking age was raised. The authors concluded that public information had a major impact on changing attitudes about drunk driving. Likewise, Holder and Blose (1987) recommended instituting a community education effort simultaneously with increasing prices and limiting advertising exposure in an effort to reduce alcohol abuse and to moderate alcohol use.

TIPS

Other unique approaches have been devised for improving quality of life by reducing alcohol abuse. Russ and Geller (1987) described TIPS (Training for Intervention Procedures), which was designed to help servers of alcohol in public taverns and restaurants recognize behavioral cues of impending intoxication (lowered inhibitions, slower reactions, impaired coordination, diminished judgment), and to intervene in appropriate ways to lower the BAC of offending patrons (e.g., by offering them food and water, slowing the delivery of alcoholic beverages, and encouraging moderation). Corey (1987) suggested applying Skinner's operant conditioning theory, the basic principle being that "it is the anticipated consequence of a behavior which is the primary factor in determining whether that behavior actually gets performed or not" (p. 38). His contention was that the actual consequence of drunk driving is often death; in this country there are about 25,000 deaths each year from drunk driving. Corey suggested that, as a part of the licensing procedure in this country, every new driver be required to witness an autopsy resulting from drunk driving because "nothing works nearly as well in altering human behavior as downright fear" (p. 38).

AEP

Eckert (1980) reported on the Alcohol Education Project (AEP), the core concept of which is *responsible* drinking. The program assumes a nonmoralistic, nonjudgmental attitude toward the use of alcohol, centered on four assumptions:

- People have the right to choose to drink or not to drink.

- Whether one drinks or not should be a conscious, carefully considered choice.
- Wherever alcohol use contributes to a person's hurting of self or others, it becomes alcohol abuse.
- People are accountable for their behavior when under the influence of alcohol.

This represents an excellent summary of my personal values regarding alcohol. Freedom and responsibility always go hand in hand. Freedom to use alcohol must be accompanied by responsibility for avoiding harm to others.

SUMMARY

Alcohol may bring more pleasure and more pain to human lives than any other substance. To use it for pleasure without abusing it is neither easy nor certain. Authorities disagree on the distinction between alcohol use and abuse. But simply stated, when alcohol produces negative effects for the consumer or anyone associated with the consumer, its purpose has been abused.

A blood alcohol content (BAC) greater than .05 percent places one legally "under the influence," which is one form of abuse. A BAC of .10 percent constitutes legal intoxication, a more serious form of abuse. Two or three drinks consumed in an hour may place a person under the influence, especially if the stomach is empty. BAC is also affected by the weight of the drinker—a small person is more affected by two drinks than is a larger person.

Authorities distinguish among social drinking, problem drinking, and alcoholism. A social drinker typically stops well short of intoxication, while a problem drinker often does not. Accidents and irresponsible acts are more frequent during intoxication. Alcoholism is a disease that prevents the consumer from drinking in moderation. Genetic differences make some people more susceptible to alcoholism than others. The alcoholic is more likely to drink every day and at any time of day and is incapable of responsible drinking, whereas the problem drinker might drink often or infrequently, moderately or to intoxication. Alcoholics Anonymous has proven very beneficial for alcoholics who wish to change their behavior. Despite alcohol's potential dangers, it continues to be widely used because it can reduce social anxiety and enhance relaxation.

Examining Your Values

Goodstadt (1978) advocated a value-based program for alcohol education, which included consideration of ethical values, social values, health values, individual differences, and educational methods for clarifying values and enhancing self-esteem. Based on the Ajzen-Fishbein model, Goodstadt believed that getting people to talk about how they *intend* to behave is an important step in the direction of behavioral change. Based on that assumption, do the following:

1. Describe how you intend to avoid irresponsible use of alcohol.
2. Describe how you intend to protect your value of health while using alcohol responsibly.
3. Describe how you intend to fulfill your social values through responsible use of alcohol.
4. Describe how you intend to accommodate others whose values regarding alcohol are quite different from your own.
5. Describe how you intend to enhance your self-esteem through use of or abstention from alcohol.
6. Use the values clarification process to make a statement about your intent to use or abstain from alcohol.
7. Use the values clarification process to justify a change in your use of alcohol.

CHAPTER 9
Smoking and Smokeless Tobacco

It's easy to quit smoking. I should know—I've done it dozens of times.
—Mark Twain

Self-Examination Statements

Instructions: Read each statement, then circle the x in the column at the left that most closely describes your belief about that statement. (Use a pencil. After reading this chapter you may wish to come back and change some of your responses on the basis of new information or attitudes.)

SA = strongly agree   **A** = agree   **U** = undecided   **D** = disagree   **SD** = strongly disagree

SA	A	U	D	SD	
x	x	x	x	x	I value freedom of choice when it comes to smoking.
x	x	x	x	x	I think of myself as a nonsmoker.
x	x	x	x	x	At least one of my parents is a smoker.
x	x	x	x	x	My best friend smokes.
x	x	x	x	x	Most of my friends are smokers.
x	x	x	x	x	About half of all American adults smoke.
x	x	x	x	x	What others do doesn't influence my smoking habits.
x	x	x	x	x	I have experimented with smoking but am not a habitual smoker.
x	x	x	x	x	The health risks of smoking are well established.
x	x	x	x	x	I abstain from smoking primarily for health reasons.
x	x	x	x	x	Most young people start smoking due to peer pressure.
x	x	x	x	x	Most young people smoke to rebel against adult authority.
x	x	x	x	x	The reasons for starting to smoke are usually the same reasons the person is still smoking 10 years later.
x	x	x	x	x	I have an external locus of control when it comes to smoking.
x	x	x	x	x	Most smokers I know would like to quit smoking.
x	x	x	x	x	Very few people begin smoking after they graduate from college.
x	x	x	x	x	People with more education tend to smoke less.

X	X	X	X	X	There are some definite benefits to smoking.
X	X	X	X	X	Smoking is an effective form of weight control.
X	X	X	X	X	Smoking calms the nerves, at least temporarily.
X	X	X	X	X	Smoking lowers the blood pressure.
X	X	X	X	X	Smoking decreases the pulse rate.
X	X	X	X	X	Smokers are more broadminded than nonsmokers.
X	X	X	X	X	Smokers are more apt to lead enjoyable lives than nonsmokers.
X	X	X	X	X	There is some truth to the mass media portrayal of smoking as glamorous.
X	X	X	X	X	The percentage of young female smokers is rising.
X	X	X	X	X	On the average, people who smoke heavily die about 10 years sooner than nonsmokers.
X	X	X	X	X	There is no health advantage to quitting if you have smoked heavily for 10 years or more.
X	X	X	X	X	I understand the concept of epidemiologic evidence.
X	X	X	X	X	Coronary heart disease is much more common among smokers than nonsmokers.
X	X	X	X	X	Smoking is the cause of most cases of lung cancer.
X	X	X	X	X	Smoking causes forms of cancer other than lung cancer.
X	X	X	X	X	Smoking raises blood pressure, thus increasing the risk of stroke.
X	X	X	X	X	Smoking is related to increased rates of emphysema.
X	X	X	X	X	Smoking is related to increased rates of bronchitis.
X	X	X	X	X	Wrinkled facial skin is a common result of long-term smoking.
X	X	X	X	X	Smoking reduces healthy high-density lipoproteins (HDL).
X	X	X	X	X	Smoking reverses the training effect of aerobic exercise.
X	X	X	X	X	I understand the concept of synergism.
X	X	X	X	X	The synergistic effect of alcohol and smoking is much greater than the effect of smoking alone.
X	X	X	X	X	The synergistic effect of smoking and using oral contraceptives is greater than the effect of either alone.
X	X	X	X	X	Smoking mothers have a much higher risk of infant death.
X	X	X	X	X	Those who smoke heavily are much more likely than nonsmokers to be problem drinkers and/or alcoholics.
X	X	X	X	X	Those who smoke heavily are much more likely than nonsmokers to abuse drugs in general.
X	X	X	X	X	I understand the difference between active and passive smoke.
X	X	X	X	X	Passive smoke has proven detrimental to health.
X	X	X	X	X	I would vote for a law that would ban all public smoking.
X	X	X	X	X	I support the U.S. Surgeon General's goal of creating a smokeless America by the year 2000.

DEFINING TERMS AND CONCEPTS: PUTTING SMOKING IN PERSPECTIVE

To put tobacco use into proper perspective, it is instructional to look at several national reports. In 1964, the U.S. Surgeon General's report made Americans realize for the first time that the link between smoking cigarettes and lung cancer was undoubtedly causal. More than a decade later, in 1975, the Public Health Service called cigarette smoking the largest single unnecessary and preventable cause of illness and death in the United States. Davis (1987) reported, "According to the U.S. Surgeon General, cigarette smoking is 'the chief, single avoidable cause of death in our society and the most important public health issue of our time'" (p. 725). Davis also cited estimates by the U.S. Public Health Service that put the toll from cigarette smoking at about 350,000 deaths per year, about one sixth of total deaths from all causes.

Undeniable Link to Cancer

In 1979 the Department of Health, Education, and Welfare issued a 1,200-page report that presented "overwhelming proof" of the link between cigarette smoking and disease. It emphasized that, as women continue to adopt smoking habits similar to those of men, they will suffer similar health consequences. Walsh and Gordon (1986) wrote:

> As a target of opportunity for public health action, smoking stands alone. . . . The health and human costs are so clear that most of the 55 million cigarette smokers in the United States voice the wish that they could stop . . . the present lifetime value of quitting for heavily smoking men under age 45 is about $34,000 in reduced risks of lung cancer, coronary heart disease, and emphysema alone . . . (p. 127)

Walsh estimated that smoking kills about 300,000 Americans annually, which is about 100 times as many as died from AIDS in 1986 and about 6 or 7 times as many as died from motor vehicle accidents. In light of such statistics, a 1984 U.S. Senate committee voted overwhelmingly to strengthen the language on all cigarette packages, warning of the smoking-related risks of cancer, emphysema, heart disease, complicated pregnancy, and addiction.

Public Reaction to Cancer Connection

How is the American public reacting to this information? A June 1986 Gallup poll reported, "Cigarette smoking has declined to its lowest incidence in the Gallup poll's 42-year trend . . . 31 percent report having smoked cigarettes during the week prior to being interviewed" ("Cigarette Smoking is Lowest," p. 2). Thirty-five percent of the men who were polled reported smoking, down from 57 percent in 1954; 28 percent of the women reported smoking, down from 32 percent in 1954. Gallup figures indicate that education is closely associated with smoking rates: college graduates, 23 percent; high school graduates, 35 percent; high school dropouts, 45 percent. Income and smoking rates were also inversely related—as income went up, smoking rates went down. The reported smoking rate among teenagers remained constant at 13 percent for the fourth consecutive year. Finally, 75 percent of all the smokers surveyed said they would like to quit, and this percentage was identical for both sexes.

McGinnis, Shopland, and Brown (1987) conducted a thorough review of the smoking literature. Here is a synopsis of their findings:

- More than 37 million Americans are now former smokers.
- The smoking rate has declined from 52 to 33 percent for males, and from 34 to 28 percent for females.

- For those in high school and through age 24, the smoking rate is greater for females than males.
- The greatest increase in the smoking rate has been for females aged 20 to 34.
- The smoking rate for blue-collar workers is greater than that for white-collar workers.
- Smoking rates are inversely correlated with education and income.
- Most smokers start smoking before age 20. The younger a person starts, the heavier she or he is likely to smoke in later years.
- Although per capita smoking has declined, per-smoker consumption has increased (i.e., there are fewer smokers, but more cigarettes per smoker).
- Most users of smokeless tobacco are young white males.
- Smoking at the worksite is no longer the norm.
- Despite the well-known health risks, over 50 million Americans still smoke.

Two publications from the U.S. Surgeon General's office, *Healthy People* and *Promoting Health/Preventing Disease: Objectives for the Nation*, are frequently cited. Reduction of cigarette smoking is one of the Surgeon General's 15 high-priority objectives for 1990. That objective includes the intent to reduce the proportion of adult smokers below 25 percent and increase the percentage of the population that is aware that smoking is responsible for the following:

- Up to 90 percent of lung cancer and other forms of cancer
- Up to 85 percent of heart disease
- Up to 85 percent of lung diseases, bronchitis, and emphysema

The latter goal, which depends on public awareness, had already been met by 1985, according to the National Health Interview Survey, but the action-oriented goal had not; as of 1985, 31 percent of all Americans continued to smoke, 6 percent above the national objective. The definition used for a "smoker" was anyone who has smoked 100 or more cigarettes in their lifetime and is still smoking. Are you a smoker by that definition?

Habitual Smokers and Nonsmokers

Other researchers have used a variety of definitions and categories to distinguish between habitual smokers and nonsmokers. Gilchrist, Schinke, Bobo, and Snow (1986) divided their subjects into three categories: nonsmokers (never tried); experimental smokers (tried smoking but didn't develop the habit); and regular smokers (smoke weekly or more often). Chassin, Presson, Sherman, Corty, and Olshavsky (1984) used four categories: never smoked a single cigarette; tried smoking, but not in the past month; used to smoke regularly, but quit; and now smoke regularly. Bonaguro and Bonaguro (1987) used five categories to provide a slightly finer distinction: never used, experimenter, former user, occasional user, and daily user.

Because nicotine is addictive, it is difficult to be an occasional user. Nicotine is one of many potentially harmful ingredients in tobacco; the others include tars, carbon monoxide, and other toxic gases. Nicotine creates a cycle of desire for more nicotine by releasing glycogen from the liver, which serves as a stimulant but is quickly followed by depression and fatigue, which create a desire for more stimulant (nicotine). Nicotine also constricts blood vessels, placing a greater burden on the cardiovascular system and causing it to function less efficiently. Tars, on the other hand, are dangerous because they are carcinogenic (cancer-producing) chemicals. The gases in the smoke, including carbon monoxide, are highly toxic and generally reverse the effects of aerobic exercise (Table 9.1). These gases are the major health-related difference between smoking cigarettes and using smokeless tobacco and may explain why the latter seems to be more popular among athletes.

Table 9.1 Inverse Relationships Between Smoking and Aerobic Exercise

Smoking results in:	Exercise results in:
Higher resting pulse rate	Lower resting pulse rate
Higher blood pressure	Lower blood pressure
Constricted blood vessels	Dilated blood vessels
Lesser blood volume	Greater blood volume
Fewer red blood cells	More red blood cells
Less hemoglobin	More hemoglobin
Less vital capacity	Greater vital capacity
Lower working pulse rate	Higher working pulse rate
Lower HDL count	Higher HDL count
Lesser $\dot{V}O_2$max	Greater $\dot{V}O_2$max
Stimulation, then fatigue	Fatigue, then stimulation
Relaxation, then tension	Tension, then relaxation
Gastroenteritis	Better digestion
Inactivity and more fat	More activity and less fat
Lighter sleep	Sounder sleep

Smokeless Tobacco

Smokeless tobacco has advantages for nonsmokers as well as smokers, in that both passive and sidestream smoke are avoided. Mainstream smoke is inhaled directly by the smoker, but sidestream smoke comes from the lit end of a cigarette, cigar, or pipe and can be inhaled by either the smoker or a nonsmoker. Passive smoking is defined as the act of a nonsmoker inhaling air polluted by a smoker.

Smokeless tobacco, in the form of chewing tobacco, plug tobacco, and snuff, has been around for centuries but has recently gained renewed popularity. According to Dent, Sussman, Johnson, Hansen, and Flay (1987), "Over the last decade, sales of smokeless tobac-co products have increased an average of 11% per year" (p. 422). This is due at least in part to the tobacco industry's attempt to recoup some of the market lost to declining cigarette sales, an effort that has been at least partially successful. One study of 3,000 adolescent males (Ary, Lichtenstein, & Severson, 1987) reported that 60 percent had tried smokeless tobacco, 7 percent were daily users, averaging more than five uses per day, and more subjects used smokeless tobacco than used cigarettes in the previous 6 months. It is believed that there will be significant long-term health consequences from using smokeless tobacco, due to the tars and nicotine in smokeless tobacco, but its widespread use is so recent that epidemiological evidence has not yet accumulated in quantity.

SMOKING CESSATION TO PREVENT DISEASE

The evidence linking smoking to heart disease, cancer, emphysema, and other diseases is so pervasive that one wonders why millions of Americans continue to smoke. The only plausible explanation is that they do not value health as highly as they value whatever benefits they derive from smoking. Consider the increased risks of death that result from a two-pack-a-day smoking habit (Table 9.2).

Table 9.2 Increased Mortality Rates Associated With Smoking

Disease	Percent of increased risk
Emphysema	1300
Lung cancer	700
Stroke	600
Cancer of the larynx	500
Cancer of the esophagus	400
Cancer of the cervix	200
Cancer of the bladder	200
Cancer of the pancreas	100
Coronary heart disease	100

Note. From "Study Finds Smokers Who Quit Can Cut Risk of Heart Attack," February 28, 1986, *USA Today*, p. D1.

Remember that the smoker assumes all of those risks simultaneously! Then consider these supporting data (McGinnis et al., 1987):

- Smokers have a 70 percent higher rate of coronary heart disease than nonsmokers.
- Smoking combines with alcohol and oral contraceptives to further increase the risks of coronary heart disease.

- Thirty percent of all cancer deaths and 85 percent of all lung cancers are caused by smoking.
- Smoking increases bronchitis, emphysema, peptic ulcers, and arteriosclerosis.
- At every age, proportionately more smokers die annually than nonsmokers.
- Nonsmokers, especially infants, are at risk from passive smoke.
- Lung cancer among women increased by an average of 6.2 percent per year from 1960 to 1983, representing a delayed reaction to the increased smoking rate among females in earlier decades.
- Chronic obstructive lung disease (COLD) is caused by smoking in 80 to 90 percent of all cases.
- Smoking mothers have an increased risk of premature birth, underweight infants, and higher infant mortality.
- Smokers have 50 percent more absenteeism from work than nonsmokers.

Some of the evidence for risk of cigarette smoking has already been reported in chapters 3, 5, and 8, related to disease prevention, physical fitness, and alcohol, respectively.

Coronary Heart Disease

Confirming evidence is available from still other sources. For example, Willett et al. (1987) studied the incidence of coronary heart disease among more than 119,000 female nurses. During a 6-year follow-up, 65 of the women died from coronary heart disease and 242 others had nonfatal myocardial infarctions. The researchers found a positive correlation between cigarettes smoked and the risk of coronary heart disease, the risk being 5 times greater for those who smoked 25 or more cigarettes per day. Smoking fewer cigarettes reduced but did not eliminate increased risks. By contrast, former smokers had little if any increase in risks. The researchers concluded that the coronary heart disease risks of cigarette smoking are not permanent because former smokers had risks similar to those who had never smoked.

Fortmann, Haskell, and Williams (1986) examined the changes in high density lipid (HDL) cholesterol in smokers over a 3-year period. They found a significant decrease in HDL among those who had started smoking and a significant increase in HDL among those who had quit. Those changes were independent of body weight, alcohol use, or exercise level. This corroborates the information provided by Cooper, as reported in chapter 5.

Cancer

It has been difficult to use experimental and control groups to establish a cause-and-effect relationship between smoking and cancer because human lives are at stake. Koop and Luoto (1982) described five criteria that can be used to establish causal relationships in the absence of experimental studies:

- Consistency of association across samples from different investigations
- Strength of association, as evidenced by high correlations
- Specific predictive association, wherein one variable causes another
- A temporal association (i.e., the suspected cause must always precede the expected outcome)
- Coherence of association (more of the suspected cause produces more of the expected outcome)

Koop and Luoto pointed out that all five of these criteria have been met in establishing a causal relationship between smoking and cancer. A 1982 report by the Advisory Committee to the Surgeon General of the Public Health Service (Koop and Luoto, 1982), using these five criteria, concluded that approximately 30 percent of *all* cancer deaths are attributable to cigarette smoking; smoking is a major cause of cancer of the lungs, larynx, oral cavity, and esophagus; and smoking is a contributory cause of cancer of the bladder, pancreas, and kidney.

Wald, Nauchahal, Thompson, and Cuckle (1986) reviewed data from 13 epidemiological studies of lung cancer and concluded that nonsmokers living with smokers have a 35 percent increase in the risk of lung cancer compared with nonsmokers who live with nonsmokers. Likewise, Svendsen, Kuller, Martin, and Ockene (1987) discovered that men whose wives smoked have twice the coronary heart disease mortality rate of those whose wives did not smoke. None of the male subjects were smokers. They concluded that "nonsmokers may be at increased risk of death through passive exposure to cigarette smoke" (p. 783). Viewed strictly from a health standpoint, a smoke-free society would appear to benefit smokers and nonsmokers alike.

Hypertension

Bonita, Scragg, Stewart, Jackson, and Beaglehole (1986) investigated the relationship between smoking, hypertension, and stroke. They reported that the risk of stroke more than tripled for men and women smoking up to 20 cigarettes per day and was over 5 times greater for those smoking more than 20 cigarettes per day. There was also a synergistic effect (which means that the total effect is greater than the sum of the parts) between hypertension and smoking, each accounting for more than one third of all strokes. As with coronary heart disease, there was no significant difference in risk between ex-smokers and nonsmokers. For those who value health, and especially for those who have hypertension, this information should weigh heavily against smoking.

Alcohol Abuse

Kozlowski, Jelinek, and Pope (1986) explored the relationship between cigarette smoking and alcohol abuse. They discovered that alcoholics tended to smoke, and smoke heavily, more often than the general population. They reported that in 1965, 90 percent of alcoholic patients were smokers. Although that rate has dropped, male alcoholics are still more than twice as likely as the general population, and female alcoholics more than 3 times as likely, to smoke 25 or more cigarettes per day. The authors recommended smoking cessation programs for those who have alcohol problems.

Risk-Taking Behavior

There are still other risks involved in smoking. In a study conducted and reported by DiFranza, Winters, Goldberg, Cirillo, and Biliouris (1986), smokers had 50 percent more motor vehicle accidents and 46 percent more moving-traffic violations than nonsmokers. They concluded that this may reflect more risk-taking behavior on the parts of smokers.

Medical Self Care ("Smoking News Update," 1987), based on a survey of 3,700 drivers who had been involved in traffic accidents, reported that smokers are three times as likely as nonsmokers to be arrested for drunken driving, in addition to having higher accident and moving violation rates. From this evidence, the writers concluded that people who are willing to risk their health by smoking are also more likely to take risks behind the wheel. They also noted the unfairness of a federal tax system that requires nonsmokers to partially subsidize the medical research and health care made necessary by smokers.

Absence From Work

Hendrix and Taylor (1987) looked at the relationship between smoking and absence from work. They estimated that smoking causes 170,000 deaths from coronary heart disease each year, 125,000 deaths from cancer, and 62,000 deaths from chronic lung diseases. Because many of these people were employed, their smoking resulted in loss of production, increases in health care costs, and increases in medical insurance premiums. They concluded that "a smoker costs the employer somewhere between $200 and $1500 per year more than a nonsmoker, depending on the business" (p. 6). Responding to this kind of data, more than 50 percent of all workplaces now impose smoking restrictions. Nearly 80 percent of respondents to a recent Gallup poll favored restricting workplace smoking to designated areas. According to Hendrix and Taylor, in most cases employers have the right to ban smoking and to refuse to hire smokers, which they are doing in increasing numbers. If you were an employer and knew that hiring smokers would almost certainly reduce your margin of profit, how would you resolve this value-laden issue?

Foxman, Higgins, and Oh (1986) conducted a 20-year longitudinal study of men from various occupational groups including miners, chemical workers, and foundry workers. They found that the mortality rate from all causes was similar in each of their occupational groups, but that smokers had higher mortality rates than nonsmokers in each case. The overall mortality rate was approximately twice as high for smokers as for nonsmokers. They concluded that smoking had a greater impact than occupation on longevity.

APPLICATION OF THE BEHAVIORAL MODELS: WHY PEOPLE VALUE SMOKING

Seffrin (1977) wrote, "No problem facing the health education discipline today is any more related to personal values than that of cigarette smoking'' (p. 197). Despite all of the evidence against smoking based on risks to good health, Seffrin suggested there may be many reasons for people to smoke regardless of health consequences. "That is, they value something that smoking does for them enough to offset the disadvantages which they *perceive*" (p. 197). Among the reasons offered were these:

- Emulation—acting like one's role model
- Curiosity—experimentation and risk-taking
- Advertising—portrays smoking as fun, sexy, and glamorous
- Paired association—smoking is linked with a work break, a cocktail, or a good meal
- Peer group influence—especially among adolescents

The perceived rewards of smoking include peer acceptance and short-term satisfaction. Most beginning smokers are too young to perceive the long-term effects smoking may have on their health. For them, smoking seems to be consistent with the adult credit-card mentality of "buy now, pay later."

Values and Priorities

Kristiansen (1985, 1987) has extensively studied the relationships between smoking, health behavior, and personal values. Based on her review of literature and her own data, she concluded that smokers and nonsmokers have different values priorities. Nonsmokers reported valuing their health more than heavy smokers. Based on the Rokeach Values Survey, nonsmokers also valued self-discipline and obedience significantly more than smokers, whereas smokers placed significantly higher value on freedom, independence, and broadmindedness. Conroy (1979) also reported that smokers valued broadmindedness more than ex-smokers, whereas those who had successfully quit smoking valued self-discipline significantly more than broadmindedness. In one of Kristiansen's studies (Kristiansen, 1985c),

the value of being broadminded was inversely related to *general* health behavior. In this context, broadmindedness apparently connotes an openness to risk-taking behavior. You may want to check chapter 1 at this point to see where you ranked broadmindedness and self-control.

In her 1987 study, Kristiansen learned that smokers tended to value the relaxation and enjoyment they associated with smoking, and nonsmokers were more concerned with the health risks, dirt and odor, and monetary costs associated with smoking. Although both smokers and nonsmokers recognized the health risks from smoking, the smokers perceived the benefits of smoking to outweigh the risks or costs. This is certainly a legitimate choice, provided that smokers do not put other persons at greater risk with their behavior and provided that nonsmokers are not financially disadvantaged by smokers' health care costs. To date, we have not been able to establish those provisions.

Social, Personal, and Behavioral Variables

Botvin and McAlister (1981) identified four groups of factors associated with smoking:

- Sociodemographic variables—smoking attitudes and habits of family and friends
- Personal attitudes and beliefs toward smoking
- Personality variables—self-image, locus of control, impatience, extroversion, and so on
- Behavioral variables—employment, academic performance, leisure interests and activities

Botvin and McAlister reported that smokers, compared to nonsmokers, were more likely to have at least one parent who smoked, have a best friend who smoked, have a poor self-image, have an external locus of control, and be impulsive or impatient to grow up.

Many of the same reasons for initiating smoking were cited by Chassin et al. (1984). They concluded that the adolescents most likely to begin smoking were those who had:

- Close friends who smoked
- Parents who smoked
- An external locus of control
- More positive attitudes toward smoking
- Higher intentions of smoking
- Lower expectations of academic success
- More tolerance of deviant behavior

The authors also found that the Ajzen-Fishbein model of reasoned action was the best predictor of which subjects would move from experimental to regular smoking.

An English study by Banks, Bemley, and Bland (1981) also used the Ajzen-Fishbein model to study smoking attitudes and behavior. They found that smokers had a significantly more positive attitude about the smoking habit than nonsmokers and that smokers tended to think that smoking was bad for you only if you smoked a lot or when you got older. Young smokers were significantly more influenced by peers than were nonsmokers. They believed that others would make fun of them if they did not smoke and that they should smoke when with smoking friends.

Attitudes, Beliefs, and Intentions

A third study using the Ajzen-Fishbein model was conducted by Grube, Morgan, and McGree (1986). These authors examined smoking attitudes, beliefs, intentions, and behaviors, and reported that the best predictors of intentions were parental smoking, peer smoking, and peer approval. Although attitudes had the greatest influence on intentions, peer smoking had the greatest influence on actual smoking behavior. Thus, for someone who needs and values affiliation more than health, the choice to smoke is quite understandable, providing that one believes that failure to smoke will result in the loss of valued friendships.

Gottlieb (1982), in a study involving students from 34 New England colleges, reported that more women (33 percent) than men (23 percent) smoked. She reported that, for female subjects, having a mother or a female friend who smoked were significant influences on initiating smoking, frequency of smoking, and difficulty in quitting. Having a father or a male friend who smoked was not a significant influence on females. She concluded that having a same-sex role model is a predictor of smoking behavior by college women.

Golding, Harpur, and Brent-Smith (1983) collected data from college students in England that supported what they referred to as a "poly-drug model." They related that smokers used more alcohol, marijuana, coffee, and other drugs than did nonsmokers. Smokers were also more likely to have a close friend who smoked. Apparently smoking behavior is normally consistent with a larger overall risk-taking behavior pattern.

The intent and effect of advertising is to influence patterns of consumption of a particular product or brand. Hunter et al. (1986) provided data that verified the effectiveness of advertising. They studied black and white students in Louisiana schools, whom they reported to have been "clearly influenced by advertising and promotional campaigns" (p. 194). This statement was based on the correlation between advertising dollars spent and sales of particular brands. Marlboro, Virginia Slims, and Salem cigarettes, all among the national leaders in advertising, were the leading choices among their male, female, and black subjects, respectively. Marlboro ads featured white "macho men," and ads for Virginia Slims featured white females. The leading advertiser for a single brand in 1980 was Salem, which presumably accounted for its popularity among all subjects, particularly blacks.

Weight Control

Undoubtedly one of the reasons given most often for beginning or continuing to smoke is weight control. According to Greenberg (1985), "A century of studies indicate that cigarette smokers weigh less than comparably aged nonsmokers and that many smokers who give up cigarettes gain weight" (p. 369). Some individuals are willing to take health risks because of the high value they place on the aesthetic appeal of ideal weight and because it seems easier to smoke than to exercise. Although there has been speculation that smoking controls weight by accelerating metabolic rate, Greenberg concluded that the evidence does not support that belief. His data refuted the notion that ex-smokers eat more than smokers, but he did find an inverse correlation between the consumption of sugar and cigarette consumption; that is, ex-smokers consumed more sweets. One plausible explanation is that smokers derive pleasure from the taste and smell of tobacco, and ex-smokers substitute the taste and smell of sweets.

Tuomilehto, Nissinen, Puska, Salonen, and Jalkcnen (1986) reported 11 studies supporting the contention that weight increases after cessation of smoking. In their study, involving over 2,000 Finnish subjects, males who stopped smoking gained a significant amount of weight (an average of about 8 pounds), but females did not. Nonsmokers reported more leisure-time physical activity than smokers. No explanation was offered, but I would speculate that the increased activity among the males who stopped smoking was not as great as it was among the females, which would perhaps explain why the men gained more weight than the women.

Albanes, Jones, Micozzi, and Mattson (1987) acknowledged that smokers tend to weigh less and have less body fat than nonsmokers, based on data from over 12,000 U.S. men and women. They cautioned, however, that mortality rates were higher for underweight than for average-weight individuals (just as they were higher for obese persons), perhaps because lean individuals were more likely to be smokers. Although you may not agree with the logic of using smoking to control weight, it is a rationale that appeals to those who believe they are not very susceptible to disease and who prefer to avoid vigorous exercise. Does this explain the increased rate of smoking among young women?

APPLICATION OF THE BEHAVIORAL MODELS TO SMOKING CESSATION

Many similarities exist between the decision-making processes that lead to smoking or not smoking. As with other health matters, we can trace these processes through an examination of personal values and priorities.

Values and Priorities

Smith (1982) studied the relationship of values to a decision to stop smoking. Smith hypothesized that values are an important aspect of the decision-making process and that values change during the quitting process. Over 300 subjects enrolled in a cessation program listed their reasons for quitting at the time of the initial decision and again after 3 weeks of the cessation program. Their original reasons for quitting, in descending order of value, were these:

- Health
- Aesthetics
- Modeling (to be a better role model for someone else)

- Economics
- To demonstrate self-control

Later, their reasons in rank order were these:

- Aesthetics
- To demonstrate self-control
- Health
- Modeling
- Economics

These findings should help us realize that there are important reasons, other than health, for people to smoke and to quit smoking.

Weinberger, Green, Mamlin, and Jerin (1981) used Hochbaum's Health Belief Model to explain smoking-cessation behavior. They learned that ex-smokers perceived smoking to be a more serious problem than did smokers and that ex-smokers felt more personally susceptible to the ill effects of smoking. They concluded, "In order to quit, it is not sufficient for persons to believe smoking is a serious health problem; they also must see themselves as personally susceptible to any adverse effects" (p. 1254).

Social Support

Studies in chapters 2 and 3 alluded to the importance of social support in making and implementing health-related decisions. Sorensen and Pechacek (1987) found evidence of this phenomenon related to smoking behavior. They studied over 400 workers from 10 Minnesota worksites. The percentage of smokers at each worksite varied from a high of 53 percent to a low of 15 percent. This significant difference is not likely due to change but is more likely due to the influence of peers in the respective social networks. The authors observed that their male subjects were more interested in quitting for health reasons, whereas their female subjects expressed greater concern about weight gains and job pressures related to quitting.

Becker et al. (1986) studied the smoking behavior and attitudes toward smoking of more than 1,300 registered nurses. They noted, "Several studies have suggested that visible smoking by the health professions imposes a negative influence on the smoking behavior of patients" (p. 1449). Their own study revealed that 22 percent of the nurses were smokers, a majority of whom indicated an intent to quit within the next year. Still, the nonsmoking nurses were found to have attitudes that made them more helpful to patients who were trying to quit smoking. The consensus of opinion is that a person is more likely to quit smoking when surrounded by nonsmokers who provide social and emotional support.

Physical Health and Appearance

There are often practical reasons for quitting smoking. Pomerleau et al. (1987) observed the smoking habits of members of a running club who averaged 35 miles per week. While 35 of the 141 club members had been smokers when they joined, only three were still smoking at the time of the study. Although this does not establish a cause-and-effect relationship, the authors pointed out the apparent incompatibility of smoking and vigorous aerobic exercise and suggested that exercise be given serious consideration for inclusion in smoking-cessation programs.

Physical appearance, especially youthful appearance, is an incentive for many to stop smoking. Cooper (1982) identified three factors which were most likely to speed up the aging process. They were, in order of importance, smoking cigarettes, inactivity, and obesity. For those who value a youthful appearance, the wrinkled features, caused by constriction of arterioles in the facial skin that inevitably follows prolonged smoking, are a powerful incentive to quit. It is ironic that many adolescents begin to smoke because it makes them appear older and that many middle-aged Americans attempt to quit for that same reason!

Financial Incentives

When all else fails, financial incentives may not. Oster, Colditz, and Kelly (1984) described the economic costs of smoking and the economic benefits of quitting. They estimated that a 40-year-old man who smokes two packs a day could save $56,000 during the remainder of his life by quitting, based on the statistical probability of lung cancer, emphysema, and coronary heart disease, and the value of work loss due to those illnesses. The researchers concluded that "the results of this study have shown that, at any age, it literally pays to stop smoking, since the benefits of quitting are also sizable" (p. 387). For this reason, economic factors may be more powerful incentives to quit than health factors for some people.

APPLICATION OF THE BEHAVIORAL MODELS TO CESSATION METHODS

There are nearly as many methods for quitting as there are writers on the subject. Different techniques seem to work for different people, depending on the motivation for smoking in the first place and the motivation for quitting. For those who smoke to stay awake or alert, substituting exercise or some other activity may be helpful. For those who smoke to occupy their hands and appear busy, less risky objects may be substituted for cigarettes. For those who find pleasure in the taste or smell of tobacco, the substitute may be food or gum. Those who smoke to reduce stress may benefit from learn-ing relaxation techniques (see chapter 11). Hypnosis is advocated for those who have a positive attitude toward quitting but lack the willpower. Quitting suddenly or "cold turkey" seems to work best for those who are motivated by fear or have simply tired of the cost and inconvenience of the habit (Farquhar, 1978).

According to Flay (1987), 90 percent of those who currently smoke would like to quit but prefer to do it without professional help. During the past 20 years, approximately 35 million adults quit smoking, and most of these did it on their own without benefit of an organized clinic. In Flay's study, awareness, information, and motivation provided by a mass media campaign were combined with informal social support and proved to be more effective than either the media campaign or social support alone. Schachter (1982) also believes in the efficacy of self-help without professional assistance. His data and other studies "indicate that long-term self-cure of smoking, obesity, and drug use are relatively common events" (p. 436).

Katz and Singh (1986) found that 64 percent of those who tried to quit smoking on their own succeeded in doing so, but that many had tried several times before succeeding. This experience has been reported by many former smokers. Among the factors that influence the effectiveness of smoking-cessation efforts are the following:

- Self-control skills (locus of control)
- Self-efficacy
- Problem-solving skills
- Perceived costs and benefits of quitting

Kaplan and Cowles (1978) hypothesized on the basis of social learning that individuals with an internal locus of control and a high value of health would be most successful at changing their smoking behavior. Their data supported that hypothesis. During pre-testing, Wallston's Health Locus of Control scale and a modified version of the Rokeach Value Survey, which included "health," were administered. All subjects then met weekly for seven weeks for a smoking cessation program. Post-testing data supported the hypothesis that subjects who had both an internal locus of control and a high value of health were most successful in changing their smoking behavior and maintaining cessation or lower smoking rates. Internal locus of control was an important factor in initiating a smoking cessation program, but after the training phase ended health values became a better predictor of subsequent smoking behavior than was locus of control. The researchers speculated that involvement in exercise and diet programs would make such individuals even more health conscious and would further strengthen their resolve to stop smoking.

Castro, Maddahian, Newcomb, and Bentler (1987) pointed out that most prevention/ cessation programs emphasize the following:

- Learning to resist social influence (peer pressure)
- Developing decision-making skills
- Improving coping skills (see chapter 11)

Because young people often start smoking in an attempt to cope with peer pressure, family pressure, or other stresses, it is important to learn alternative methods for dealing with stress. The Marlatt and Gordon model is the method advocated by Davis and Glaros (1986) and includes the following elements:

- Learning to cope with high-risk behavior
- Learning problem-solving skills to improve self-efficacy
- Learning to alter expectancies about cigarette use
- Learning to deal with relapse by applying problem-solving skills
- Using behavioral contracts to cover relapse situations

Smith (1982) is another writer who has suggested a health behavior contract as a useful tool for changing smoking behavior. It is an application of the values clarification process to require individuals to prize and *publicly affirm* their behavioral choice. Once a decision to quit has been made, reinforcement from the social support of significant others is crucial.

Edwards (1986) has suggested three primary strategies for reducing tobacco use in general:

- Legislation—Restrict tobacco advertising and sales, restrict smoking in public places and worksites, limit tar and nicotine content, and require health warnings on all tobacco products.
- Education—Media promotion of a smoke-free society, free public smoking-cessation programs, and educational programs designed to help potential smokers cope with peer pressure and avoid starting the smoking habit.
- Economic—Eliminate government subsidies of the tobacco industry, raise taxes on tobacco products, and make the cost of buying cigarettes prohibitively expensive.

Walsh and Gordon (1986) offered many of the same suggestions and added the incentive of lower health, auto, and home-owners' insurance premiums for nonsmokers.

Smokers who can't, or won't, quit can reduce their health risks by smoking fewer cigarettes per day, inhaling less smoke or none at all, smoking less of each cigarette (leaving longer butts), smoking filter cigarettes or milder brands with fewer tars, or substituting a pipe or some other pleasure that does not involve inhaling smoke.

SUMMARY

The proportion of Americans who smoke has declined from about one half the population in the early 1950s to less than one third in the late 1980s, suggesting that people are both aware of and concerned about the effects of smoking. The U.S. Surgeon General intends to further reduce the proportion of adult smokers to under one quarter by 1990 and to produce a smokeless society by the year 2000.

Fewer Americans smoke than use alcohol, but it is more difficult to smoke in moderation than to drink in moderation because of the addictive qualities of nicotine. Adolescents often cite peer pressure and a desire to appear older as reasons they smoke. Most come to recognize these reasons as invalid after reaching adulthood and try to quit, sometimes repeatedly.

The first and second leading causes of death in the U.S. are directly influenced by smoking: The carbon monoxide in smoke creates a high risk of heart disease, and the tars in tobacco are responsible for cancer. The unhealthy effects of smoking on the cardiorespiratory system are virtually a mirror image of the healthy effects of aerobic exercise, namely, a reversal of the training effect.

A recent trend among young males is substituting smokeless tobacco for smoking when it meets the same need for peer approval. Early research efforts indicate that the health risks for smoking and smokeless tobacco are similar. Another trend is more young female smokers, perhaps because they use cigarettes to help control weight. Probably the best that can be said for tobacco use is that it provides temporary pleasure for many, despite its ultimate health hazards.

Examining Your Values

Do you value good health? Are you a smoker? If you answered yes to both of those questions, there is a serious inconsistency between your values and your health behavior (a cognitive dissonance). If you would like to quit, ask yourself these questions:

1. Why did I start smoking? (List the reasons.)
2. Are any of these reasons still valid? If not, why am I still smoking?
3. What are the potential costs of continuing the habit?
4. What are the benefits of continuing the habit?
5. What are the benefits of quitting now?
6. Am I willing to assume responsibility for my decision and for the consequences?
7. If someone else influenced me to start smoking, are they likely to accept responsibility for the consequences?
8. Will my self-concept be better as a smoker or as a nonsmoker?

CHAPTER 10
Drug Use and Abuse

If I accept the sunshine and warmth, I must also accept the thunder and rain.

—Kahlil Gibran

Self-Examination Statements

Instructions: Read each statement, then circle the x in the column at the left that most closely describes your belief about that statement. (Use a pencil. After reading this chapter you may wish to come back and change some of your responses on the basis of new information or attitudes.)

SA = strongly agree **A** = agree **U** = undecided **D** = disagree **SD** = strongly disagree

SA	A	U	D	SD	
x	x	x	x	x	I have conflicting values regarding drugs.
x	x	x	x	x	My self-concept is not that of a drug user.
x	x	x	x	x	I understand the distinction between drug use and drug abuse.
x	x	x	x	x	My self-concept is not that of a drug abuser.
x	x	x	x	x	The risks of drug abuse are not worth the benefits of drug use.
x	x	x	x	x	I don't believe I am susceptible to drug abuse.
x	x	x	x	x	I have an internal locus of control for drug use.
x	x	x	x	x	I understand the distinction between legal and illegal drugs.
x	x	x	x	x	I use legal drugs but not illegal ones.
x	x	x	x	x	I use over-the-counter drugs to safeguard my health.
x	x	x	x	x	I value what prescribed drugs and medicines can do for my health.
x	x	x	x	x	I am willing to use any legal drug that makes me feel better.
x	x	x	x	x	I place higher value on an exciting life than on health.
x	x	x	x	x	I use recreational drugs for their social value.
x	x	x	x	x	I like to think of myself as a risk-taker.
x	x	x	x	x	The social value of recreational drug use outweighs any negative health impact it might have.
x	x	x	x	x	Most of my friends smoke marijuana.
x	x	x	x	x	My friends would approve of my using marijuana.
x	x	x	x	x	My family would approve of my using marijuana.
x	x	x	x	x	Smoking marijuana poses no greater threat to health than smoking cigarettes.

X	X	X	X	X	I believe the health risks from alcohol are greater than those from marijuana.
X	X	X	X	X	Weekly recreational use of marijuana does not pose a significant health risk.
X	X	X	X	X	I believe the legal risks of smoking marijuana outweigh the health risks.
X	X	X	X	X	I would vote in favor of legalizing marijuana.
X	X	X	X	X	One unhealthy aspect of drug use is the synergistic effect.
X	X	X	X	X	People who abuse drugs are more likely to abuse alcohol.
X	X	X	X	X	People who use any drug illegally are more likely to use other illegal drugs.
X	X	X	X	X	People who abuse drugs become prostitutes more often than people who don't abuse drugs.
X	X	X	X	X	The crime rate is higher among drug abusers than among the general population.
X	X	X	X	X	Making all recreational drugs legal would lower the crime rate.
X	X	X	X	X	I would vote to legalize cocaine.
X	X	X	X	X	Cocaine is the drug of choice among my friends.
X	X	X	X	X	Cocaine would be my preferred drug if it were legal.
X	X	X	X	X	I would prefer cocaine to marijuana if they cost the same.
X	X	X	X	X	Cocaine use is a source of esteem because it is expensive.
X	X	X	X	X	Risk of addiction is the primary health risk from cocaine use.
X	X	X	X	X	More people are addicted to prescription drugs than to cocaine.
X	X	X	X	X	I refuse opiate-based medications because of their potential for addiction.
X	X	X	X	X	Risk of addiction is the primary reason I would not use heroin.
X	X	X	X	X	I am not aware of any heroin use within my social network.
X	X	X	X	X	If my friends frequently used heroin I would probably use it as well.
X	X	X	X	X	What others do does not affect my use of drugs.
X	X	X	X	X	Psychedelic drug use is common in my social circle.
X	X	X	X	X	I have a negative attitude toward psychedelic drug use.
X	X	X	X	X	I have a positive attitude toward use of any recreational drug that is legal.

DEFINING TERMS AND CONCEPTS

Drugs are chemicals or substances other than food that affect the functioning of the body or the mind. Using that definition, alcohol and tobacco are prime examples of drugs. They have been treated separately in this book only because of their widespread use and the extent to which they represent health problems in our society. According to data from several national studies, as reported by Wallack and Corbett (1987), cigarettes are used on a daily basis more than twice as often as any other drug, and alcohol is used once a month or more at least twice as often as any other drug (that is, far more people smoke daily than drink daily, but far more people drink at least monthly than smoke monthly). Although these data came from high school seniors, they are reflective of drug use among adults as well.

Distinguishing Between Use and Abuse

It is important to distinguish between drug *use* and drug *abuse*. Far more people use legal drugs than illegal ones. The question is not whether people will use drugs—almost everyone does and will. The issue is when, for what purposes, at what risk, and with what consequences. The challenge is to maximize constructive use of drugs and minimize destructive aspects.

Drugs are usually taken for one of two reasons, social or medical. Social drugs are usually taken for their mood-altering effects, and medical drugs are usually taken to ease pain. Either may be used to advantage, and either may be abused. Drug abuse (as opposed to drug use) is taking a drug in a way that could damage one's health or ability to function (LaPlace, 1984). That definition applies to both legal and illegal drugs. For example, aspirin might be both the most widely used and the most widely abused drug in the United States today. According to Mayer (1974), there are no toxic substances, only toxic concentrations—that is, any drug is safe if taken in small enough dosages—and any drug can be lethal or harmful if taken in sufficiently large quantities.

Dixon (1978) identified a problem of increasing concern: the reliance of the American people on medicine and drugs, which Dixon called "magic bullets," to try to maintain a high level of health and wellness. As *Time* magazine wrote in 1981, "Americans inhabit a society in which they are conditioned from infancy to believe that 'there is a pill for every ill' " ("Cocaine: Middle Class High," p. 78). We want to avoid stress and pain whenever possible. We have come to value the "quick fix," the short-term effects of drugs, with too little regard for the long-term dependence and addiction that may result.

The Federal Comprehensive Drug Abuse Prevention and Control Act of 1970 established five classes of drugs differentiated according to potential use and abuse:

- Schedule I   High potential for abuse, and without legitimate medical use (heroin, cocaine)
- Schedule II   High abuse potential, but currently used in medicine (methadone, Valium)
- Schedule III   Used in medicine, but potential for psychological dependence (amphetamines, barbiturates)
- Schedule IV   Prescription required, but low abuse potential (birth control pills, codeine-based cough syrup)
- Schedule V   Low abuse potential, no prescription required (vitamins, antihistamines)

Schedule I drugs are illegal; the others can be legal or illegal, depending on their sources and uses.

Identifying Legal and Illegal Drugs

Illegal drugs may include stimulants, depressants, hallucinogens, and other psychoactive drugs such as marijuana, cocaine, and heroin. It is important to remember, however, that although illegal drugs may be more troublesome from the standpoint of maintaining law and order, many more adults are likely to abuse legal over-the-counter drugs (OTCs) and prescription drugs. According to Pekkanen (1984), many of the leading prescription drugs—Valium, Seconal, Miltown, Nembutal, Percodan—are more addictive than psychoactive drugs.

Over-the-Counter and Prescription Drugs

Legal drugs are often subdivided into over-the-counter drugs (OTCs) and prescription drugs. OTCs are so named because they are legal and may be purchased without a prescription. Aspirin is the most common form, but most cold medicines, cough syrups, and laxatives also fall into this category, as do most nose drops, eye drops, and suppositories. Vitamin and mineral supplements are sometimes included in this classification as well. OTCs may encourage people to diagnose and treat their own ailments rather than seek medical advice, but there is a definite element of risk in carrying this procedure too far.

Alcohol and tobacco can be legally purchased over the counter by individuals who are old enough. OTCs also include products containing caffeine, notably coffee and cola drinks. The collective market for OTCs is much greater than the market for prescriptive or illegal psychoactive drugs. Although many OTCs are put to good use, most of them are abused at one time or another. For example, laxatives and diuretics may be used to induce weight loss, or cough medicines may be taken because of their alcohol or codeine content.

The same might well be said for prescription drugs, most of which fall under the headings of amphetamines, barbiturates, or tranquilizers. Dexedrine and Benzedrine are two brand names of amphetamines, which are otherwise referred to as "uppers," "pep pills," or "bennies." They are used to stimulate the central nervous system, overcome fatigue, or suppress hunger. At the other extreme, barbiturates, also called sedatives or "downers," and tranquilizers are used to depress the central nervous system. Valium is reportedly the most commonly prescribed tranquilizer and is used to control anxieties. Seconal and phenobarbital are commonly prescribed to induce sleep, and lithium is prescribed to combat depression, whereas Thorazine and Haldol are more likely to be prescribed for the treatment of other mental illnesses. Seemingly there is a pill for everyone and every need. Unfortunately, once prescribed, drugs are often taken in amounts and combinations not anticipated by the prescribing physician. Some physicians prescribe drugs more readily than others, and some fail to stress the importance of reading labels carefully and taking medical prescriptions only as directed. Drugs prescribed to diminish physical or mental anguish are sometimes used for social purposes, leading to drug abuse.

Synergy, a major problem with drug use, is a phenomenon that occurs when various drugs are taken in combination, where the cumulative effect is far greater than additive. The word "sets" has been used to describe various combinations of drugs taken in synergy in an attempt to produce effects not intended by medical personnel. The combination of Doriden, a depressant, and prescription Tylenol, which contains the narcotic codeine, is an example of a set that has proven lethal. As mentioned in previous chapters, alcohol and tobacco act synergistically to increase the risk of oral cancer, and alcohol and oral contraceptives act synergistically to increase the risk of coronary heart disease. The most deadly combination of all, alcohol and barbiturates, is sometimes used by those with suicidal intentions; when the two drugs are combined naively, they may produce death without suicidal intent.

Marijuana and Cocaine

Marijuana (also known as pot, reefer, hash, and grass) is America's most widely used illegal drug, and trails only alcohol and tobacco in popularity as a social or recreational drug. Like most other drugs, marijuana has the potential to do good or harm, depending on how it is used. It has been used as a medicine for over 2,000 years (Angier, 1981) and has proven somewhat effective in the treatment of glaucoma, epilepsy, multiple sclerosis, and migraine headaches, and for patients undergoing chemotherapy. It has proven less effective in a variety of other medical applications, including rheumatism, gonorrhea, and leprosy. Although chemically more complex, marijuana cigarettes are similar to tobacco cigarettes in that both contain tars and produce carbon monoxide. A primary difference is that cigarettes contain nicotine, which creates physical dependency and addiction, whereas the principle psychoactive ingredient in marijuana is delta-9-tetrahydrocannabinol (THC), which is not addictive.

Cocaine is the second most widely used illegal drug in the U.S. Its popularity has been growing during the past decade, although the University of Michigan's Institute for Social Research reported that use by high school seniors dropped in 1987 for the first time since the mid-1970s ("Some Teens Seem to Get the Message on Drugs," 1988). According to this same source, the National Institute on Drug Abuse estimates that there are more than 4 million regular users and 15 million who have experimented with cocaine. Once used only by the rich because of its expense, cocaine has become affordable in its diluted form, "crack"; when combined with sodium bicarbonate or other fillers, it produces a crackling noise as it is smoked. Unlike other narcotics, cocaine is a stimulant rather than a depressant; it increases the pulse rate, raises the blood pressure, and prepares the body for "fight or flight" in much the same way as adrenalin or amphetamines, giving its user a short-lived feeling of mental and physical power. Once an individual has had that feeling, there is a tendency to want to repeat it, thus risking psychological dependency.

Cocaine may be sniffed, snorted, smoked (free-based), or injected. If it were used only occasionally and in moderate quantities, it might be no more harmful than similar use of alcohol or marijuana. Because of the pleasure it provides, however, users tend to increase their use, until euphoria and exhilaration turn into nausea, insomnia, and convulsions. Using cocaine is a high-risk behavior that can also lead to social risks, including loss of employment, alienation from family, and higher rates of crime in order to maintain the habit.

Hard Drugs and Fad Drugs

The ultimate in drug abuse is resorting to the so-called hard drugs, especially heroin. Heroin's properties of physical dependence, addiction, and related withdrawal are so well known that it is much less widely used than social drugs like alcohol, marijuana, and cocaine. Like morphine and codeine, heroin is a derivative of opium and an effective pain killer and depressant. Methadone has been widely used in the treatment of heroin addicts because it reduces the effects of withdrawal symptoms. Belatedly, it has been discovered that methadone creates an addiction of its own. Naltrexone is a newer synthetic, analgesic drug that is being used in place of methadone in the treatment of heroin addicts because it is very potent and has longer duration of action and oral effectiveness.

The list of drugs with a smaller user base is extensive. At one time hallucinogens were among the favored social drugs. They include LSD, or "acid," and PCP, or "angel dust." Both were thought to have mind-expanding properties, but their use diminished as it became more evident that they were extremely dangerous, distorting senses and judgment in unpleasant and unpredictable ways. Inhalants are also used from time to time to produce a "high" or mood alteration. Glue sniffing was popular during one era, as was the sniffing of solvents, paint thinners, and aerosol sprays. A relative newcomer to the drug scene is anabolic steroids, which have the ability to promote rapid muscular growth and thereby enhance athletic strength; we will return to steroids later in this chapter.

Defining Levels of Use

As with alcohol use and abuse, there are many ways to label the various levels of drug use and abuse. For example, Kane (1985) distinguished the following five categories:

- Experimental
- Occasional
- Situational
- Intense
- Compulsive

The experimental user is motivated by curiosity. The risk of drug abuse is lowest for this individual. The occasional user is also referred to as a "social" user; just as a social drinker consumes alcohol only when with friends who are drinking, an occasional user of pot or cocaine would not think of using such drugs when alone. The third category, situational use, is quite different. Anyone who requires a sedative every night in order to sleep, uppers to get through every major exam, or alcohol to survive every weekend, is a situational user. Whereas occasional use is social, situational use is functional; the user has become dependent on a drug to tolerate an otherwise difficult situation. The primary risk is that such situational use may lead to the fourth category, intense use. Unlike the situational user, who only uses drugs to cope with a specific situation, the intense user tends to use drugs to cope with a wider variety of occasions and personal problems. Drugs may be used to combat every ache or pain, mental or physical. One characteristic of intense use is that it becomes private rather than public.

The fifth category is that of compulsive use. The primary difference between an intense user and a compulsive user has to do with control. The compulsive user has lost control of his or her ability to make a decision about whether or not to use the drug; use has become habitual and addictive. For example, a problem drinker would fall into the intense category, whereas the alcoholic would fall into the compulsive category. Compulsive users are incapable of making rational judgments about their habit, and

that habit is unlikely to change without professional assistance.

Which of these five categories, if any, best describes your drug use behavior?

PREVENTING DRUG ABUSE: CAUSES AND EFFECTS

Kittleson and Sutherland (1982) defined three levels of drug abuse prevention using the same terms (primary, secondary, and tertiary) as were used in chapter 4 to describe health care generally. They characterized primary prevention as actions taken prior to the onset of drug abuse, dealing with causes rather than effects. Secondary prevention includes early intervention activities following identification of a drug abuse problem. Tertiary prevention includes efforts to rehabilitate someone who has already suffered physical or mental illness as a result of drug abuse. The authors noted that governmental funds earmarked for drug abuse treatment are used predominantly for tertiary prevention, to the detriment of primary prevention. We now turn our attention to *causes* and *effects* of drug use, which might be considered a form of primary prevention.

High School Drug Abuse

Yamaguchi and Kandel (1984) conducted a three-part study that examined the drug use patterns of high school students and their habits 10 years later as young adults. The authors distinguished among five classes of drug use:

- Alcohol
- Cigarettes
- Marijuana
- Other illicit drugs
- Abuse of prescription drugs

A slightly different progression of drug use and abuse was discovered for males and females. Typically, alcohol was the first drug used by males, followed by marijuana, other illicit drugs, and abuse of prescribed psychoactive drugs; this was true independently of whether or not cigarettes were used. For women the pattern was the same except that cigarettes were substituted for alcohol use; that is, smoking cigarettes was likely to be followed by smoking marijuana, using illicit drugs, and abusing prescribed psychoactive drugs, whether or not alcohol was used. Here is a further elaboration on the order in which drug use was initiated:

- About two thirds of all subjects used alcohol before cigarettes.
- About two thirds used cigarettes before marijuana.
- Nearly 90 percent used alcohol before marijuana.
- Over 90 percent used marijuana before other illicit drugs.
- About 95 percent used alcohol before other illicit drugs.

The researchers also identified predictors of future drug use:

- People who use both alcohol and cigarettes are much more likely to use marijuana.
- People over age 22 are much less likely to begin using marijuana than those under age 20.
- Friends' use of marijuana is the best predictor of marijuana use.
- Involvement in delinquent activities is a significant predictor of overall drug use.
- Belief that marijuana is not harmful is a significant predictor of its use.
- Alcohol use before age 18 is a predictor of future drug use.
- Marijuana use is a strong predictor of use of other illicit drugs.

- Prescribed psychoactive drug use is a strong predictor of use of other illicit drugs.
- Of persons who have never used marijuana, only about 2 percent will ever use illicit drugs.
- Women who use cigarettes before age 15 and continuously thereafter are 3 times more likely to progress to illicit drug use (beyond marijuana) than other women.

They concluded:

The findings in this paper suggest potentially important policy implications for the development of preventive and educational efforts, namely that prevention of early involvement in legal drugs would reduce the use of marijuana, and that prevention of early involvement in marijuana use would reduce involvement in other illicit drugs. (p. 680)

Based on these predictors, what is your future drug use likely to be?

Bry, McKeon, and Pandina (1982) hypothesized that extent of drug use is dependent on six risk factors they had identified, no one of which independently proved highly predictive of drug use; any combination of four, however, was predictive of heavy drug use or abuse among their high school–age subjects. These are the six risk factors:

- Low self-esteem
- A perceived lack of parental love
- A lack of any religious affiliation
- Psychological distress
- Low grades (Ds and Fs) in school
- Younger age at first use of alcohol independent of family

Note that the first two factors relate to basic human needs in Maslow's hierarchy. Note also the emotional and spiritual dimensions of health that influence and are influenced by drug abuse.

The authors observed that drug abuse behavior is similar to other behavioral problems in that there is no simple solution when causation is multifaceted.

Newcomb, Maddahian, and Bentler (1986) also studied risk factors that correlated with increased drug use in a high school sample. These were the best predictors:

- Drug use by peers
- Deviant behavior
- Drug use by adult role models
- Early alcohol use

These authors concurred with Bry and his colleagues that drug abuse results from a complex interaction of factors. They observed that experimental use of alcohol and other drugs by adolescents is not surprising but cited statistics from the National Institute on Drug Abuse to make the point that the 18 percent of teenagers who report at least weekly use of marijuana are no longer experimenting but are habitual users, nor are the 43 percent who reported consuming five or more alcoholic drinks on one occasion merely experimenting. It is a thin and wavering line that separates experimental drug use from habitual drug abuse.

Age-Related Experimental Drug Abuse

It is a well-documented fact that experimental drug use and abuse are age-related. According to Kandel and Logan (1984):

> The period of major risk for initiation to cigarettes, alcohol, and marijuana is completed for the most part by age 20, and to illicit drugs other than cocaine by age 21. Those who have not experimented with any of these substances by that age are unlikely to do so thereafter. (p. 660)

According to their data, the majority of 18-year-olds have experimented with alcohol (95 percent), cigarettes (68 percent), and marijuana (54 percent), but fewer than 20 percent have experimented with any other drug. Use of cigarettes and psychoactive drugs continues to increase from age 20 to 29, but use of alcohol and marijuana peaks earlier and declines during the mid-20s as individuals marry, have children, and assume other adult roles.

The findings of Raveis and Kandel (1987) lend credence to the above report. They observed that the use of illicit drugs peaks during the 18- to 22-year-old age span but use of medically prescribed psychoactive drugs continues to increase into the mid-20s. They reported that "there is no initiation of use of cigarettes and alcohol after age 24-25" (p. 608). Men are more likely to use cocaine, and women are more likely to use tranquilizers and sedatives. By age 29, men had accumulated almost twice as any months of illicit drug use as women. Apparently drug use is affected by both age and sex.

Stress and Abuse

Bruns and Geist (1984) examined the relationship between stressful life events and drug use and abuse. They pointed out that adolescence is a time when methods are being chosen for coping with stressful events. If drugs are chosen as a preferred coping method at that time, alcohol and drug addiction are more likely to occur during adulthood. The authors sorted more than 500 high school students into the following categories: abstainers, alcohol users, marijuana users, polydrug (both alcohol and marijuana) users, and drug abusers (those already in treatment). They found that the drug abusers reported significantly more stressful life events than any other group, and the frequency of such events was directly associated with drug use in each category; abstainers reported the fewest stressful events.

Which category would you place yourself in? How often do you resort to alcohol or drug use as a primary means of coping with stress? Alternative coping strategies, other than drugs, will be presented in the next chapter.

Smart and Murray (1985) reported on the level of drug abuse in 152 countries, each of which was classified as either a "developed" or a "developing" nation. They found that only 14 countries had a serious drug problem, that the U.S. was one of them, and that the U.S. was the only developed nation among the 14. In general, countries with the lowest level of drug abuse tended to have the lowest socioeconomic status, the lowest literacy rates, the lowest life-expectancy rates, the fewest physicians per population unit, and the highest infant-mortality rates. Although the authors offered no explanation of this, I would hypothesize that there is a price to be paid for industrial advancement, and that it undoubtedly has to do with stress. The Ajzen-Fishbein model of reasoned action suggests that our drug-related behavior is at least partially due to our perception of societal norms. The Rokeach system of beliefs and general social learning theory suggest that perhaps we are the victims of our cultural values that emphasize achievement, and that fragile self-concept is damaged when achievements fail to match expectations. How do *you* explain the fact that a country with one of the highest standards of living in the world also has the greatest drug abuse problem among developed nations?

Adult Consequences of Adolescent Drug Use

Kandel, Davies, Karus, and Yamaguchi (1986) spent 9 years following the adulthood consequences of adolescent drug use among more than 1,000 subjects. They found that use of a particular drug was the best predictor of its future use, that illicit drug use was predictive of drug-related health problems, and that adolescent drug use was predictive of delinquency, unemployment, abortions, and divorce during adulthood. They concluded that every aspect of young people's lives was affected by drug use and abuse. Similarly, Newcomb and Bentler (1986) did a study of nearly 500 high school students, then did a follow-up study 4 years later. They reported that frequent use of cigarettes, alcohol, marijuana, and hard drugs correlated positively with lower high school grades, lower rates of entrance into college, lower rates of involvement in college activities, and higher rates of unemployment. Clearly there are both health and nonhealth risks related to a general pattern of drug use and abuse.

Marijuana

As has been mentioned, marijuana is the most commonly used illicit drug. According to Glantz (1984), it took 50 years to establish the harmful effects of cigarette smoking, and it may take as long before we know the results of heavy, continued marijuana use. Because its widespread use dates back only about 2 decades, it is too early to be certain of long-term effects. Glantz's survey indicated that 60 percent of high school seniors had experimented with marijuana but fewer than 7 percent of people over age 25 reported using marijuana even once in the past month; he concluded that marijuana is a "young person's drug" (p. 3).

Angier (1981) suggested that the psychological dangers of marijuana exceed the physical ones. Intellectual abilities, particularly memory, may be affected; motivation to work, study, or exercise may be diminished; and chronic marijuana use may have devastating effects on the personality. Glantz (1984) similarly reported that effects on mental capacities include impaired short-term memory, fragmented speech, disjointed thinking, and loss of concentration. He also noted that heavy use of marijuana is often preceded by low self-esteem and that heavy users tend to value independence more than achievement and peer associations more than parental associations. Does this fit with your observations?

Excessive use of marijuana tends to slow reaction time and reduce motor coordination. Glantz noted that physical effects include decreased vital capacity of the lungs, comparable to the effects of smoking tobacco. Marijuana use may also have a deleterious effect on the reproductive system, lowering the fertility rate in males by lowering the testosterone level and sperm cell count, and causing irregular menstrual cycles for females. In addition, doctors consistently advise pregnant women to avoid the drug (Angier, 1981). Hatch and Bracken (1986) identified good reasons for this. They found that women who used marijuana regularly during pregnancy were at increased risk of delivering low birth-weight infants, and that marijuana users were also significantly more likely to use tobacco, alcohol, and caffeine, all of which increase the risks associated with birth.

Kaplan, Martin, Johnson, and Robbins (1986) acknowledged that most young adults have tried marijuana, and that experimentation with it has become a social norm. "Continued use of marijuana, however, has more serious health, economic, and behavioral implications . . . In the case of marijuana, the distinction between trying marijuana and escalating to regular use is important" (pp. 44-45). They studied more than 1,200 high school students, and then surveyed them again as young adults (23 to 25 years old). Their data led them to conclude that the use of marijuana is escalated by the following factors:

- Initially using marijuana at a younger age
- Trying marijuana at a time of psychological distress

- Trying marijuana in the absence of peer motivation
- Weakened ties with significant others
- Lack of peer acceptance

They also noted that individuals committed to a conventional value system (e.g., parent and teacher approval, good grades, good manners, honesty, kindness) were less likely to exhibit deviant behavior, experiment with marijuana, or escalate its use into adulthood.

Cocaine

Use of cocaine is also value-related, according to philosopher Sidney Hook, who was quoted by *Time* magazine ("Cocaine: Middle Class High," 1981) as saying, "We have abandoned our old-fashioned values . . . People want things to come easily, they no longer want to work hard, to suffer any pain, to feel any stress or anxiety" (p. 78). Professional athletes and entertainers who have large discretionary incomes have been widely publicized abusers of cocaine. Some have received lifetime suspensions from their sport, some have been imprisoned, and still others have died or been injured as a result of cocaine abuse.

According to Morningstar and Chitwood (1987), men are more likely to be involved in dealing cocaine, using their profits to support their own habits and those of their female friends. Hence, men tend to be the primary source of cocaine for both men and women. Women are more apt to be manipulative in getting their supply, often trading sexual favors for it, thus earning the label of "coke whore." A coke whore does not consider herself to be a prostitute, since no firm price is set for her sexual favors and no money changes hands. Still, more than 60 percent of the respondents in the study admitted that cocaine ultimately created money problems for them because their average monthly expenditure for coke was nearly $1,000. The net effect is a high crime rate among those who push cocaine or develop the coke habit. The risks of cocaine abuse ought to be carefully weighed against any benefits of social use.

Heroin

The causes and effects of heroin abuse are in many ways parallel to those for marijuana and cocaine. Anglin, Kao, Harlow, Peters, and Booth (1987) reviewed the literature on general narcotic addiction and heroin addiction in particular. They reported that addicts have lower self-esteem and self-worth than the general public, are less likely to form intimate and trusting relationships, and are less likely to be sexually active. Heroin use often replaces sexual activity. Deren (1986) reported that opiate-addicted women are typically unemployed, have low self-esteem, and suffer from anxiety and depression. As with marijuana, opiates are known to interfere with the normal menstrual cycle, and children born to addicts have a lower average birth weight and a higher infant mortality rate than the general population. Women addicted to heroin or methadone are also more likely to smoke cigarettes, use alcohol excessively, use cocaine, and be prostitutes. Each of these behaviors adds an element of risk for the health of both the mother and her offspring.

Methadone

Methadone is currently the predominant form of treatment for chronic heroin addiction. This drug itself is highly addictive and therefore can be expected to create problems for its users. Rosenbaum and Murphy (1987) have described some of the problems and "side effects" related to its use. Patients complain of many physical effects, including weight fluctuation, and of emotional instability—that is, they feel that methadone is in control of their lives. Another often-heard complaint from both men and women is that methadone diminishes sexual desire. It

is difficult to determine how many of these problems are due to methadone rather than other factors because most patients on methadone are also heavy cigarette smokers and users of alcohol, Valium, and other drugs. Methadone users will also have poor overall quality of health if they continue the typical heroin addict's practice of consuming mostly junk food and seldom getting regular exercise.

Multiple Drug Use

According to Clayton and Ritter (1985), "More often than not, the persons who are using drugs frequently are *multiple* drug users" (p. 83). For example, they reported that 86 percent of the daily users of marijuana in their study had used other illicit drugs (e.g., tranquilizers, amphetamines, cocaine) during the previous year, in addition to cigarettes and alcohol. The two most powerful predictors of multiple drug use were use of drugs by friends and use of alcohol and cigarettes by friends. Likewise, 74 percent of the subjects in a study reported by Barr and Cohen (1987) admitted multiple drug use. There was a universal feeling of "loss of control" on the parts of these subjects, which seems to be a recurrent theme among individuals abusing alcohol or other drugs.

Steroids

According to *American Health Magazine* ("Rambo Drugs," 1987) and *Sports Illustrated* (Neff, 1987), the most recent drug craze in the United States is abuse of steroids, sometimes referred to as "Rambo drugs." Long-used by football players and weight lifters in their efforts to increase muscular strength and size, steroids are now increasingly being used by women and teenagers who have also become enamored with the search for the "body beautiful" hyped by mass media and advertisers. These groups use steroids because the drug changes body composition by increasing the percentage of muscle tissue and reducing percent body fat. There are legitimate medical uses for steroids, including treatment for osteoporosis, some forms of cancer, and correcting hormonal imbalances. However, the risks of steroid abuse include cardiovascular disorders, hypertension, sterility, and liver and kidney problems. As with so many health-related decisions, short-term gains must be weighed against long-term risks.

WELLNESS AND USING DRUGS TO IMPROVE QUALITY OF LIFE

Why do people use drugs at all? Obviously there are perceived benefits; otherwise there would be no users. Our behavior usually represents a balancing act between perceived benefits and perceived risks. The fact that more people use over-the-counter drugs than use heroin suggests that either the benefits are greater for OTCs or the risks are fewer. Each drug user must decide where to draw the line: to use drugs for medicinal purposes only, to use only prescribed medicines, to use social drugs, or to use illegal drugs. Which drugs we choose to use, and the circumstances in which we find them acceptable, is a function of our system of personal values.

Values and Social Norms

Epstein (1985) summarized this dilemma: "The use of drugs or abstinence from them is a value statement. . . . values play a significant role in how we view chemicals and what we do to them and with them as well as without them" (pp. 795-796). He suggested that any drug-intervention plan should include a values-intervention model. The critical factor, however, is not changing individual values in isolation but considering support group, community, and societal values as well. It is important to under-

stand that values may differ substantially from one generation to the next, and from one sub-culture to another. It is not realistic to expect an individual to adopt "healthy" values related to drug use that are markedly different from perceived social norms. Some researchers (Dembo, Schmeidler, & Koval, 1976) believe that it is actually healthier to accept the social norms of drug use than it is to risk alienation from one's peer group by clinging to peripheral values.

Society's Responsibility to Change

Drug use is normally a reflection of the larger society, and it becomes incumbent on the *society* to initiate change before asking individuals to do so. Macdonald (1987) has described an important societal initiative, the Anti-Drug Abuse Act of 1986. Enacted by Congress, it provided $1.7 billion for 1987, including provision for the Office of Substance Abuse Prevention (OSAP), which was activated in November 1986, to sponsor prevention and rehabilitation projects for high-risk groups. Six goals were established:

- To achieve drug-free workplaces
- To develop drug-free schools
- To improve and expand drug abuse treatment
- To increase public awareness and prevention of alcohol and drug abuse
- To improve international cooperation
- To strengthen law enforcement against drug abuse

Macdonald concluded, "The year 1987 will be recognized as the year the nation decided that alcohol and drug abuse would no longer be tolerated—neither among our youths nor the adult population—and started to reestablish a truly 'drug-free' society" (p. 123). The 1988 establishment of a federal Cabinet-level position to lead the battle against drug abuse supports Macdonald's assertion that the nation intends to take action.

CHAPTER 11
Stress Management

Grant me the strength to change what I can, the courage to bear what I cannot and the wisdom to know the difference.

—Reinhold Niebuhr

Self-Examination Statements

Instructions: Read each statement, then circle the **x** in the column at the left that most closely describes your belief about that statement. (Use a pencil. After reading this chapter you may wish to come back and change some of your responses on the basis of new information or attitudes.)

SA = strongly agree   **A** = agree   **U** = undecided   **D** = disagree   **SD** = strongly disagree

SA	A	U	D	SD	
x	x	x	x	x	My self-concept is positive regarding my ability to cope with stress.
x	x	x	x	x	I have an internal locus of control when it comes to stress management.
x	x	x	x	x	I take pride in being in control of my own destiny.
x	x	x	x	x	I feel challenged by major changes in my life.
x	x	x	x	x	I feel threatened by major changes in my life.
x	x	x	x	x	Coping with stress has never been a serious problem for me.
x	x	x	x	x	Stress is not harmful, but uncontrolled stress is.
x	x	x	x	x	My immediate family would describe me as "easily stressed."
x	x	x	x	x	My best friend would describe me as "easily stressed."
x	x	x	x	x	I would like to live a stress-free existence.
x	x	x	x	x	I like to think of myself as an achievement-oriented person.
x	x	x	x	x	I am committed to living a rewarding and productive life.
x	x	x	x	x	Without stress there would be little productivity.
x	x	x	x	x	It is stress that makes my adrenalin flow, and that is when I perform best.
x	x	x	x	x	I understand the difference between distress and eustress.
x	x	x	x	x	I can think of three examples of eustress—good stress.
x	x	x	x	x	Stress is more likely to frustrate me than anger me.
x	x	x	x	x	I have destroyed valuable property while angered by a stressful situation.
x	x	x	x	x	People tend to stress me more than events.
x	x	x	x	x	There are certain techniques that I consciously use to cope with stress.
x	x	x	x	x	I value exercise as an effective means of coping with stress.

x	x	x	x	x	I have used yoga or meditation to cope with stress.
x	x	x	x	x	I know how to use biofeedback or relaxation techniques to cope with stress.
x	x	x	x	x	Prayer helps me to cope with stressful situations.
x	x	x	x	x	Smoking relaxes me and helps me cope with stress.
x	x	x	x	x	Drinking alcohol is my favorite way to cope with stress.
x	x	x	x	x	I often use sedatives or tranquilizers to cope with stress.
x	x	x	x	x	I understand the differences between Type A and Type B behavior.
x	x	x	x	x	I think of myself as more Type A than Type B.
x	x	x	x	x	My best friend would describe me as a Type A.
x	x	x	x	x	My family would describe me as a Type A.
x	x	x	x	x	Given a choice, I would rather be a Type B.
x	x	x	x	x	Type B people are generally too "laid back" to be productive.
x	x	x	x	x	I know that I am a Type A because I tend to be very competitive.
x	x	x	x	x	For me to act hostile toward others would be out of character.
x	x	x	x	x	I can usually see the humorous side of difficult situations.
x	x	x	x	x	I believe that "laughter is the best medicine."
x	x	x	x	x	I routinely feel hurried and harried by life's events.
x	x	x	x	x	I often do two things at once to save time—for instance, eat and read, or read and watch TV.
x	x	x	x	x	I am familiar with the concept of the Type C personality.
x	x	x	x	x	Daily hassles stress me more than major life events.
x	x	x	x	x	I am familiar with the concept of "hardiness" as it relates to stress management.
x	x	x	x	x	I believe that I have a hardy personality.
x	x	x	x	x	I often feel that my life is totally out of control.
x	x	x	x	x	I believe that I am in good spiritual health.
x	x	x	x	x	Spiritual health is more dependent on faith in the human spirit than on religion.
x	x	x	x	x	I am committed to helping others find love and peace in life.

DEFINING TERMS AND CONCEPTS

Homeostasis is a state of body balance. Our bodies are constantly adjusting to internal and external changes. Alvin Toffler's books *Future Shock* (1970) and *The Third Wave* (1980) describe difficulties people encounter in coping with societal changes. Some of the difficulties described in the books are encountered by our present society:

- Loss of family support due to rising divorce rates
- Rising birth rate among unwed mothers

- Splitting of immediate and extended families as members seek better employment opportunities in other geographic areas
- Diminished social network beyond the family, resulting from greater mobility
- Insecurity that arises as it becomes apparent that computers and other technology will replace many workers
- Lack of a feeling of permanence about most things in life, a result of planned obsolescence and throw-away products
- Threat to health imposed by AIDS, drug use, and alcohol, as societal values change

Whenever the changes are greater than the body's ability to adjust, stress results. Kasl (1984) noted that "the relationship between stress and health is complex and multidimensional" (p. 319). The source of stress may be internal, as when we try to maintain our self-imposed standards of academic excellence; environmental, as when inclement weather forces cancellation of a picnic; situational, as when a check bounces due to insufficient funds; or relational, as when a loved one does not reciprocate our feelings.

Psychological Stress and Physical Responses

Lazarus and Folkman (1984) wrote, "Psychological stress is a particular relationship between the person and the environment that is appraised by the person as taxing or exceeding his or her own resources and endangering his or her own well-being" (p. 19). Thus, in the classic stimulus-response relationship there are at least three variables:

- The environmental stimulus/stressor
- The individual's appraisal or perception of that stimulus/stressor
- The individual's physical or emotional response to that stimulus/stressor

Researchers assure us that the crucial factor generally is not the amount of stress we face but how we perceive it and cope with it. Lazarus and Folkman distinguish four types of stressors:

- Acute stressors, which are 1-time events (e.g., the death of one's mother)
- Sequential stressors, such as events leading up to marriage or divorce
- Intermittent stressors, like monthly bills
- Chronic stressors that occur daily or regularly, such as driving through rush-hour traffic

Selye (1976) defined stress, in slightly broader terms than Lazarus and Folkman did, as the non-specific response of the body to any demand made upon it. One of the prominent early researchers in stress management, Selye believed that the body reacted to each and every source of stress in three stages: alarm, resistance, and exhaustion. He referred to this sequence as the General Adaptation Syndrome:

- Alarm stage—physiological changes
- Resistance stage—fight, flight, or emotional coping
- Exhaustion state—illness or death

We are all familiar with the signs and symptoms of the alarm stage. The adrenalin begins to flow freely, the heart beats more rapidly, perspiration and respiration rates increase, the mouth and throat become dry, the palms and hands become clammy, and the nervous and muscular systems are generally tense and on edge. If the cause of stress is a physical danger, the body becomes ready for resistance in the form of "fight or flight."

In our modern world the source of stress is more likely to be mental or emotional than physical, in which case it is not so easy to resist by fighting or fleeing. Other mechanisms must be found for coping with emotional stress, so we resort to anger, denial, repression, and other defense mechanisms, that will be discussed later in this chapter. If the coping mechanism is successful, the body gradually returns to its original homeostatic state. If stress continues unabated, despite our efforts to cope, the body eventually enters Stage 3, exhaustion. Loss of physical and psychic energy may result in such psychosomatic illnesses as headaches, backaches, ulcers, allergies, insomnia, arthritis, colitis, and, in extreme cases, death (Singsank & Singsank, 1984).

Eustress, Distress, and Recent Life Events

Selye further distinguished between positive (eustress) and negative (distress) forms of stress. He emphasized that the body's physiological adaptations during the alarm stage are similar under both eustressful and distressful circum-

stances. Based on this premise, Holmes and Rahe (1967) developed the Social Readjustment Rating Scale (Table 11.1) in the form of a schedule of recent life events. The most stressful event was arbitrarily given a score of 100, and other events were given lower scores in accord with the lesser amounts of stress produced. Criteria for measuring stress included onset of illness or depression, physiological changes (e.g., weight gain or loss), and the amount of energy that subjects perceived to be required to cope with the situation.

According to this scale, the most distressful life events are the death of a spouse, divorce, marital separation, a jail term, or the death of a close family member. Among the most eustressful life events are marriage, a marital reconciliation, graduation, a promotion, or retirement. Each recent life event, whether distressful or eustressful, requires *change*, and it was the

Table 11.1 Social Readjustment Rating Scale

Rank	Life event	Mean value
1	Death of a spouse	100
2	Divorce	73
3	Marital separation	65
4	Jail term	63
5	Death of close family member	63
6	Personal injury or illness	53
7	Marriage	50
8	Fired at work	47
9	Marital reconciliation	45
10	Retirement	45
11	Change of health of family member	44
12	Pregnancy	40
13	Sex difficulties	39
14	Gain of new family member	39
15	Business readjustment	39
16	Change in financial state	38

Rank	Life event	Mean value
17	Death of close friend	37
18	Change to different line of work	36
19	Change in number of arguments with spouse	35
20	Mortgage over $10,000	31
21	Foreclosure on mortgage or loan	30
22	Change in responsibilities at work	29
23	Son or daughter leaving home	29
24	Trouble with in-laws	29
25	Outstanding personal achievement	28
26	Spouse begins or stops work	26
27	Begin or end school	26
28	Change in living conditions	25
29	Revision of personal habits	24
30	Trouble with boss	23
31	Change in work hours or conditions	20
32	Change in residence	20
33	Change in schools	20
34	Change in recreation	19
35	Change in church activities	19
36	Change in social activities	18
37	Mortgage or loan less than $10,000	17
38	Change in sleeping habits	16
39	Change in number of family get-togethers	15
40	Change in eating habits	15
41	Vacation	13
42	Christmas	12
43	Minor violations of the law	11

authors' contention that change itself is one of the chief sources of stress.

Undesirable Change

Mueller, Edwards, and Yarvis (1977) challenged Holmes and Rahe's claims, asserting instead that the key dimension of stress is undesirable or threatening change. They interviewed more than 360 adults and, based on evidence from four studies, concluded that undesirable events were more stressful than desirable ones. They found a certain level of anxiety for positive events, but it was milder than for negative events and milder than that attributed to eustressful events by Holmes and Rahe.

Jacobsen (1986) offered three alternative stress models:

- Transition model—stress stems from change.
- Transaction model—stress occurs when perceived demands exceed perceived resources.
- Needs model—stress results from failure to meet a basic human need (e.g., security or affiliation).

Jacobsen's primary thesis was that social and emotional loneliness are especially stressful, and that well-timed social support is perhaps the best coping mechanism we can have.

Hassles and Uplifts Scale

Kanner, Coyne, Schaefer, and Lazarus (1981) also believed that the "life events" approach, as outlined by Holmes and Rahe, placed an undue emphasis on change and did not prove to be a good predictor of health outcomes. They found that the average correlation between recent life events and health outcomes, based on many studies, was only about 0.12, which suggests that there are other important considerations involved in mental and emotional health. In an effort to identify those other factors, they developed a Hassles Scale and an Uplifts Scale.

Lazarus (1984) defined daily hassles as "experiences and conditions of daily living that have been appraised as salient and harmful or threatening to the endorser's well-being," and daily uplifts as "experiences and conditions of daily living that have been appraised as salient and positive or favorable to the endorser's well-being" (p. 376). Lazarus concluded, on the basis of a series of studies, that daily hassles and uplifts are more capable of explaining physiological and somatic health than recent life events. Because daily hassles affect all of us on a regular basis, whereas life events occur irregularly, daily hassles correlate more closely with measures of health (e.g., hypertension and weight control). The most common hassles and uplifts were identified by Miles (1986) and appear in Table 11.2. The numbers in the right-hand column refer to the percentage of respondents who reported experiencing each respective hassle or uplift.

Table 11.2 Ten Most Frequent Hassles and Uplifts

	Hassles	
Rank		Percent
1	Misplacing or losing things	75
2	Troubling thoughts about your future	64
3	Not getting enough sleep	60
4	Filling out forms	54
5	Concerns about weight	53
6	Social obligations	48
7	Concerns about physical appearance	48
8	Not getting enough rest	48
9	Concerns about meeting high standards	48
10	Being lonely	47

Uplifts

Rank		Percent
1	Being visited, phoned, or sent a letter	78
2	Visiting, phoning, or writing someone	77
3	Having fun	77
4	Socializing (parties, being with friends, etc.)	74
5	Recreation (sports, games, hiking, etc.)	74
6	Making a friend	73
7	Hugging and/or kissing	69
8	Getting enough sleep	67
9	Being complimented	67
10	Eating out	66
10	Having someone listen to you	66

Lazarus acknowledged that what constitutes a hassle or an uplift varies greatly from person to person and is "based in large part on individual patterns of beliefs, values, and commitments" (p. 382).

Other researchers have corroborated the conclusion of Lazarus and his colleagues. Weinberger, Hiner, and Tierney (1987) investigated the impact of hassles on the health status of elderly, low-income persons. They concluded that hassles were better predictors of health status than major life events. They found that life events increased the number of hassles, which in turn more directly influenced health. Based on their own work and that of other researchers whose subjects represented a broader age range, they divided hassles into five categories:

- Work-related—boss, customers, fellow employees, actual work
- Sexual or family—birth control, pregnancies, physical health
- Money-related—debts, taxes, educational expenses
- Self-development—fears, prejudices, inner conflicts
- Others—traffic, pollution, smokers, wasted time

Which of these are major sources of stress in your life?

Daily Stress Inventory and Problems Scale

Brantley, Waggoner, Jones, and Rappaport (1987) developed a Daily Stress Inventory, a self-report instrument designed to measure relatively minor stressful events. Similarly, Burks and Martin (1985) developed an Everyday Problems Scale. Both sets of researchers concluded that *daily* problems, as opposed to major life events, are a more significant source of stress. Table 11.3 provides a consensus list of frequent sources of such stress and some common coping strategies, not all of which lead to health and wellness.

Table 11.3 Everyday Problems

Stressor	Coping mechanism
Low self-esteem	Alcohol, drugs, promiscuity
Failures	Drop out, give up, drugs, alcohol
Finances	Charge it, do without, new job
Family	Rebel, move out, alcohol, drugs
Friends/Lovers	Move in, move out, promiscuity
Time management	Reduce commitments, change priorities
Weight management	Dieting, miss meals, caffeine
Work/School	Complain, change, quit

STRESS AND DYSFUNCTION

Having more stress than one can cope with leads to dysfunctional behavior, including various forms of mental illness. Whaley (1982) identified five levels of dysfunction:

- Worry
- Neurosis
- Aggressive behavior
- Psychosis
- Suicide

Worry

Worry is "normal." However, people respond to worry in very different ways. Some respond in physical ways by smoking, drinking, overeating, or popping pills. Others cope by using a variety of defense mechanisms, such as the following:

- Regression (child-like behavior)
- Repression (pretending the problem doesn't exist)
- Rationalization (blaming circumstances beyond our control)
- Projection (blaming others)
- Conversion (psychosomatic illnesses)

We all worry, and we all occasionally use defense mechanisms, sometimes to good advantage, but we should recognize that they are only a temporary solution to what may be a long-term problem.

Neurosis

Neuroses include a variety of phobias (fears), anxieties, obsessions, and compulsions. The most common form of neurosis is depression, which is often caused by loss—the loss of a friend, family member, job, grade, self-confidence, or self-esteem. Neurotic behavior is generally considered to be the mildest form of mental illness. Like mild forms of physical illness, it is something we must all confront from time to time. It is thought that many "accidents," suicide attempts, and actual suicides result from depression and other forms of neurosis.

Aggressive Behavior

Aggressive behavior is usually directed at others. The neurotic tries to cope with stress by turning his attention inward, but the aggressive person attempts to cope by turning his attention outward. Child abuse, spouse abuse, and rape are examples of dysfunctional behavior. Unlike the neurotic, the aggressive person typically ends up in legal trouble. Our American heritage is rich with examples of individuals and groups who have "taken the law into their own hands" in an attempt to deal with stressful situations. One example is the "wild west" mentality, where justice was often rendered with a rope rather than a courtroom trial. The Ku Klux Klan is still making decisions about guilt and punishment outside the legal system, most often victimizing black Americans. Street gangs are another example of groups that mete out their own form of justice when someone arouses their anger.

Psychosis

Psychosis is an even more serious level of dysfunction. A psychotic is out of touch with reality and often requires extensive therapy on an outpatient basis or confinement to a mental health institution for treatment. The most common forms of psychosis are schizophrenia and affective manic-depression. Schizophrenia typically includes hallucinations, delusions, or other departures from logical thinking. Manic-depressives experience severe mood swings, ranging from extreme sadness and melancholia to uncontrolled exuberance. In theory, such conditions are as responsive to treatment and rehabilitation as most forms of physical illness or injury. Psychiatrists tend to agree that many psychotics are at least initially responsive to therapy. The stigma we sometimes attach to mental illness makes the therapist's task more difficult. We cling to the false notion that physical illness is beyond our power to prevent and is therefore acceptable, but that mental illness can be avoided by strong-willed people and is therefore unacceptable. The evidence suggests that people who value good health can be at least as effective in preventing physical illnesses as in preventing mental illnesses.

Suicide

Suicidal tendency is a level of dysfunction in which the individual no longer has the will to live and has ceased to look for ways to cope with stressful situations. Suicide is often the preferred solution at this level of dysfunction. Such individuals, if they have rational thoughts at all, feel lonely, helpless, rejected, and totally lacking in control of their own lives. Lack of control and loss of a feeling of self-worth are critical. According to Kane (1985), the key to good mental health rests with our ability to cope with stress in ways that preserve our sense of control and self-worth.

PERSONALITY TYPES AND STRESS

The research of Rosenman and Friedman (1974) identified two major personality types, which they labeled Type A and Type B. These two types of persons differ significantly in how they handle stressful situations. Here is a summary of traits and behaviors associated with Type A personalities:

- Angry, aggressive, hostile
- Obsessed with time and deadlines; doing more and more in less and less time
- Competitive and achievement-oriented
- Short-tempered; lacking patience and tolerance
- Hard-driving, explosive personality
- Accelerated speech and pace of living
- Undertakes two or more activities simultaneously
- Little time for, or interest in, hobbies or leisure pursuits
- Few intimate friendships

Type B personalities are quite different from Type As. They are more relaxed, speak more softly, are less obsessed with success, and tend to deal more effectively with stressful situations.

Type As "burn their candles at both ends" and are always searching for more candles, whereas Type Bs learn how to make their candles last longer.

Matteson, Ivancevich, and Gamble (1987) outlined the Price model of Type A behavior pattern, which was built on Bandura's social learning theory. It rests on three assumptions that form the nucleus of Type A behavior: that one must constantly prove oneself or risk being judged unworthy and unsuccessful; that no universal goal or principle exists, and good might not prevail; and that life is a zero-sum game with competition for all resources and insufficient time, achievement, and recognition to go around.

The Type A person believes that, as in any zero-sum game, one person's gain is another person's loss. The authors concluded that such beliefs are typically formulated in childhood, based on the values, behavior, and role-modeling of parents, especially parents who were unloving, achievement-oriented, and severely critical. Type A behavior has become associated with increased risk of many diseases.

STRESS AND DISEASE

According to Silverman, Eichler, and Williams (1987), there is no precise or universally agreed-upon definition of stress, yet whatever definition is used, "researchers consistently find relationships between stress and disease, health, and daily functioning" (p. 47). They reported results from the 1985 National Health Interview Survey, which included 78 million respondents! About 49 percent of the women and 38 percent of the men who responded reported that stress had "some" or "a lot" of effect in their health in the previous year. Respondents who reported the highest levels of stress were more likely to do the following:

- Rarely or never eat breakfast
- Sleep fewer than 6 hours per night
- Be less physically active than their peers

- Drink more alcohol than their peers
- Be smokers or ex-smokers (females only)

How many of these stressors describe your behavior? Did you note the similarity between these factors and those associated with longevity by Breslow and Belloc reported in chapter 3?

Stress and Coronary Heart Disease

Rahe (1979) drew an interesting parallel between coronary heart disease (CHD) and mental health. His analogy equated the build-up of cholesterol in the blood vessels with the build-up of stress in the form of life-change events, the former causing physical illness and the latter causing mental illness. In each instance disease may or may not occur, but the risk becomes greater as cholesterol and stress, respectively, increase.

Suls and Mullen (1981) wrote, "A large body of recent research has accumulated which indicates that the risk of physical and psychological illness increases in direct proportion to the accumulation of recent life changes" (p. 30). Their own research, however, concluded that "an accumulation of recent life events perceived as undesirable and uncontrollable was most likely to predispose the individual to subsequent illness" (p. 31).

Flannery (1986) found agreement in the literature that "stressful life change events may impair health" (p. 485). His research reported significant correlations between both major life events or daily hassles and anxiety or depression. Emotional stress also leads to many physical illnesses. Jemmott (1987) reported:

A confluence of evidence supports the view that psychological stress occasions reactions in the individual that may contribute to the development of a wide range of disease and physical conditions, including infectious diseases, cardiovascular disease, gastrointestinal disorders, and perhaps even cancer. (p. 267)

DeMense (1985) observed that stress caused by life events has been widely researched and has been found to be associated with heart attacks, tuberculosis, diabetes, and ulcers, in addition to depression.

Anger and Hostility

Siegel (1984) noted that epidemiological research has identified seven primary factors associated with cardiovascular health, one of which is Type A behavior pattern. Greenglass (1987) wrote that "anger and hostility have been reported to be critical components of the Type A behavior pattern which contribute to coronary heart disease" (p. 639). According to her review of previous studies of Type A behavior, hostility is related to atherosclerosis, suspicion and jealousy are related to CHD, anger is associated with higher diastolic blood pressure, and stress increases secretion of norepinephrine, a suspected precursor of coronary heart disease. In her own study of managerial women, Greenglass found that her subjects were equally hostile whether Type A or B, but Type As were more likely to outwardly express their anger and hostility.

According to Burke (1984), "Type A behavior has been shown to be associated with coronary heart disease when other known risk factors are held constant" (p. 174). Longitudinal studies with large samples have indicated the following:

- Type As have over twice the risk of premature death from CHD as Type Bs.
- The more extreme the Type A behavior, the more likely is CHD.
- Type As are more likely to have *severe* heart attacks.
- If they survive the first, Type As are more likely than Type Bs to have a second heart attack.

Friedman, Hall, and Harris (1986) asserted that the critical element in the development of heart disease is hostility. They identified two subgroups of Type A individuals. In the more healthy of the groups, individuals were described as charismatic, expressive, dominant, fast-moving, sociable, in control, and capable of coping with stress. Persons in the less-healthy group were characterized as hostile, competitive, and negatively expressive and dominant.

Ortega and Pipal (1984) declared that Type A subjects sought greater degrees of challenge than did their Type B counterparts. When faced with four choices involving incrementally more difficult problems, Type A subjects chose the more difficult problems significantly more often than Type Bs. Type As also scored higher on a self-report measure of challenge-seeking. Smith and Anderson (1986) reached a similar conclusion, writing, "Type A persons do not simply respond to challenges and demands; they seek and create them" (p. 1166).

Gender

For many years it was assumed that Type A behavior was typical for men but not for women. However, Sorensen et al. (1987) found that Type A behavior related to long work hours, high occupational mobility, and nonsupportive interactions with coworkers, irrespective of gender. When they controlled for these factors, their female subjects had higher Type A scores than males. They concluded that "environment acts as a catalyst or 'fuse' for Type A behavior" (p. 324). Likewise, Dearborn and Hastings (1987) discovered that employed women were more prone to Type A behavior than homemakers, although it is uncertain whether employment causes Type A behavior or Type A women are more disposed toward seeking employment. The authors pointed out that coronary heart disease is the number 1 killer of females as well as males, and that Type A women have 4 times greater risk of CHD than Type Bs. When they controlled for education, occupation, and socioeconomic status, female subjects were as prone to Type A behavior as males. Further, they found that the employed Type A women, when compared to Type Bs, had more demanding jobs, felt more stress on the job, and reported poorer health. They were also more likely to express time urgency, competitiveness, and anger or hostility.

Job Dissatisfaction

According to Howard, Cunningham, and Rechnitzer (1986), "There have been a number of studies suggesting that job satisfaction may be associated with coronary heart disease" (p. 95). They studied managers from 12 corporations and found that 61 percent were Type As. The Type As smoked more and had significantly higher blood pressure. For Type As, but not for Type Bs, ambiguity on the job raised blood pressure and intrinsic job satisfaction had a moderating effect on high blood pressure. Apparently it is helpful to fit the personality of the worker to the demands of the job. Another illustration of this was reported by Evans, Palsane, and Carrere (1987). They found that Type A bus drivers had more accidents, absenteeism, and official reprimands, and reported more occupational stress than did Type Bs. There was a rise in adrenalin and blood pressure during working hours for both Type A and Type B drivers, but the differences between the two groups in these two measures were not significant.

Hypertension

Several other researchers have reported an association between hypertension and Type A behavior. Diamond (1982) wrote, "Anger and hostility appear to play an important role in the development of hypertension, though the mechanism is not yet clearly specified" (p. 410). Anger was attributed to blocked goals or unfulfilled needs, and hostility appeared to emanate from a mixture of anger, disgust, indignation, contempt, and resentment. Hypertensives were described as likely to be outwardly submissive but inwardly resentful.

Matthews, Cottington, Talbott, Kuller, and Siegal (1987) tested the hypothesis that "stress-ful work conditions were related to elevated diastolic blood pressure" (p. 287). They found that overall job dissatisfaction was related to higher diastolic blood pressure, perceived job insecurity, little influence in decision-making, little opportunity for promotion, and unsupportive coworkers. As with earlier studies, they found that anticipating job loss had a particularly negative effect on blood pressure, causing it to rise significantly.

Stress and Cancer

Kasl (1984) reviewed the related literature and found that Type A behavior is related not only to cardiovascular disease but also to cancer. Although the exact reasons for this are not known, Kasl speculated that stress increases the incidence of smoking, alcohol consumption, and promiscuous sexual behavior, all of which are known to increase the risks associated with certain kinds of cancer.

MANAGING STRESS TO IMPROVE QUALITY OF LIFE

Scheier and Carver (1987) reviewed the research that links optimism to a number of positive health-relevant outcomes and concluded that "beneficial effects are partly due to differences between optimists and pessimists in the strategies that they use to cope with stress" (p. 169). Optimists are more likely to score high on the hardiness factor associated with Type C personality (which is discussed in a later section of this chapter), to have high self-efficacy, and an internal locus of control. Pessimists are more likely to resort to anger and hostility, characteristic of Type A behavior. In Scheier and Carver's terms, optimists are more likely to use problem-focused coping, whereas pessimists are more likely to use emotion-focused coping. Cousins (1977) described the healing powers of laughter and a good sense of humor in his personal battles with a massive heart attack and other serious illness.

Social Support

LaRocco, House, and French (1980) studied the buffering effect of social support on occupational stress, using over 600 male subjects in 23 different occupations. Their findings supported the view that social support has a buffering effect on both mental and physical health symptoms like anxiety, depression, and irritation, especially reducing anxiety and depression. It failed to support the buffering hypothesis, though, in regard to job-related stress with its more location-specific symptoms, like boredom with the job or dissatisfaction with workload. Suls, Becker, and Mullen (1981) measured social insecurity among college males and found it to be associated with negative stress experiences. They concluded that "individuals scoring as both Type A and socially insecure reported the greatest degree of stress" (p. 29).

Cohen and Wills (1985) did a lengthy review of dozens of studies related to social support and found not only that people with more social contacts are in better physical health but also that "several prospective studies using mental health outcome measures have shown a positive relation between social support and mental health" (p. 311). In other words, social support can both directly provide reinforcement for healthy behaviors and indirectly buffer the disappointments that would otherwise lead to excessive stress. How effective is your social support network in this regard?

Age and Productivity

Burke and Weir (1980) detected an age relationship between Type A behavior and health. Un-like younger subjects, subjects 45 and older suffered from poorer physical and emotional health. Overall, Type As reported more stressful life events at work, greater interference of work with home and family life, and less marital satisfaction. On the positive side, the Type As reported more self-esteem at work, greater life satisfaction, and less depression, and they were less likely to be smokers or moderate or heavy drinkers.

Strube, Berry, Goza, and Fennimore (1985) hypothesized an age relationship, believing that the achievement-oriented lifestyle of Type As would be better suited to younger people and that the more relaxed lifestyle of Type Bs would be better suited to old age. Their findings generally supported that thesis. For Type As, the ability to maintain a hard-driving lifestyle diminished with age, and reports of poorer health increased with age.

Such findings raised the suspicion that Type A persons are productive despite the health risks involved, and Type B persons give up productivity for better health. But such is not the case, according to Jamal (1985), who studied career progression patterns among more than 200 white-collar employees. No significant differences were found in quantity of work produced by Type As and Bs, or in promotions; but Type Bs (males and females) received higher ratings on the *quality* of their work. Jamal noted that these findings were consistent with previous studies in which Type Bs typically outperformed Type As. The rationale offered was that Type As tend to rush through tasks regardless of their importance, but Type Bs have more patience, concentration, and broader perspectives. As important as personality is to managing stress, it is not the only factor that determines mental health. Many elements contribute to a balanced life, including eating well, developing and maintaining an effective system of social support, feeling personally competent and in control, and doing meaningful work.

Nutrition

Girdano and Everly (1986) pointed out that consumption of certain foods can compound stress by causing fatigue and irritability. This is especially true for individuals who are eating many meals away from home, missing some meals, and eating others on the run. The most likely culprit is caffeine; more than 250 milligrams per day may create an adverse effect. Common sources are coffee (100 mg/cup), colas (50 mg/can), and chocolate (100 mg/candy bar). Refined sugar is another stressor. It robs the body of B-complex vitamins without replacing them, inducing anxiety, depression, and insomnia. Refined sugars also predispose toward hypoglycemic conditions, leading to fatigue and failure to cope with stressful conditions. Too much salt increases fluid retention, raises blood pressure, and increases nervous tension. Finally, Girdano observed that nicotine, while not a food, does release hormones that elicit the stress response. He concluded:

> Research in the last several years has offered strong evidence that two common 'oral' habits, cigarette smoking and caffeine consumption, may be highly deleterious to your health either singly or when combined, and that much of this effect is attributable to excessive stress. (p. 82)

Four Basic Coping Mechanisms

Flannery (1987) reviewed coping strategies of people who adapted successfully to stressful situations. He reported that "four factors repeatedly emerge as coping strategies in stress-resistant persons and are associated with a lower incidence of physical illness, lower amounts of anxiety and depression, and increased longevity" (p. 26). Flannery identified the following factors:

- Personal control (developing an internal locus of control; feeling in charge of one's life)
- Task involvement (doing something that is "important" and "meaningful")
- Lifestyle choices (modifying diet to reduce caffeine, nicotine, and white sugar; adding aerobic exercise and relaxation activities)
- Social support (developing a social network that includes helping and being helped by other people)

As a postscript, Flannery also noted that a sense of humor and a commitment to religious values are tools that many find helpful in coping with stress. Certainly this framework of stress management is consistent with the research literature that has been reported in previous chapters.

The one aspect of the Flannery strategy that has not been addressed in depth is "task involvement." That concept came primarily from research on "hardiness" by Kobasa, Maddi, and Courington (1981) and Kobasa, Maddi, and Pucetti (1982). These researchers reported that four traits guard one's future health: personal health practices, social support, absence of Type method, which relies on checks of basal body temperature and the cervix—including cervical of the three Cs:

- Commitment—A sense of purpose in life; belief in the importance and value of what one is doing (Flannery's "task involvement"). "Committed persons have both the skill and the desire to cope successfully with stress" (Kobasa, 1982, p. 7).
- Control—Belief that one can influence events and outcomes.
- Challenge—Believing that change, not stability, is normal; perceiving change as opportunity rather than threat.

Kobasa's early research yielded low correlations between stress and illness, indicating that many highly stressed individuals managed to cope effectively without becoming ill. She concluded that such persons were "hardy."

The Type C Personality

Based on Kobasa's research, Kriegel and Kriegel (1984) identified the Type C personality, so named because it encompasses the three Cs of the hardy personality described previously. Type C behavior is neither as aggressive as Type A nor as laid back as Type B behavior. Expanding on Kobasa's research, the Kriegels asserted that Type Cs learn to cope with stress by using the *five Cs*: control, confidence, commitment, challenge, and courage. A Type C person's locus of control is more likely to be internal than external. Such a person is more likely to accept the challenge presented by higher education, to remain committed to it, and to become more confident as a result. Type Cs welcome change and feel challenged rather than threatened by it, which helps them climb the career ladder of success. They think positively and adapt quickly—traits that are especially desired in managerial and professional positions. They manage stress through a combination of the following:

* Planning
* Goal-setting
* Problem-solving
* Risk-taking

It is a formula that has considerable merit for all of us.

Kobasa, Maddi, and Courington (1981) reported on a 5-year longitudinal study of male executives. They found that those who lacked hardiness were significantly more likely to have an external locus of control, to have a sense of powerlessness (lack of control), and to feel alienation from self and work. They concluded that "commitment, control, and challenge are interrelated components of hardiness" (p. 375).

Exercise

Kobasa, Maddi, and Pucetti (1982) examined the relationship of exercise and hardiness to stress and illness. Again their subjects were male business executives. They found that despite a lack of significant correlation between exercise and hardiness, per se, "personality hardiness and exercise emerge from this study as empirically distinct variables that preserve health in the face of stressful life events. Their buffering effects seem additive in that persons who are both hardy and exercise are the healthiest" (p. 401). Also of note was the fact that subjects with an internal locus of control scored higher on hardiness.

Cooper (1982) also recognized the relationship of exercise to stress management, describing exercise as the perfect antidote to stress. Some writers have referred to exercise as "active coping." It can be as strenuous as aerobic exercise or as mild as deep muscle relaxation, as convenient and inexpensive as walking around the block or down a country road. Those who are physically active all day may prefer a relaxed approach; those whose work is sedentary will discover that vigorous exercise is a more effective antidote for stress.

Self-Esteem

Cronkite and Moos (1984) studied factors that moderate the effects of stress. Like so many other researchers, they found that self-esteem is positively related among both men and women to resisting stress. Stress tends to lead to poorer functioning, which in turn leads to more stress.

> Conversely, people who are in good health generate resources that protect them against the likelihood of experiencing certain stressors. For example, employees who are energetic and optimistic are less likely to be reprimanded or fired. More generally, persons in good health may develop healthful lifestyles and be able to effectively manage their lives so as to prevent stress. (p. 374)

It seems that people who feel good about themselves and want what is best for themselves are most likely to establish healthy lifestyle habits.

Further, it is difficult to like and respect others if we do not like and respect ourselves.

Mental Intervention

Barton (1986) reviewed the literature related to stress management and distinguished cognitive, physiological, and social interventions. These included time management, cognitive restructuring, values clarification, autogenics, biofeedback, progressive relaxation, social networking, and assertiveness training. A growing number of health educators are of the opinion that mental intervention is at least as valuable a method of coping with stress as physical intervention. Prayer is commonly used to enhance spiritual well-being. Yoga and meditation combine the physical and mental elements; each is most effective when practiced in a quiet and peaceful setting. It is helpful to breathe slowly and deeply, maintaining a quiet state of mind that is void of problems.

Worksite Stress Management

Pelletier and Lutz (1988) reviewed the literature related to stress management programs in the workplace. They indicated that "medical care costs and benefits are currently about a third of the average person's salary" (p. 5) and a large percentage is for stress-related disorders such as heart disease, hypertension, headaches, backaches, and gastrointestinal disorders. A single employee heart attack may cost an employer $60,000, so it is little wonder that stress management programs are the most prevalent form of health promotion program requested by corporate managers.

Pelletier and Lutz concluded that prepackaged stress management programs are ineffective. The key components of successful stress management programs for the worksite were identification of high-risk individuals by qualified health professionals, symptom-oriented treatment with appropriate follow-up, and evaluation of both health and cost effectiveness. "It is also essential to modify hazardous working conditions to avoid the paradox of 'healthy people in unhealthy places' " (p. 12). Evidence from studies beyond worksite settings also indicates that it is cost effective for corporations and industries to provide effective stress management programs for their employees.

Problem Solving

Farquhar (1978) believes that managing stress effectively is a learned skill of vital importance to our well-being. He advocates this six-stage problem-solving approach not unlike the scientific method you probably learned in a biology or chemistry class:

- Identify the problem—know the primary sources of your stress.
- Consider the alternatives—learn what changes might reduce stress.
- Gather data—keep a record of your responses to stressful situations.
- Decide on a plan of action—set a realistic long-term goal and intermediate objectives.
- Implement your plan of action—include mental and physical stimulation and relaxation.
- Evaluate—measure your progress toward your goal and objectives.

Keeping a checklist of the most frequent stressors in your life, and your most frequent responses to those stressors, will tell you a great deal about your self-concept, values, and attitudes. Knowing what causes stress in your life is the first step toward controlling it.

Time Management

Another common form of stress management is time management, which involves planning in order to achieve more in less time without feeling overworked or overcommitted. Lakein (1973) expressed the opinion that we find the time to do everything we really want to do, and offered these suggestions for using time more efficiently:

- Write down your lifetime goals.
- Based on your goals, establish priorities for reaching them.
- Schedule weekly and daily activities according to priorities.
- Spend most of your time on your highest priorities.
- Always do the most important things first.

This process requires a series of value judgments, based on the goals and priorities you choose. For example, if you value making the Dean's List, you may have to turn off the television set until you have written an English composition paper. If you value a college degree, buying a Porsche may have to wait.

There are other variations on the theme of stress management. In *Games People Play* (1964), Eric Berne recommended *time structuring* as a long-term coping process. He explained that the quantity and quality of time we spend with others ranges from withdrawal to intimacy. Although withdrawal is sometimes necessary to reduce immediate stress, its long-term effect is to increase stress. Conversely, intimacy, the highest level of one person caring for and about another, may create momentary stress but its long-range effect is to ameliorate stressful conditions. Between these two extremes there are various levels of interaction, many of which lead to devious and manipulative relationships, that he describes as "playing games." See if you recognize, or have played any of these games:

- Playing the affections of one parent against another to gain an advantage
- Dating someone you really don't care for because no one else is readily available
- Accepting a date with one person to make another jealous or take notice
- Dating someone at college without telling that you are emotionally committed to someone back home
- Cheating on a partner just because the two of you are physically apart
- Getting what you want from someone who is emotionally attached to you, then quickly losing interest

Those of you who are other-oriented, rather than self-centered, are most likely to develop the intimate relationships and social support networks that are such a critical part of stress management.

Self-Actualization

Maslow (1970) concluded that people who engage in the ongoing process of self-actualizing are the most mentally healthy. Self-actualizing people are those who enjoy the self-satisfaction of doing their best and fully utilizing their potential without suffering the frustrations that come from setting unrealistic or perfectionistic goals. Such people seem best able to overcome problems and still remain productive. They tend to see life as a series of opportunities rather than as a series of problems. Mentally healthy people are able and willing to accept changes in their lives and to adapt accordingly. Neurotics and psychotics have difficulty dealing with change. To resist change is to invite stress; to accept change and cope with it is what stress management is all about.

Kane (1985) emphasized the importance of developing a personal value system, including a set of principles and a code of conduct that give meaning to life. He also emphasized the role of self-concept in achieving mental well-being. This is consistent with the Rokeach system of beliefs, in which self-concept is central to the development of values and attitudes that ultimately determine behavior.

Lazarus and Folkman (1984) wrote, "Commitments are an expression of what is important to people, and they underlie the choices people make'' (p. 80). What Maslow called needs and Rokeach called values, Lazarus and Folkman referred to as commitments. They observed that people with what Rosenman and Freedman termed Type A behavior are an example of a set of values and a corresponding lifestyle, while Type B personalities represent a contrasting lifestyle and set of values. Which of these lifestyles you choose should tell you a great deal about what you really value.

SUMMARY

Emotional stress is inevitable and not necessarily harmful. Some people respond well to the challenges associated with stress and become more productive. Others feel threatened by it and allow it to negatively affect their interpersonal relationships or productivity.

Major life events are significant stressors that occur only infrequently—the death of a spouse or parent, marriage, or divorce, for example.

Other, more frequent stressors include such events as missed sleep, unpaid bills, and rush-hour traffic. People learn to cope with major life events and daily hassles in a variety of ways. Common coping strategies include the use of cigarettes, alcohol, and other drugs. Healthier strategies, also widely used, include exercise, relaxation, meditation, and effective time management. One way to offset daily hassles is to give and receive daily uplifts such as compliments, hugs, or phone calls.

Three general personality categories have been labeled as Types A, B, and C, according to how people typically cope with stress. Those who are impatient and become angry or hostile when things go wrong are classified as Type As. Type Bs are more relaxed—polar opposites of Type As. Type Cs, often referred to as ''hardy,'' accept changes as challenges, feel they are in control of their lives, and have a strong commitment or purpose in life. The risk of disease, particularly of coronary heart disease, is significantly greater for the angry Type A person. For that reason, stress management programs have become increasingly popular and can probably be considered true lifesavers.

Examining Your Values

Return to chapter 1 and reexamine the way you rank-ordered your instrumental and terminal values.

1. Are your instrumental values reflective of a Type A or Type B behavior pattern?
2. Are your terminal values reflective of a Type A or Type B lifestyle?
3. Are your values consistent with your self-concept as a Type A or Type B person?
4. Are you a Type C person in terms of stress management?
5. Does your lifestyle have ''hardiness''? Have you made a commitment to something or someone? Are you in control of your life? Do you accept the challenges of change?
6. Do you have an action plan for stress management? Is it consistent with your values? Is it consistent with a wellness lifestyle?

CHAPTER 12
Human Sexuality

Sex is like fire: properly controlled, it is good; uncontrolled, it can be devastating.

—Albert Meisenbach

Self-Examination Statements

Instructions: Read each statement, then circle the x in the column at the left that most closely describes your belief about that statement. (Use a pencil. After reading this chapter you may wish to come back and change some of your responses on the basis of new information or attitudes.)

SA = strongly agree   **A** = agree   **U** = undecided   **D** = disagree   **SD** = strongly disagree

SA	A	U	D	SD	
x	x	x	x	x	I am content with my self-concept as it relates to my sexuality.
x	x	x	x	x	My sexual values are clear in my mind.
x	x	x	x	x	I am proud of my sexual values.
x	x	x	x	x	I am willing to publicly affirm my sexual values.
x	x	x	x	x	My sexual values are compatible with those of my parents.
x	x	x	x	x	My sexual values are compatible with those of my best friend.
x	x	x	x	x	The sexual values of my peers are compatible with the sexual values of my parents.
x	x	x	x	x	Sexual behavior is one way I express personal values.
x	x	x	x	x	My sexual behavior is consistent with my values.
x	x	x	x	x	I know what my primary sex role is.
x	x	x	x	x	I am pleased with my sex role at the moment.
x	x	x	x	x	Sexual intimacy is a more basic need than love.
x	x	x	x	x	Love should be a prerequisite for sexual intimacy.
x	x	x	x	x	I value mature love more than "an exciting life."
x	x	x	x	x	It is healthy to express one's love physically.
x	x	x	x	x	I consider my sexual behavior to be healthy.
x	x	x	x	x	My values are a stronger influence on my sexual behavior than any possible health risk.
x	x	x	x	x	Some risk-taking in sexual behavior adds to my enjoyment.
x	x	x	x	x	Two people with similar values are more likely to be sexually compatible.

x	x	x	x	x	The ''double standard'' of acceptable sexual behavior is an unhealthy basis for a relationship.
x	x	x	x	x	I avoid promiscuous sex because of the health risks involved.
x	x	x	x	x	I believe that the risk of sexually transmitted diseases (STDs) increases as the number of sexual partners increases.
x	x	x	x	x	I am willing to accept the increased risk of STDs that comes with increased promiscuity.
x	x	x	x	x	I would feel guilty about having sexual relations with more than one person, knowing the possible health risks to them.
x	x	x	x	x	I know how to avoid sexually transmitted diseases.
x	x	x	x	x	If I had an STD, I would tell my most recent sexual partner.
x	x	x	x	x	If I had an STD, I would tell all my sexual partners within the past 12 months.
x	x	x	x	x	I would know if I had an STD because the symptoms would be obvious.
x	x	x	x	x	I know at least three common symptoms of such STDs as pelvic inflammatory disease and nongonococcal urethritis.
x	x	x	x	x	The only STD that really concerns me is AIDS.
x	x	x	x	x	AIDS does not concern me because I am not a male homosexual or intravenous drug user.
x	x	x	x	x	Using condoms and other barriers greatly reduces the health risks of promiscuous sexual activity, for both males and females.
x	x	x	x	x	Using condoms and other barriers greatly reduces the health risks of promiscuous sexual activity, whether homosexual or heterosexual.
x	x	x	x	x	''The Pill'' is a reasonably safe and healthy form of contraception.
x	x	x	x	x	The Pill is not a healthy form of contraception for smokers.
x	x	x	x	x	I would rather risk unwanted pregnancy than use artificial means of contraception.
x	x	x	x	x	Unwanted pregnancy is more damaging to mental than to physical health.
x	x	x	x	x	I know how to avoid unwanted pregnancy.
x	x	x	x	x	I believe that I have a good working knowledge of human sexuality in general.
x	x	x	x	x	The surest way to avoid unwanted pregnancy is abstinence from sexual intercourse.
x	x	x	x	x	I am willing to accept the risk of unwanted pregnancy that comes with unplanned intercourse.
x	x	x	x	x	I can't think of anything more stressful than deciding whether or not to have an abortion.
x	x	x	x	x	My values would preclude any consideration of an abortion.
x	x	x	x	x	Masturbation is not an acceptable sexual behavior in my system of values.

x	x	x	x	x	Homosexuality is not an acceptable sexual behavior in my system of values.
x	x	x	x	x	Premarital sexual intercourse is not an acceptable behavior in my system of values.
x	x	x	x	x	Extramarital sexual intercourse is not an acceptable behavior in my system of values.
x	x	x	x	x	Oral sex is not an acceptable behavior in my system of values.
x	x	x	x	x	Any sexual activity is acceptable so long as it does not compromise the values of those involved.
x	x	x	x	x	I never feel guilty about my sexual behavior.
x	x	x	x	x	Choosing between a career and a traditional wife/mother role represents a conflict in values for me.
x	x	x	x	x	Acceptable sexual roles and behavior involve value judgments that ought to be agreed on before any two people make a lasting commitment to each other.
x	x	x	x	x	I would compromise my values in order to be sexually compatible with someone I love.

DEFINING TERMS AND CONCEPTS

Clearly defined terms are more important than ever when the topic is as controversial and value-laden as human sexuality. In its broadest sense, sexuality is the entire gamut of how people deal intimately with themselves, members of the same sex (homosexuality), and members of the opposite sex (heterosexuality). In its physical dimension, the most obvious aspect of sexuality relates to sexual intercourse, including when to have it, with whom, whether to use birth control, who should assume responsibility for birth control, and what methods should be used. From the standpoint of maintaining physical health, sexually transmitted diseases (STDs) are a very significant component of human sexuality, as are decisions related to abortion and sterilization. But these and other decisions pertaining to human relationships have even greater ramifications for mental, social, and spiritual health.

Sex Roles

Sex roles are an important aspect of these relationships, and differ from culture to culture, and from generation to generation within the same culture. Sex roles have to do with expected and acceptable behavior for husbands, wives, children, and same-sex and opposite-sex intimates. Many of life's most stressful conditions (e.g., puberty, courtship, sexual preference, marriage, divorce, parenting, and sibling rivalries) are intimately related to changing sexual roles.

According to McCary (1979), physical human sexuality expresses itself most commonly in one of five ways: nocturnal orgasm, masturbation, homosexual relations, heterosexual petting, and heterosexual intercourse. Which of these outlets is appropriate for you is largely a matter of your own personal judgment and values, and may not be the same for you during puberty as during adulthood.

Puberty

Puberty is a time when secondary sex characteristics (e.g., beard or breasts) begin to appear, and it brings with it an awakening sex drive. Due to better nutrition and higher standards of living, puberty tends to occur at earlier ages now than ever before; at the same time, changing cultural norms, especially extended education and the accompanying delay in achieving earning power, has made early marriage a less viable option. Hence, for an increasing percentage of the population, many years may pass between the onset of sexual urges and their fulfillment in marriage. Each of us has a different impression of what constitutes acceptable behavior during that time span.

Masturbation

Our society has become more tolerant of a variety of sexual expressions, notably including masturbation and homosexuality. According to Ensor, Hunkel, and Means (1978), masturbation should be considered a normal part of life for both males and females, and for both individuals who do not have sexual partners and those who do. Some physicians even recommend it as a form of therapy, a way to learn about your sexual preferences and responses. Medical experts agree that masturbation causes no mental or physical harm, and that it actually helps sexual development by providing a release from sexual tension when no sex partner is available. Despite medical acceptance, social norms have not always shared this view.

Homosexuality

In the early 1970s in response to pressure from the American Psychological Association, the American Psychiatric Association removed homosexuality from its official list of mental disorders and by so doing recognized it as a sexual preference rather than an illness. In some cultures homosexuality is considered normal practice, and other cultures condemn homosexuality, but in the United States homosexuality is either more widespread or less hidden than in previous generations. Masters and Johnson (1966, 1970) concluded that homosexuality is learned behavior, but there is no unanimity on this point. From the standpoint of physical health, the greatest risk for male homosexual behavior is the higher incidence of STDs (especially herpes and AIDS). Lesbians experience fewer STDs than any other sexually active group.

Sexually Transmitted Diseases

A sexually transmitted disease (STD) is any disease spread primarily through sexual contact with infected persons. Such contact may be either homosexual or heterosexual. Most cases occur among unmarried persons, and the primary reason is promiscuity. Strictly speaking, promiscuity means having more than one sexual partner, although it has connotations of being indiscriminate in one's choice of partners; many sexually promiscuous individuals take as partners individuals whose habits are not well known to them. This is commonly referred to as "casual sex," and is one of the areas where values and health behavior become most closely intertwined.

The following have been the most prevalent STDs in the United States during the 1980s:

- Chlamydia, which takes the form of nongonococcal urethritis (NGU) among males, and pelvic inflammatory disease (PID) among females
- Gonorrhea
- Herpes
- Syphilis
- Trichomoniasis
- Genital warts

Less common, but more deadly and thus more prominent in the news, is acquired immuno-deficiency syndrome (AIDS). Specific causes and effects of STDs will be discussed later in this chapter.

Unwanted Pregnancies and Birth Control

Along with STDs and decisions about sexual preference, another aspect of human sexuality that can create physical and emotional health problems is unwanted pregnancies. Having to deal with an unwanted pregnancy can be extremely stressful. Before engaging in hetero-sexual intercourse, one has a responsibility for understanding how to prevent unwanted preg-nancies and how to deal with a pregnancy, should it occur. For this reason it is critical for sex education to begin prior to puberty, with explanations of the anatomical functions of the male penis and female vagina, as well as the human sexual response.

Birth control may be defined as any action taken to prevent an unwanted birth (Kane, 1985). When one thinks of birth control, one normally thinks of contraceptives, including pills, condoms, intrauterine devices (IUDs), dia-phragms, cervical caps, sponges, spermicides (foams, creams, jellies), and chemicals. Tech-nically, contraceptives prevent a sperm from meeting an ovum, whereas birth control includes all means of preventing a live birth. There are three common forms of birth control beyond use of contraceptives: abstinence, sterilization, and abortion. However, none of these options is an acceptable solution to the problem of birth control for the majority of people.

Abstinence

This means avoidance of sexual intercourse. It is the most effective method of birth control, but also is the least acceptable in terms of fulfilling whatever heterosexual sex drives a person may have.

Sterilization

This involves a vasectomy for males and a tubal ligation for females. This option is also a highly effective form of birth control, and it is reputed to be the most common form among married people in the U.S. It is obviously an unaccept-able solution to birth control for young people who plan eventually to have a family, because it is almost always permanent.

Abortion

This term refers to the removal of a live embryo or fetus from a female's uterus. Although legal-ized by the 1973 Supreme Court Roe versus Wade ruling, it is a last resort for most women and is often fraught with moral and emotional complications, as discussed in chapter 4. Al-though having an abortion is usually a stressful event, having an unwanted child may be even more stressful. It is for this reason that most knowledgeable, conscientious, sexually active individuals carefully select some form of contra-ception as a primary means of preventing an un-wanted pregnancy. Contraception is for people who value their human sexuality and plan to have heterosexual intercourse, but who also value maintaining control over whether and when they will have children.

Contraception

The two primary categories of contraception are natural and mechanical birth control methods. In general, mechanical methods are more effec-tive, but some people still prefer natural methods for personal or religious reasons. The Roman Catholic Church, for example, permits only natural methods of contraception. For natural methods, there is a significant difference between their theoretical and practical effectiveness (Whaley, 1982). For example, coitus interruptus (withdrawal of the penis just before ejaculation) is theoretically almost 100 percent effective, but the power of sexual urges makes it much less reliable in actual practice.

Unlike the outdated rhythm method, which relied on past ovulation to indicate "safe" times for intercourse, the modern sympto-thermal method, which relies on checks of basal body temperature and the cervix—including cervical mucus—can be as effective as any other method of contraception. Like coitus interruptus, this method depends heavily on human willpower and conscientiousness. You need to weigh your values carefully if you are considering using a natural method of birth control. Is upholding religious beliefs more important to you than avoiding pregnancy, or is the opposite true? How important to you is freedom from the risk of side effects from mechanical methods of birth control?

Mechanical methods of contraception have the disadvantage of a variety of side effects that may endanger health. Oral contraceptives—"the Pill"—are the most common mechanical form and the most effective in preventing pregnancy. However, in addition to many other side effects, oral contraceptives can so disrupt the menstrual cycles of some women that these women can find it difficult to conceive later if they choose to become pregnant. Further, taking the Pill is especially risky for the one quarter to one third of sexually active women who smoke, for reasons described in chapter 9.

Use of an intrauterine device (IUD) was, until recently, the next most common and effective mechanical contraceptive. It is effective because, after being inserted into the uterus by a physician, it remains there indefinitely, preventing implantation of a fertilized ovum. Thus, the need for additional precautions immediately prior to intercourse is eliminated. However, not all women can use an IUD, because it causes internal bleeding and pelvic inflammatory disease (PID) among some and is expelled by others. Its long-term use is now in question, and many brands have been removed from the market.

The diaphragm (for females) and the condom (for males) are also widely used, and they are quite effective *if* used properly and regularly; because they must be put in place immediately prior to intercourse, however, they are often *not* used regularly enough to avoid all unwanted pregnancies. Hendricks (1987) observed that for most men, wearing a condom while making love is like wearing earplugs to a concert! Her analogy helps us understand why those who intend to use condoms as a primary form of birth control are sometimes willing to risk intercourse without one. For diaphragms, a variety of spermicides in the form of foams, jellies, and suppositories are available, and new ones are being marketed all the time; although they are generally effective, they are often criticized for being "messy," inconvenient, and expensive.

Understanding the Reproductive Process

Infertility is a health problem related to human sexuality at the other end of the spectrum. Although it is a lesser concern for the average person than unwanted pregnancy, infertility—the inability to conceive and bear children when wanted—has become a growing problem in this country.

An understanding of the reproductive process is helpful to both those who want to conceive a child and those who wish to avoid it. Insertion of the penis into the vagina, and ejaculation of sperm therein, is not always sufficient (or necessary) to produce a pregnancy. Knowing the menstrual cycle, the frequency of ovulation, the most fertile time for conception to occur, and the life span of sperm inside the uterus and fallopian tubes may help create or prevent a pregnancy as desired. If pregnancy does not occur when desired, a thorough medical examination is in order, because the problem may be physiological. Furthermore, men and women whose families have a history of unhealthy hereditary traits may wish to seek genetic counseling, a medical procedure that can tell them before the birth whether or not their offspring may inherit a disease or disorder or if a high-risk pregnancy is likely.

Some childless couples resort to fertility drugs, but there is some risk of unhealthy side effects, especially multiple births. Other couples or single individuals choose to adopt rather than remain childless, which seems to be a healthy alternative. Some opt for artificial insemination (use of another man's sperm if the male partner is infertile) or surrogate motherhood (use of another female's womb if the female partner is infertile), although a recent New Jersey court ruling makes the legality of surrogate motherhood questionable, at least in some states. Decisions of this magnitude involve value judgments and ought to be made carefully and in keeping with one's overall system of values.

PREVENTING SEXUAL DISEASE

Meisenbach (1987) distinguishes two aspects of human sexuality, the pragmatic and the ethical/moral. In chapter 1, we discussed ethics and morals in order to differentiate them from values. It is Meisenbach's contention that health educators ought to avoid making moral judgments about sexual behaviors because this is the rightful province of family and religious influences. Remember, though, that the moral point of view means being considerate of how your actions may affect others and of doing what would be acceptable to you if you reversed roles with another person. Nowhere is such behavior more appropriate than in the area of human sexuality. Whether or not one accepts monogamy and fidelity (the opposite of promiscuity) as a moral imperative, the pragmatic fact is that such behavior has the health benefit of being the best protection (short of complete celibacy) against sexually transmitted diseases, including AIDS.

Current Information

More than in almost any other health-related area, there is a great gap between what we know and what we do regarding STDs. Although penicillin, tetracycline, and other antibiotics are relatively effective in the treatment of the most common STDs, the number of cases continues to grow. According to Parra and Cates (1985), "The problem of sexually transmitted diseases (STDs) in the United States has been growing, in both scope and complexity, at an alarming rate" (p. 261). There are many reasons why this is so, two of which are ignorance and apathy—lack of awareness or involvement, if you are still applying Dennison's Activated Health Education model. Other reasons include changes in sexual values and behavior (e.g., greater sexual freedom, and increased use of oral contraceptives instead of barriers like condoms).

Syphilis and Gonorrhea

Parra and Cates reported some progress since the Surgeon General's 1980 designation of STDs as one of the 15 priority areas for improving the health of the American people. They noted that the reported cases of syphilis have been dropping for 35 years, an example of what can be done when public awareness is coupled with medical advances. Likewise, the gonorrhea rate has been dropping since 1980, and it seems likely that the stated goal for 1990 will be reached (fewer than 650,000 cases annually).

Chlamydia

According to Swinker (1986), chlamydia has replaced gonorrhea as the most common STD in the U.S. today. Nongonoccocal urethritis (NGU) is caused by chlamydia and is most prevalent among males; its counterpart among females is pelvic inflammatory disease (PID). Both NGU and PID tend to occur without visible symptoms in their early stages, and thus often go untreated until after they have been spread.

Regular medical screening is recommended for anyone who is sexually active with more than one partner.

Age- and Gender-Related Behavior

Perine, Handsfield, Holmes, and Blount (1985) confirmed that the highest rates of STDs occur among 20- to 24-year-olds because they are the most sexually active in terms of both number of partners and frequency of sexual activity. Further, STDs are more common among men than women, nonwhites than whites, poor individuals than affluent, male homosexuals and bisexuals than heterosexuals, single individuals than married, and promiscuous individuals than single-partner. Most of these factors are beyond your control, while others are very much subject to choice (see the chapter-opening quote).

It is believed that widespread use of "the Pill" as a primary form of birth control has led to increased rates of STDs. Previous generations relied more heavily on condoms for birth control; not only did condoms serve to prevent pregnancy, but they also reduced the skin-to-skin contact that facilitates the spread of STDs. The Pill was so effective in reducing the risk of pregnancy that it created a false illusion of safety, which encouraged multiple sexual contacts among young, unmarried people. Greater mobility has also been a factor. When people move frequently from one geographic location to another, it becomes more difficult to track and treat infected sources, and thus more difficult to slow the spread of the disease.

Genital Herpes

Unlike the STDs just mentioned, genital herpes has become more prominent during the 1980s because antibiotics are an ineffective form of treatment and there is no known cure. Approximately half a million new cases are reported in the U.S. each year, and it is often the first form of STD acquired. VanderPlate and Aral (1987) noted that, because of its recurring nature and its repulsive appearance, "For many individuals, the disease produces an alteration in sexual attitudes, sexual identity, and behavior. . . . A critical issue for sexually active individuals who contract genital herpes virus is that of informing potential sexual partners of the disease" (p. 63). Orally administered acyclovir seems to reduce the severity of herpes symptoms, but it is not a cure. The authors offered three suggestions for preventing herpes: choose sexual partners carefully, abstain from sexual contacts when the visual symptoms of herpes periodically occur, and use rubber barriers.

AIDS

Without question, the most sensational news about STDs in the 1980s has been that of acquired immunodeficiency syndrome (AIDS). The first reported case in the U.S. was in 1979 or 1980 or 1981, in New York City or San Francisco or Los Angeles, depending on one's source of information. Panic was created by the discovery that many victims of AIDS die in 1 to 3 years and the realization that no cure was available. Further, according to Surgeon General Koop (1987), more than 1.5 million people who have been infected by the AIDS virus, don't know they have it, and thus are unknowingly spreading the disease to others.

Women

The risk of getting AIDS has not been as great for women as for men. Mondanaro (1987) reported that only 7 percent of people with AIDS are women and almost all of these women engaged in the high-risk behaviors of prostitution or injecting drugs with used needles. Morgan and Curran (1986) noted that over 90 percent of those with AIDS are either homosexual or bisexual males, their sexual partners, or intravenous drug abusers. Thus, for women, prevention appears to be largely a matter of avoiding IV drug use and male partners who are promiscuous, especially if the male is also bisexual.

Male Homosexuals

The promiscuous norm for many male homosexuals is well documented, and it is a critical factor in the spread of AIDS, according to Kaslow et al. (1987) and Moss et al. (1987). The former study reported that over two thirds of their nearly 5,000 male homosexual subjects reported having had more than 50 sexual partners each, and over 80 percent reported engaging in receptive anal intercourse, both of which are high-risk behaviors. The latter study reported that AIDS was 52 times more prevalent among men with 100 or more sexual partners (not uncommon) than among men with 1 to 5 partners. The risk went up 5 times or more for those who were rectal recipients of a penis. There was no evidence of transmission of AIDS through oral-genital sex. Monogamous relationships between two male homosexuals, which are less frequent than promiscuity, appear to be similar to monogamous heterosexual relationships in terms of risk of AIDS.

Transmission

Cowell (1985) wrote, "It is important to remember that there are two methods of transmission: sexual activity involving the exchange of body fluids and contact with blood or blood products" (p. 254). Homosexuals are at high risk when the penis of one partner tears the rectal tissue of another, allowing the semen of an infected person to enter the bloodstream of a previously uninfected individual. Another method of transmission, blood transfusions, represents only about 2 percent of all reported cases of AIDS in the U.S., and that number will probably dwindle as testing procedures for blood donors become more rigorous.

Pierce, Benke, Gislason, and Broski (1986) interviewed Dr. Otis Bowen, Secretary of the Department of Health and Human Services, who said about AIDS:

> The scientific evidence is that it is not a disease passed along through casual contact. And there has not been one single case shown that it has been by any other way except through sexual contact, through shared use of needles for drug users, and through birth of a baby from one who has AIDS. It is not probable that it can be passed on in any other way; therefore we try to hold down panic in these areas. (p. 287)

This assertion was corroborated by Surgeon General C. Everett Koop (1987), who declared, "AIDS is not spread by casual, nonsexual contact. It is spread by high-risk sexual and drug-related behaviors—behaviors that we can choose to avoid" (p. 1). (Here is an opportunity for you to apply the values clarification process described in chapter 1.) Koop emphasized these points:

- The risk of AIDS increases with the number of sexual partners.
- The best protection from AIDS is sexual abstinence or, barring that, use of a condom.
- To quarantine a person infected with AIDS is pointless because AIDS is not spread by casual contact.
- Compulsory blood testing is unnecessary, inaccurate (too many false positives and negatives), and prohibitively expensive.
- The drug azidothymidine (AZT) may slow the effects of AIDS, but it is *not* a cure.

PREMARITAL SEX AND PREGNANCY

Heterosexual activity brings with it the problem of possible unwanted pregnancy. Kovar (1979) reported, "The social and economic consequences of early childbearing in the United

States have been documented repeatedly" (p. 115). These consequences include lower educational levels, lower family income, and greater expenses from larger families. The STD rate is also higher in this early-childbearing group. Gerrard, McCann, and Fortini (1983) observed, "There are basically four choices open to the unmarried woman who conceives: abortion, marriage, keeping the child without marrying, and giving the child up for adoption" (p. 154). They noted that there are problems associated with each option. Their 15-year longitudinal study compared couples who married after conception with socioeconomically matched couples who married before conception. At the end of 15 years the couples who "had to get married" reported less education for both husband and wife, lower family income, more unemployment, and more subsequent unplanned children.

The authors concluded that premarital pregnancies could be cut in half if sexually active women would *consistently* use the best and most reliable forms of contraception available. Their data indicated that there was no difference in knowledge about contraceptives between women who were effective and ineffective users of contraceptives, respectively. However, the ineffective users were more likely to have an external locus of control and to attribute pregnancy to bad luck or chance.

Guilt and Contraception

Many studies have reported that guilt about premarital sex is a significant factor in both choice of contraceptive method and consistency of use. Herold and Goodwin (1981) observed that attitudes toward contraceptives were more important in determining behavior than knowledge about contraceptives. Their data indicated that "non-users are 5 times more likely to become pregnant than consistent users" (p. 249). Guilt was

often the factor that accounted for nonuse of contraception among sexually active women. High-guilt women were significantly more likely to do one of the following:

- Not want to appear that they were planning to have sex
- Not expect intercourse to happen
- Be too embarrassed to buy contraceptives
- Be concerned that their parents would find out that they were using contraceptives
- Feel guilty about actually using contraceptives
- Expect their partners to provide contraceptives
- Not know how to use contraceptives properly

Are any of these attitudes toward contraception descriptive of you or your partner?

Mosher and Vonderheide (1985) hypothesized that greater guilt about premarital sex would correlate with less effective use of contraceptives, and that greater guilt about masturbation would correlate with ineffective use of a diaphragm. Women who feel guilty about masturbating are generally uncomfortable touching their genitals, and either fail to use a diaphragm on a regular basis or insert it hastily to minimize genital contact. The data they gathered from single college women confirmed both of these hypotheses. Further, women who relied on the Pill or an IUD, which are generally considered to be among the more reliable forms of contraception, scored lower on sex guilt than women who relied on less reliable contraceptives such as foams and condoms.

Perhaps the most persistent researcher in the area of sexual guilt has been Meg Gerrard (1987), who has studied the sexual behavior of heterosexual college women on three separate occasions at 5-year intervals (1973-74, 1978-79, 1983-84). She reported that, although sexual activity increased dramatically during the 1970s, it decreased from 51 percent of her 1978-79 subjects to 37 percent of her 1983-84 subjects. She found that sexually inactive subjects had significantly higher sex guilt scores, which presumably accounted for their inactivity. The next-highest sex guilt scores were reported for those subjects who used no or ineffective contraceptives, even though they were sexually active. Those who reported the lowest sex guilt scores were also the most effective contraceptive users.

Gerrard concluded that guilt inhibits women from proper planning and use of contraceptives. She also noted that her samples provided "evidence of a definite shift in sexual values and sexual behavior among college women" (p. 979). She attributed the decrease in sexual activity to the influence of changing social norms, primarily the greater fear of contracting a sexually transmitted disease.

It was Gerrard's contention that the risk for premarital pregnancy is greatest for those females whose guilt is not sufficient to prevent sexual activity but is sufficient to prevent them from thoughtfully and logically protecting themselves from unwanted pregnancy. That hypothesis seems to be borne out by the review of literature conducted by Yarber (1986), who concluded the following:

- Unwanted pregnancy among single women is a major social health problem.
- About half of all unwanted pregnancies among teenagers occur in the first 6 months of sexual activity.
- Nearly two thirds of unwed mothers use no contraception, or use contraceptives inconsistently.
- Adolescents typically delay first use of medical contraception for more than a year following first coitus.
- For unwed women ages 20 to 29, the average delay from first coitus to first use of contraceptives is about 6 months.
- A third of the unwed women ages 20 to 29 have been pregnant at least once.

It should be noted, however, that given the variety of personal values in our society, some unwed women probably choose to become pregnant, choose not to use contraception, and do so without guilt.

Contraceptives and Behavioral Models

Yarber (1986) found no significant relationship between locus of control and use of contraceptives, which is not surprising in the absence of some consideration of health values. However, the subjects who were interested in safety reported the shortest delay between first coitus and first use of contraceptives. Those who were most interested in exercise or fitness reported the longest delay; Yarber speculated that they may have avoided prescription use of contraceptives because of health-related side effects.

Ewald and Roberts (1985) applied the Ajzen-Fishbein model to sexual behavior, hypothesizing that beliefs about condoms would influence attitudes, attitudes about condoms would influence intent to use them, and intent to use condoms would influence actual use. They found that all three hypothesized relationships were significant, supporting use of the Ajzen-Fishbein model for predicting this health-related behavior.

Hester and Macrina (1985) used the Health Belief Model to explain differences in the adequacy of contraceptive use by college women. They found that, although contraceptives were readily available on most college campuses, risk-taking behavior was startlingly high, resulting in a pregnancy rate among unmarried females of 6 to 10 percent at most campuses and as high as 22 percent at one university. Based on the Health Belief Model, it was hypothesized that contraceptive behavior would be a function of perceived susceptibility to pregnancy, perceived seriousness of such an outcome, perceived benefits of taking preventive action, and perceived barriers or costs to taking such action. Although each of the 171 subjects in this study claimed not to want to become pregnant, over a third were engaging in intercourse at least once a week, and nearly half of those (1 out of 6 of all subjects) were identified as "inadequate users" of contraception. Inadequate users differed significantly from "adequate users" in the following ways:

- They were more embarrassed about asking for contraceptives.
- They perceived contraceptives to be more difficult to get.
- They perceived that using contraceptives made intercourse less enjoyable.
- They found it more inconvenient to use contraceptives.
- They found intercourse to be less emotionally satisfying when protected by contraceptives.
- They found it more awkward to talk to a partner about means of contraception.

The authors concluded that the best predictor of contraceptive use was the costs and barriers variable.

Smoking and Contraception

Zabin (1984) studied the risk-taking behavior of 1,200 young women and found a significant relationship between smoking and sexual behavior. Those who smoked were more likely to avoid using contraceptives altogether, or to use less reliable forms of contraception (e.g., withdrawal, rhythm method, condoms, or spermicides). The lower the smoking rate, the more effective the contraceptive method chosen and the more frequently contraceptives were used. Zabin concluded that females who prepared for coitus in advance were significantly less likely to smoke. "The evidence clearly suggests that those who initiate sexual activity in early adolescence demonstrate levels of smoking well beyond the norm" (p. 262). They also discovered

that the majority of those who used prescribed methods of birth control chose oral contraceptives, a high-risk choice, given the relationships between smoking, oral contraceptives, and coronary heart disease.

CURRENT SEXUAL NORMS AND VALUES

There is little doubt that a change in sexual values, attitudes, and behaviors of young Americans occurred during the 1970s. The evidence indicates that young people became more sexually active, more promiscuous, less inhibited, and less responsible. This was referred to as "the sexual revolution." Now there is support for Gerrard's contention that the pendulum is swinging back toward more conservative norms. Sherwin and Corbett (1985) studied the sexual norms among college students in 1971, 1978, and 1984. The percentage who reported that sexual intercourse was the norm prior to marriage increased in each successive sample, but the number of male and female students who reported themselves to be virgins was higher in 1984 (28 percent for males and 43 percent for females) than in 1971 or 1978. They also reported the norm for a casual dating relationship was far from "anything goes," with only 7 percent expecting intercourse on a casual date. Like Gerrard, they concluded that sexual values and behaviors are becoming more conservative in the 1980s.

Attitudes About Premarital Sex

Singh (1980) also studied trends in attitudes toward premarital sexual relations. He reported significantly more permissive attitudes toward premarital sex among the following groups:

- Easterners and Westerners, as compared to "Bible Belt" residents of the South and Midwest

- Those who seldom attend religious services
- Those who live in urban and metropolitan areas
- Those who are single or divorced
- Those with higher education or more income
- Those who are age 25 or younger

It should also be emphasized that there is often a significant difference between attitudes and behavior; as Rokeach observed, the cognitive dissonance created by such differences is a source of unhealthy levels of emotional stress.

McCary (1979) described differences in attitudes toward premarital sexual intercourse related to age and sex role. The percentage of those who have a favorable attitude toward premarital sex is highest among single college-age individuals. The percentage declines somewhat for older single adults, further declines for married adults without children, is lower still for married people with children, and is lowest of all for married people with teenage children. It appears that people's values shift toward conservatism as their roles change from lover to spouse to parent and as greater experience and responsibility add to their level of maturity, and that shift causes them to change their attitudes toward premarital sex.

Identify Appropriate Sex Roles

Identifying an appropriate sex role is a significant problem for most young people and potentially a great source of stress. This is especially true for females whose education has prepared them for a career and who then feel they must choose between the conflicting values of a professional position and the roles of wife or mother. Sacrificing either role may result in depression, anger, or loss of self-esteem. The late Congresswoman Clare Booth Luce (1983) wrote:

You have to make your mind up! Are you going to have a highly successful career? In which case, you are *not* going to have a highly successful marriage—probably won't have that anyway—and you will be *forever* getting there, and on the way you will have to make another decision: do you want an illegitimate child, or do you want to go childless into the future? What is it? What is it you want? . . . Women are torn by their feeling that they cannot establish their 'identities' until they've decided on a career or a sex life—if they find themselves pregnant, should they get married? Have an abortion? Have a child and bring it up without a father? Women's liberation has liberated *men*—they have far less commitments than they did before. (p. 5)

Avery-Clark (1986) studied more than 200 working and nonworking married women and found that women who were pursuing a career were twice as likely to complain about inhibited sexual desire, characterized by "a low level of initiatory sexual behavior and receptivity to the initiation of sexual behavior" (p. 102) by a spouse. One possible reason is the high level of stress associated with the dual roles of marriage and career; men can pursue a career without fear of it being interrupted by pregnancy, and nonworking women can become pregnant without it interrupting a career. Another is the change in attitude that sometimes occurs when increased earning power makes a woman more independent and more likely to reject the traditional values of male dominance.

This same issue was studied by Hardman and Gardner (1986), who noted that "inhibited sexual desire (ISD) is the most common and pervasive of all the sexual dysfunctions" (p. 55). One of the primary reasons they cited was fear of loss of control and use of sex to maintain control over a relationship. Being committed to a sexual relationship without giving up control of one's individuality is typical of the challenges that confront both men and women. It is easier to resolve such difficulties when both partners value each other's independence as well as each other's companionship.

WELLNESS THROUGH HUMAN SEXUALITY

The terminal values identified by Rokeach suggest that at least two kinds of human relationships are important: true friendship (close companionship) and mature love (sexual intimacy). People may experience both true friendship and mature love within a single relationship, or may have one relationship in which they find and express true friendship and a separate one in which they find and express mature love. Both fall under the heading of human sexuality, however, according to our definition at the beginning of this chapter.

Intimate, Nonsexual Relationships

Levinson, Darrow, Klein, Levinson, and McKee (1978) wrote a perceptive book about establishing intimate, nonsexual friendships with members of the same and the opposite sex. The authors observed that adult American men seldom have a really close friendship with either a man or a woman unless it involves a sexual relationship. An American woman is much more likely to have a female confidante with whom she shares her innermost thoughts. Men typically settle for a social network that includes many friends but no confidante. This is a cultural norm that has evolved over the years, but it is not necessarily a healthy one. Go back to chapter 1 and see where you ranked "true friendship" among your terminal values. Do you have a true friend, someone with whom you have shared your personal beliefs, attitudes, and values in recent months? Having one may contribute more to your social and emotional health and to the quality of your life than will any of the physical health behaviors we have discussed so far.

True friendship is especially important because it provides the soundest base from which mature love (sexual intimacy) may develop. This is not to say that your friend will be your lover, but

that the state of mind that allows true friendship to exist will also be appropriate for a healthy sexual relationship. Both relationships depend for their success on refusal to exploit another person.

Healthy Sexuality

Reiss (1981), who has written extensively about human sexuality, defined exploitation as "use of someone for one's own advantage or to take more than one is giving" (p. 273). It is his belief that any sexual act where neither person feels taken advantage of cannot be considered exploitative and should therefore be considered socially acceptable. Not everyone would agree with him on this point. For example, is incest acceptable when one party is too immature to *feel* exploited? He observed that the double standard of acceptable sexual behavior for men and women (i.e., it is less acceptable for women to voice an interest in sex or to be sexually active than it is for men) is still much in evidence in this country and that it is responsible for much unhealthy guilt related to sex. He pointed out that no culture in the history of the world has maintained a norm of sexual virginity for males at age 21, and he advocated a guilt-free acceptance of responsible sexual expression for both males and females.

The values we have learned from our families and from any religious affiliations we have had probably have a greater influence over our premarital sexual attitudes and behavior than any concern we might have for health-related issues. If we approach the matter from the standpoint of social and emotional health, however, there are only four possible interactions of attitudes and behavior (Figure 12.1). Two involve feelings of guilt, and two do not. It is my belief that it is emotionally healthier to choose either of the guilt-free behaviors than either of the guilt-laden choices. You are urged to use the values clarification process described in chapter 1 to make decisions pertaining to not only premarital

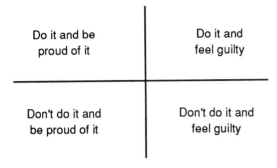

Do it and be proud of it	Do it and feel guilty
Don't do it and be proud of it	Don't do it and feel guilty

Figure 12.1. Sexual attitudes and behaviors.

sexual behavior but the entire range of decisions that will allow your human relationships to contribute to the quality of your life.

Gilgun and Gordon (1983) nicely summarized the relationship of morals to decisions about sexual behavior, in or out of marriage: "Concern for the well-being of others and a willingness to help others flourish are characteristic of a morally excellent person" (p. 28). Such a person neither exploits others nor allows himself or herself to be exploited by others, sexually or otherwise. Gilgun and Gordon recognized the central importance of self-concept, just as Rokeach did, declaring, "Persons with good self-esteem believe they are equal to other human beings. They believe they are worthy of dignity and respect, and they extend this regard to others" (p. 29).

Mature Love

Mature love, defined by Rokeach as sexual and spiritual intimacy, may include heterosexual and homosexual cohabitation. However, the fact that America has one of the highest marriage rates of any country in the world seems indicative of the value we place on marriage as a primary expression of mature love. According to Wattenberg (1985):

- Nineteen of every 20 American adult women were or had been married as of 1983.

- Over 90 percent of married women have children at some point in their marriage.
- Although the divorce rate doubled between 1960 and 1980, peaking in 1981, it declined 8 percent between 1981 and 1985.
- Eight of 10 men and 7 of 10 women remarry within 5 years of divorce, which seems to indicate that even divorced people value family life.

The fact that our divorce rate is among the highest in the world may suggest that we have high expectations, a low tolerance for imperfection, and poorly developed skills for building human relationships.

Kane (1985) concluded that "a good marriage is one that makes both partners happy, one that is characterized by mutual love, respect, support, and sharing" (p. 204). To make marriage or any other intimate relationship last, both partners must be committed and willing to compromise for the common good; it helps if partners share certain basic human values. Love, unfortunately, does not guarantee a successful marriage. Those who "fall in love" quickly are just as likely to fall out of love quickly (Peck, 1978). The ultimate test will be whether or not two people like each other enough to be willing to continue as companions in spite of obvious imperfections. Each partner must be willing to listen to the other's point of view and be prepared to compromise. This is equally true for all intimate human relationships, in or out of marriage.

If you choose to marry, it is important to find out the extent to which you and your prospective partner agree on values related to human sexuality and sex roles. Do you understand and accept the "double standard" for males and females as it relates to sexual activity prior to marriage, and does this create a problem for either of you? Do you agree on the role of fidelity for each of you after marriage? Have you agreed on the expectations that each of you has for a career, and the expectations that each of you has about rearing a family? Have you agreed on the role that each of you will have in making important decisions and in performing household responsibilities? Have you discussed sexual preferences (some of which may be considered variant or deviant sex by others), and do you agree on acceptable behavior for each of you? Have you agreed on who will assume responsibility for birth control and what method will be used?

If you are a lesbian woman or a gay man considering making a commitment to another, you, too, should consider all of these questions (except birth control). Your relationship may undergo the additional pressures of homophobia (heterosexual fear and mistrust of homosexuality), which may affect your ability to sustain commitment to the relationship. The quality of any relationship, homosexual or heterosexual, will be improved by the partners' willingness to discuss and agree on these important issues before making a lasting commitment.

SUMMARY

Human sexuality includes all of life's intimate personal relationships, within and outside marriage, whether or not sexual intercourse is involved. One's sexual behavior is greatly influenced by personal values, as well as religious and cultural norms. Acceptable sexual behavior varies greatly from one country to another, from one generation to another, and from one person to another. Open and ongoing communication between loved ones is one of the surest ways to establish healthy relationships.

Casual sexual intimacy carries two significant risks: unwanted pregnancy and sexually transmitted disease (STD). An unwanted pregnancy forces a choice between marriage, single parenthood, abortion, and adoption, each of which has significant social and economic consequences. The risk of STDs rises exponentially with each new sexual partner. The consequences of contracting an STD range from the relatively temporary inconvenience of some form of chlamydia to the life-long stigma of herpes and the life-threatening presence of the AIDS virus.

While monogamous heterosexual relationships within marriage were once the norm, other patterns of sexual preference have become increasingly common in recent years. Among them are homosexuality, serial monogamy within or outside marriage, and multiple sexual partners. Homosexuality eliminates the risk of unwanted pregnancy but, without modern contrivances such as artificial insemination or surrogate motherhood, also eliminates propagation of the species and weakens the traditional family unit.

Examining Your Values

Make a list of the personal qualities (instrumental values) that you would like your "significant other" to have. Now return to chapter 1 and look at your rank-ordering of instrumental values.

1. Are the two lists consistent and compatible?
2. Do you expect your true love to possess qualities that you do not possess?
3. To what extent are you asking more than you are prepared to contribute to the relationship?
4. Are you willing to contribute more than you receive?

CHAPTER 13
Safety and Security

Risk-taking behavior is goal oriented. Man is to be educated not so that he can survive, but so that he can live.

—Kenneth Clarke & Guy Parcel

Self-Examination Statements

Instructions: Read each statement, then circle the x in the column at the left that most closely describes your belief about that statement. (Use a pencil. After reading this chapter you may wish to come back and change some of your responses on the basis of new information or attitudes.)

SA = strongly agree   **A** = agree   **U** = undecided   **D** = disagree   **SD** = strongly disagree

SA	A	U	D	SD	
x	x	x	x	x	I think of myself as a safety-conscious person.
x	x	x	x	x	Members of my immediate family are safety conscious.
x	x	x	x	x	Most of my close friends are safety conscious.
x	x	x	x	x	Family safety and security are high on my list of values.
x	x	x	x	x	National security is high on my list of values.
x	x	x	x	x	My general attitude is "better to be safe than sorry."
x	x	x	x	x	I believe that my attitude toward safety helps keep me safe from accidents.
x	x	x	x	x	I believe that I practice safe behavior most of the time.
x	x	x	x	x	I have an external locus of control when it comes to safety.
x	x	x	x	x	I believe that people with an external locus of control are more accident prone.
x	x	x	x	x	In the next 5 years I am more likely to die from an accident than from illness or disease.
x	x	x	x	x	I don't believe that I am particularly susceptible to accidents.
x	x	x	x	x	I think of myself as a risk-taker.
x	x	x	x	x	Taking risks adds excitement to my life.
x	x	x	x	x	Life devoid of all risks would be boring.
x	x	x	x	x	I am proud of my ability to cope with risky situations.

X	X	X	X	X	I enjoy taking risks when they involve only me.
X	X	X	X	X	I often take risks that involve other people.
X	X	X	X	X	When I drive an automobile, I am aware that the risks I take may affect others.
X	X	X	X	X	I believe that a traffic accident is more likely to claim my life this year than any other form of death.
X	X	X	X	X	I believe that being a defensive driver is likely to save my life.
X	X	X	X	X	Auto seat belts are proven life savers.
X	X	X	X	X	I support legislation to make seat belt use mandatory.
X	X	X	X	X	Motorcycle helmets are proven life savers.
X	X	X	X	X	I support legislation to make use of helmets by motorcyclists mandatory.
X	X	X	X	X	The majority of highway fatalities are caused by alcohol abuse.
X	X	X	X	X	For people my age, alcohol is the direct or indirect cause of most accidents.
X	X	X	X	X	The majority of fatalities from fires are related to cigarettes and/or alcohol.
X	X	X	X	X	The majority of water fatalities are related to alcohol abuse.
X	X	X	X	X	I know how to swim well enough to save my own life in an emergency.
X	X	X	X	X	I know how to swim well enough to save another person's life in an emergency.
X	X	X	X	X	I believe that I am better able to cope with emergency situations than most other people.
X	X	X	X	X	I am certified to administer emergency first aid treatment.
X	X	X	X	X	I am certified to administer cardiopulmonary resuscitation (CPR).
X	X	X	X	X	I believe that everyone should know first aid and CPR.
X	X	X	X	X	I would feel safer if more of my family and friends knew CPR and first aid.
X	X	X	X	X	I perform monthly self examinations of my breasts (testes for males) as a protection against cancer.
X	X	X	X	X	I took a driver education class because I wanted to be a safe driver.
X	X	X	X	X	I have taken self-defense classes to make me less vulnerable and more secure.
X	X	X	X	X	I own a gun because it makes me feel more secure.
X	X	X	X	X	I know how to use a gun well enough to feel safe around firearms.
X	X	X	X	X	The threat of nuclear war makes me feel unsafe.
X	X	X	X	X	I value the security I feel, knowing that the U.S. has nuclear arms to protect me from attackers.
X	X	X	X	X	The benefits of nuclear power outweigh the risks involved.

DEFINING TERMS AND CONCEPTS

When we think about healthy behavior, it is easy to overlook the importance of safety. However, according to Oleakno (1987):

Injuries are a major public health problem. In the United States, injuries are the leading cause of death in persons 1-44 years of age and are responsible for more years of potential worklife lost than that from heart disease and cancer combined. (p. 39)

Robertson (1986) explained why this is so. Half of those who die from heart disease are more than 76 years old, and half of all cancer victims are 68 or older, but half of those who die in motor vehicle accidents are less than 27 years old. Hence, an accidental death is more likely to result in lost work years than a death from heart disease or cancer.

The magnitude of this problem was made even clearer by Morelock, Hingson, Smith, and Lederman (1985), who wrote, ''Accidental injury is the fourth leading cause of death after heart disease, cancer, and stroke. Motor vehicle accidents are the leading cause of all deaths for people 1 to 34 years of age'' (p. 357). They are also a major cause of severe injuries, including paraplegia, quadriplegia, and permanent brain damage.

Risk-Taking Behavior

Many people tend to assume that accidents happen by chance or according to the law of averages. The truth is that attitudes are the most critical factor in accident rates. People who are risk-takers, and those who have an external locus of control, tend to be accident prone. Jonah (1986) asserted that certain personality traits seem to lead to higher accident rates. These include aggressiveness and low self-esteem, combined with self-centeredness and poor judgment. Self-centered people are less likely to drive defensively, for example, or to be sensitive to how their actions may threaten their own or another's safety. People with low self-esteem tend to question their own worth, and use high-risk behavior to demonstrate their ability to deal with danger, perhaps by driving at high speeds or while drunk. Accidents are caused by ignorance, carelessness, and negligence. Of the 160,000 Americans who die each year, many could have been saved by a change in attitude.

For purposes of this discussion, accidents have been divided into four major categories:

- Motor vehicle
- Occupational
- Home
- Public

Motor vehicles account for the most accidental deaths, but the other causes are also of great concern. For example, occupational safety and health is one of the 15 priority areas identified in *Healthy People: The Surgeon General's Report on Health Promotion and Disease Prevention* (U.S. Department of Health, Education, and Welfare, 1979). Regardless of cause, accidents do not occur randomly, but are fairly predictable, based on age, sex, geography, occupation, and lifestyle. Culture also plays a role in accident rates. Some cultures, including our own, value speed, competition, and risk-taking. When these traits prevail, higher accident rates are inevitable. Many of these traits are often considered to be ''macho,'' which may help explain why males are involved in far more accidents than females.

Risk-Taking and Values

Risk-taking is an indication of values. Historians are fond of pointing out that Americans have a rich tradition of risk-taking, from those who sailed on the Mayflower, to the pioneers who settled the West, to those who volunteered to serve their country in armed battle during World Wars I and II. Most observers of human behavior understand that a life devoid of all risk would not be worth living.

Streufert (1986) pointed out that all of us engage in risk-taking, but some of us confine it to situations where the risk is low and the results are of little consequence; smoking a first cigarette just to experiment is typically perceived as low-risk behavior. Others engage in risky behavior only when the perceived benefits are great. For example, a nonswimmer might instinctively jump into deep water in order to save a loved one from drowning. Almost everyone would avoid a situation where the risks are great and the consequences are severe. Most people avoid using heroin because the consequence may be addiction or death. Individual differences are immense, and what one person considers risky might simply be "exhilarating" or "fun" for another. At what point along the risk-taking continuum a person draws the behavioral line says much about his or her values. Streufert reported that a person with Type A behavior is more likely to accept risks if the payoff, in terms of achievement or winning, is high enough; such a person also tends to be more attentive to the details of the task at hand, thus reducing risks. Type B persons are generally less likely to take great risks merely to achieve a goal but may be more willing to take small risks where the penalties are not severe.

Perceived Hazards and Benefits

Clarke and Parcel (1975) used Hochbaum's Health Belief Model to explain risk-taking behavior. They contended that it is ineffective to ask people to limit smoking, alcohol, drugs, or promiscuous sex merely because of the health hazards involved because this is a negative approach. Rather than measure risk on a continuum, with hazards at one end and benefits at the other, they proposed a double continuum (Table 13.1), one measuring hazards and the other measuring benefits.

Their formula was Calculated Risk (CR) = hazards ÷ benefits. Some behaviors are high in both risks and benefits, whereas others are low in both. In either instance, it was Clarke and Parcel's contention that a behavior is not based on the risk involved as much as on the difference between perceived hazards and perceived benefits. The qualifier "perceived" is critical because we often lack objectivity about the real hazards and benefits. The authors concluded that there is nothing unhealthy about taking risks as long as the benefits are real and valued. This concept is worthy of your consideration, especially if you believe, as I do, that health and safety are not ends but means to achieving a higher quality of life.

Culture and Risk

Callois (1955), a French sociologist, offered another theory regarding risk-taking behavior. He observed that the people of every culture throughout history have engaged in various forms of play, which he divided into four categories: games of chance, games of mimicry (play-acting), games of competition, and games of vertigo (risk-taking). It was his belief that the healthiest and most productive societies were those where games of competition prevailed. Decadent or declining societies, on the other hand, preferred vertigo or risk-taking activities (e.g., bullfighting, auto racing, abuse of alcohol or mind-altering drugs). He pointed out that people living in a healthy society typically prefer to incur risks by engaging in competitive sports, whereas members of a decadent society who enjoy risk-taking activities are more likely to participate in them vicariously, letting the paid gladiators take the actual physical risks. Using this criterion, do you perceive the society in which you live to be healthy or decadent? How do you explain the popularity of professional football and professional wrestling? How do you

Table 13.1   Calculated Risk-Taking Continuums

Benefits	Score	Hazards
	0 — 0	
Kicks	10 — 10	Negligible
	20 — 20	
Immediate satisfaction	30 — 30	Controllable
	40 — 40	
Worthwhile	50 — 50	Formidable
	60 — 60	
Long-standing satisfaction	70 — 70	Serious
	80 — 80	
Life preserving	90 — 90	Life threatening
	100 — 100	

account for the fact that so many people watch sports on television rather than actively engaging in them? What is your primary role, that of participant or spectator?

PREVENTING MOTOR VEHICLE ACCIDENTS

Driving causes more accidents than any other risk-taking activity, and the highest risk of such accidents exists among young male drivers. There are several reasons for this. Comparing minimum drinking ages among states reveals that alcohol has been a major factor in vehicular accident rates. Statistics indicate that 18- and 19-year-olds have had the worst driving records, especially in states where the legal drinking age was 18.

Drinking, Driving, and Demographics

When an inexperienced driver is also an inexperienced drinker, the combination too often proves lethal. One wag suggested raising the legal driving age and lowering the legal drinking age so that beginning drivers would be more experienced as drinkers! Perhaps a better solution would be to allow 16-year-olds a choice between drinking and driving, knowing they would have to wait at least 3 years for their second choice. As was pointed out in chapter 8, every state now has a minimum legal drinking age of 21, in an effort to avoid this serious safety problem—and to avoid losing federal funds for failure to comply.

According to Jonah (1986), vehicular accident rates are higher as miles-driven increases, at night, on highways, when drivers are inexperienced, and as risk-taking behavior increases. His summary of other studies revealed that younger drivers typically drive faster, allow smaller margins for error, and get more speeding tickets per distance traveled. These studies ''unequivocally support the contention that young drivers take greater risks by driving faster than older drivers'' (p. 259). It was his contention that the primary effect of alcohol on young drivers was not to impair their physical skills or reaction time as much as to impair the decision-making process and specifically to disinhibit risk-taking. It was also his conclusion, based on the data available, that failure by the driver and passengers to wear seat belts places the driver *and every other occupant of the vehicle* at greater risk of injury should an accident occur. (More on this controversial "rights versus responsibilities" issue later in the chapter.)

About two thirds of all traffic fatalities occur at night, with the highest rates occurring between 1 and 4 a.m. on Saturdays and Sundays. As you might expect, alcohol is a factor in more of these deaths than is true for deaths that occur during daylight hours or on weekdays. Fatigue also accounts for some late-night accidents. Increased speed results in more motor vehicle accidents, more severe accidents, and more fatalities. The rate of auto accidents is higher in urban than rural areas, but there are relatively more fatal accidents in rural areas, where people drive faster. The highest auto accident fatality rates per unit of population are in sparsely-populated rural states—Wyoming, New Mexico, and Nevada (Kane, 1985).

Speed Limits

In 1974 the national speed limit was dropped from 65 mph to 55 mph in an attempt to conserve fuel and save lives. The auto fatality rate dropped by 17 percent, and the number of persons killed annually in auto accidents declined from a peak of about 55,000 prior to 1974 to under 44,000 in 1985. In a Gallup poll ("Fifty-five mph," 1986), 79 percent of those questioned conceded that the 55-mph speed limit saved lives. Despite this, mounting public pressure caused a return to the 65-mph speed limit on many rural interstate highways in 1986 and 1987, following federal approval. How would you side on this classic example of a values conflict, between health and safety on the one hand, and achievement, "an exciting life," and individual freedom on the other?

An interesting sidelight of the same Gallup poll provides considerable insight into the discrepancy between self-perceptions of our behavior and our perceptions of the normative behaviors of others. Fifty-four percent of those queried indicated that they obeyed the 55-mph speed limit "most of the time," but their perception was that only 30 percent of other people complied with this law most of the time." Respondents also perceived that 62 percent of others complied "not very often," but only 20 percent admitted that they complied "not very often." This same phenomenon repeats itself in most of the gray areas of human behavior, in that we tend to believe that we are more successful in abiding by society's rules and laws than most others, which provides some rationalization for our occasionally breaking those rules and laws. Who among us has not justified our action at one time or another with the comment, "Everyone else does it"?

Safety Reform

Returning to the problem of traffic accidents, there are other ways to lower these rates. Ralph Nader spearheaded auto safety reform for several decades, one result of which was the National Traffic and Motor Vehicle Safety Act of 1966. Safety belts, infant seats, and rubber bumpers were outgrowths of that legislation. Wearing seat belts is estimated to save 10,000 to 20,000 American lives per year, but unless use is mandated by law, most drivers continue to ignore them. This tendency appears to be changing, however, as older drivers who learned to drive before seat belts existed are gradually being replaced by younger drivers who were accustomed to using them from the very beginning of their driving experience.

Morelock and his associates (1985) reported, "Less than one fifth of the U.S. population consistently wears automobile seatbelts" (p. 357). However, a Gallup poll ("Auto Seat Belt Use," 1986) revealed that "the use of auto seat belts has doubled in the last 2 years" (p. 29). When they asked people whether or not they used a seat belt the last time they got into a car, in 1984 25 percent said yes, whereas 52 percent said yes in 1986. Of college graduates, 72 percent said yes in 1986. Clearly, public awareness of the benefits of seat belt use is growing, and attitudes and behaviors are changing; as usual, those with more education tend to make healthier choices. This was confirmed by Morelock et al. (1985), who found that the following were least likely to use seat belts or to support a law requiring their use:

- Drivers with little education and low income
- Those who risk driving after abusing alcohol or marijuana
- Those who believe that seat belts are ineffective or uncomfortable
- Those who believe they have a low probability of crash involvement
- Those who have been cited more often for moving traffic violations

Of those with two or more tickets for moving violations, 70 percent opposed seat belt laws; of those with no moving violations, only 39 percent opposed such laws.

Williams and Lund (1986) similarly observed that the people who were most likely to need seat belts—males, teenagers, speeders, and heavy drinkers—were least likely to use them. They reported that half of the 50 states had mandatory seat belt laws in place as of July 1986, covering 73 percent of the nation's population; a federal mandate would have required air bags in all new automobiles unless at least two thirds of the United States population lived in states with mandatory seat belt laws by 1987. The authors' data indicated that laws requiring seat belts definitely increase usage and decrease accidents and fatalities. For example, in Great Britain, use rates above 90 percent have been reported, with fatalities reduced by more than 20 percent; in Canada, use rates exceed 60 percent. Altogether, more than 30 countries have enacted mandatory seat belt laws with reported reductions in accidents and injuries ranging from 20 to 50 percent.

Eiser and Harding (1983) compared the perceived health risks of smokers and nonsmokers, and users and nonusers of seat belts. They found similar attitudes among smokers and nonusers of seat belts, both of whom were more willing to take risks and inclined to see more benefits and fewer costs in their risk-taking behavior. This attitude also carried over into other health-related behavior. Nonusers of seat belts, for example, as compared to users, expressed more negative attitudes toward use of contraceptives, preventive vaccinations, and organ transplants.

Driver Education

Another action that reduces risks is taking driver education. Insurance companies offer lower rates for drivers who have had a course in driver education because statistics have indicated that these drivers have a lower accident rate. Defensive driving is emphasized in such courses and is one of the keys to highway safety. Driving defensively means anticipating problems. It means assuming that many others on the highway will be inexperienced, intoxicated, sleepy, or high-risk–takers. Accidents can be prevented by anticipating the dangers represented by such drivers.

Robertson (1980) questioned some of those assumptions, based on a study of students from Connecticut high schools that had dropped driver education. He concluded that driver education encouraged more adolescents to become drivers at earlier ages, and that the absence of driver education discouraged some of them from driving at ages 16 and 17, thus reducing the total number of traffic accidents for this age group. Although this reasoning might hold true for his urban Connecticut population, it seems dubious to assume that 16-year-olds across the nation would stop seeking driving privileges simply because driver education became unavailable.

Here is another source of values conflicts: At what point do we have the right to deny young people the opportunity to drive, knowing that their inexperienced driving will increase risks for the rest of us?

Other Vehicles

Autos are not the only cause of traffic accidents. Motorcycles, bicycles, and other forms of transportation contribute to the death and serious injury counts. As with auto seat belts, about half of the 50 states have laws requiring motorcyclists to wear helmets. As Goodrow (1982) reported, the two laws have been controversial for similar reasons. Advocates of both laws have argued that human lives will be saved; opponents have decried the loss of personal freedom and the intrusion of government into what they believe to be private decision-making. Watson, Zador, and Wilks (1980) found that 26 states had repealed or weakened their helmet-use laws for motorcyclists and that there was a corresponding increase in deaths in 23 of those states, which they estimated at about 40 percent. Muller (1980) observed a reduction of nearly 50 percent in actual use of helmets following repeal of mandatory-use laws, which he estimated cost the nation $61 million in additional medical care, money that ''could be saved annually if all motorcyclists were to use helmets'' (p. 586).

Kiburz, Jacobs, Reckling, and Mason (1986) reported that ''bicycling accidents comprised the greatest recreational source of Emergency Room visits last year, numbering over 500,000'' (p. 416). Weiss (1986) determined that most serious injuries were caused by bicyclists falling after losing control and that head trauma resulting from those falls was the most frequent cause of death and serious injury among cyclists. As bicycles have become more technologically advanced, they have become faster and a more common form of regular transportation. Both of these changes have resulted in more cycling miles, more accidents, and a greater need for wearing helmets to protect against head injuries. Kiburz et al. (1986) surveyed nearly 500 adult cyclists, almost half of whom reported having been involved in a cycling accident, and concluded, ''The use of riding helmets decreased the severity of injury and hospitalization time'' (p. 416).

Alcohol

Perhaps the most common denominator of accidents in all categories is alcohol. Parker, Shultz, Gertz, Berkelman, and Remington (1987) reported the percentages of deaths from various alcohol-related causes as follows: 50 percent from motor vehicles, 42 percent from fires, 42 percent from homicides, 35 percent from watercraft accidents, and 30 percent from drownings. In addition, 31 percent of injuries from all causes were alcohol-related. Williams, Peat, Crouch, Wells, and Finkle (1985) analyzed the causes of death for 440 male drivers, aged 15 to 34, and discovered that alcohol was present in 70 percent of the corpses, often in combination with other drugs, raising to 81 percent the total in whom one or more drugs were detected. They concluded that because blood alcohol concentrations of 0.10 or more were found in about 50 percent of fatally injured drivers, ''the major role of alcohol (ethanol) in motor vehicle crashes is well established'' (p. 19).

PREVENTING ACCIDENTS IN THE HOME

The second most common category of accidental injuries is those that occur in the home, and alcohol is a factor in those as well. Among the causes of such injuries are falls, fires, and firearms.

Alcohol

Oleakno (1987) reported that the three leading causes of unintentional non-motor–vehicle injuries (UNVIs) were falls, cuts and piercing wounds, and striking against, being struck by, or being caught against or between objects. After examining the cause of hospitalization for over 200 victims of such accidents, he concluded that drinkers were "about 3 times as likely as nondrinkers to have had a UNVI" (p. 41) even after controlling for sex, age, race, and employment status. Essentially the same was true for smokers as compared to nonsmokers. He concluded that drinking and smoking behavior were significant risk factors for accident rates among young adults.

Hingson and Howland (1987) reported that 13,000 deaths occur annually as a result of falls; only motor vehicle crashes and firearms surpass falls as causes of injury deaths in this country. They reviewed 21 studies that analyzed the role of alcohol consumption in falls and found that "there is a striking unanimity among the papers reviewed that alcohol use contributes to falls" (p. 217). Reported estimates of fatal falls related to alcohol consumption ranged from 21 to 77 percent. Alcoholics were several times more likely to die from falls than the general population, and the blood alcohol concentration of victims of falls was typically several times higher than that of other patients.

Howland and Hingson (1987) conducted a similar study of alcohol as a risk factor for injuries or deaths due to fires and burns. Their review of 32 studies revealed that "nearly half of those who die in fires are legally drunk at the time of death" (p. 480). They reported that fires and burns rank fourth as a cause of unintentional deaths from injuries, trailing motor vehicles, falls, and drownings. (Firearms rank lower because many of the deaths they cause are homicides or suicides and thus are not considered unintentional.) Again, the combination of smoking and drinking adds to the risk; when a cigarette started the fire, the smoker was likely to have been drinking as well and may have fallen asleep or simply been careless.

A more recent study by Howland and Hingson (1988) estimated that 7,200 people drown each year in the U.S., some in bathtubs and home swimming pools, others in public waters. They reviewed 36 studies of the relationship between drownings and alcohol and concluded that somewhere between 25 and 50 percent of adult drownings involve alcohol. They cited several reasons:

- Alcohol impairs judgment, making risk-taking more frequent.
- Alcohol impairs balance, causing victims to fall into water.
- Alcohol impairs vision, so potential dangers go unseen.
- Alcohol creates an illusion of warmth, encouraging victims to stay in cold water too long.

They noted that those are concerns not just for swimmers, but for anyone engaged in boating, fishing, and other water activities where alcohol is present.

Firearms

Firearms are both a source of, and a threat to, our safety and security. According to McGinnis (1987a), the three leading causes of death for adolescents and young adults are accidents, homicides, and suicides; firearms are a contributing factor to all three. He reported that the death rate from accidents for 15- to 24-year-olds has dropped 7 percent in the past 30 years, but the death rate from homicides has doubled over that same time span, and the suicide rate has nearly tripled. Many suicides are reported as accidents because it is often difficult to prove intent after a death. According to Buchalter (1988), there was a 53 percent increase in the number of female gun-owners in the United States between 1983 and 1986. Many of these women indicated that their intent was to provide for their personal safety and security, but their logic is questionable, according to Kellerman and Reay (1986). They estimated that there are 120 million privately owned guns in the U.S., three quarters of whose owners say self-protection is at least a partial motivation for their having firearms. However, their survey of Seattle area gun killings revealed that only 9 of 398 deaths were slayings of intruders; all the others were suicides (84 percent), homicides (10 percent), and accidents (3 percent). Apart from suicides, nearly 90 percent of the victims were friends or family members of the gun owner, not criminals. Based on this evidence, how do you feel about owning a gun to protect yourself? This is one more example of having to weigh risks versus benefits before making a decision that affects the health and well-being of yourself and others who may share a residence with you.

PREVENTING WORK-RELATED ACCIDENTS

The third of four primary categories is work-related accidents. On-the-job accident rates have been dropping throughout this century, primarily as a result of legislation designed to make employers responsible for safe worksites. The Occupational Safety and Health Act (OSHA) of 1971 helped to establish mandatory industrial safety standards. Despite this, roughly one third of all respondents to a National Health Interview Survey, reported by Shilling and Brackbill (1987), perceived some form of health or safety risk on their job. Many of those whose perceived risk was greatest (e.g., farmers, police, fire fighters, foresters, fishermen) were employed outside the typical factory setting where OSHA

standards prevail. Workman's compensation laws have provided an incentive for employers to maintain high standards of safety, or risk paying additional medical costs for job-related injuries. Unfortunately, this does not help the self-employed worker, who must be especially self-controlled and safety conscious.

Robinson (1988) noted that the change in industrial accident rates varied according to the type of accident. Although the incidence of amputations, burns, and cuts and punctures has declined, the number of bone fractures, sprains, and radiation accidents has actually risen. Robinson speculated that the better health benefits that are in existence today might encourage workers to report more of their accidents and to take time off from work when they are slightly injured, knowing that they will get paid. Once again, a value judgment is required as to how often one should be willing to take advantage of such opportunities and benefits.

Attribution theory may also be relevant to occupational safety. DeJoy (1985) explained:

> Attribution theory is the area of social psychology concerned with how people process information in determining the causality of an event. Central to attribution theory is the idea that an individual's perceptions of causality are important determinants of that person's subsequent behavior. (p. 61)

He observed that attribution theory is relevant to occupational safety in three ways:

- How workers perceive personal risks associated with workplace hazards
- How supervisory personnel respond to safety incidents
- How upper management influences the safety climate of the organization

DeJoy believed that workers who attribute accidents to their own carelessness are more likely to take protective action than workers who attribute accidents to unsafe working conditions over which they have no control. Likewise, supervisors who attribute accidents to careless employees are less likely to take preventive actions than when they attribute accidents to an unsafe work environment. Under the latter circumstances, supervisors typically provide safety training and incentive programs to reduce injury rates. Upper management is usually responsible for developing a safety-conscious attitude that permeates the workplace but are less likely to do so if they attribute accidents to causes other than their failure to develop such an attitude among employees. As always, it is easier to place blame elsewhere than to accept responsibility for problems and take corrective action.

PREVENTING PUBLIC ACCIDENTS

The fourth category is that of public accidents, which includes public transportation catastrophes involving airplanes and rail vehicles; natural disasters, such as floods, tornadoes, earthquakes, and lightning; drownings in public waters; and some firearm accidents, particularly hunting. Some experts add radiation as a form of public health "accident" that needs to be addressed.

It is easy to assume that we have little control over natural disasters or public transportation accidents, and for that reason it may seem pointless to discuss such issues. However, this is probably an oversimplification, because we know that high-risk–takers tend to be accident prone under any circumstances. For example, drowning victims are 5 times more likely to be males than females, and the ratio is even greater for victims of hunting accidents and crimes; undoubtedly macho attitudes held by some males are at least partially responsible. Even in the case of natural disasters, risk-takers tend to ignore weather reports and other signs of impending danger. Those who are concerned for their own safety are more likely to take the necessary precautions—for instance, wearing a life jacket while boating or skiing, seeking shelter before a storm, or avoiding high-crime areas when traveling alone.

Sports-Related Accidents

A growing number of accidents that overlap several of the categories just cited are sports related. One outgrowth of increased public interest and participation in sports and fitness activities has been the evolution of related health care, especially sports medicine. Injuries to the head and eyes have led to the manufacture of shock-absorbent helmets for cyclists, baseball players, and football players; face masks for ice hockey; and goggles for skiing, racquetball, and other sports. Knee and foot injuries have led to arthroscopic surgery, sophisticated orthopedic braces, and special footwear designed for each specific sport. None of these were in common use a generation ago. As with participants in other activities, sports enthusiasts can avoid unnecessary injuries by taking safety precautions.

Safe and Unsafe Use

Most inanimate objects—motor vehicles, guns, power tools—are safe when used safely and are potentially dangerous when used unsafely. An extreme example of this that concerns us all is radiation. Statistically, radiation is not a significant safety problem, yet its potential for disaster is mind-boggling. As Newcomb (1986) warned:

> For 40 years the world has lived with the threat of nuclear war and, recently, with the possibility of nuclear power plant accidents. Although virtually every generation must confront various national or international crises, the threat of nuclear war is unprecedented in its destructive potential. (p. 906)

Since 1979, the Three Mile Island accident in Pennsylvania and the Chernobyl debacle in the

USSR have demonstrated that the threat posed by uncontrolled radiation is real. Newcomb concluded that the threat of nuclear war or accident is related to increased distress, anxiety, less satisfaction with life, a feeling of powerlessness, and increased drug use. Thanks to concerned citizens, however, we have federal regulations that have controlled both the number and severity of such nuclear accidents to date. It is the responsibility of those concerned citizens—you and me—to insist that our national leaders take equally stringent actions to prevent military nuclear acts and accidents. If we fail to prevent these, all other acts of health and safety may be meaningless.

WELLNESS: USING SAFETY TO ENHANCE QUALITY OF LIFE

Abraham Maslow recognized how important it is for human beings to feel safe and secure, placing this need second in his hierarchy, after basic physiological needs and before such important considerations as love and self-esteem. Each of us fulfills our need for safety with a slightly different combination of activities. For some, having a family is less a matter of love and affiliation than it is a safety net against catastrophe, knowing someone will look out for them in trying times. Others use religion in much the same way, looking to God for protection against the evils of the world. Still others diligently strive to maintain good health primarily to avoid the ravages of disease and early death.

By now it should be clear to you that, indeed, healthy people are likely to live longer and that there are very specific actions each of us can take to reduce the risks for mortality and morbidity. But this focus is not in keeping with the wellness concept, which encourages us to self-actualize. The goal is not to stay healthy in order to feel safe and secure from illness. If you are intent on a wellness lifestyle, you will use good health, and the security that comes with knowing you are well, as a *means*, a springboard to greater achievements and satisfaction. And the research that has been reported reassures us that if we value our health and adopt an internal locus of control, we can by and large maintain a level of health that will be conducive to a better quality of life.

First Aid and CPR

Regardless of how carefully we plan, though, and how safely we act, some accidents are unpredictable—the result of bad luck, fate, the unsafe actions of others, or uncontrollable circumstances. In such cases we can reduce the level of risk by knowing and using appropriate first aid procedures. A first step is to keep well-stocked first aid kits in our homes, automobiles, and workplaces. The Red Cross and other social agencies provide excellent courses in first aid, cardiopulmonary resuscitation (CPR), and other lifesaving procedures. If you value your own life and the lives of others, you will avail yourself of such instruction.

Being certified in first aid and CPR means knowing how to do the following:

- Stop bleeding, using direct and indirect pressure
- Give artificial respiration, including heart palpitation and mouth-to-mouth breathing
- Immobilize broken bones and move accident victims without undue risk of further injury
- Treat for shock, heat stroke, heat exhaustion, and burns
- Use Heimlich's maneuver for victims of choking

Proficiency in these skills may save a life; but it is equally important to remember that improper use may compound the problem or even cost a life. Good instruction is a prerequisite. How can you claim to value human life if you have not prepared yourself to save a life?

Self-Defense

Learning self-defense techniques is a method of coping with the insecurities of modern living. The threat of assault is ever present, more so in urban than in rural areas, for females than for males, and for children than for adults. Self-defense may focus on learning physical combat skills, but it also involves simple precautionary measures to reduce the risk of being caught alone and unguarded. Discretion *is* the better part of valor.

Self-Examination

Another recommended precaution is to learn self-examination techniques for discovering cancer of the breasts (females) and testes (males). Walker and Glanz (1986) pointed out that far more women die from breast cancer each year than from auto accidents. How can a woman justify wearing a seat belt daily in order to be safe on the highway and not perform a monthly breast self-examination (BSE), which is less inconvenient and much more likely to save her life? Although it can be done privately and at no expense, and although it is recommended by the American Cancer Society for all women over age 20, reportedly fewer than half of adult women actually perform a monthly BSE. Because cancer of the testes occurs more often among young male adults than among older men, it is as prudent for young men to examine their testes as it is for women to examine their breasts. Free pamphlets are available from the American Cancer Society describing simple, protective procedures of breast self-examination and testicular self-examination. See Appendix B, starting on page 211, to find out how to perform these procedures.

Safety Strategies

Robertson (1986) suggested three strategies for safer use of motor vehicles, but his suggestions are equally applicable to most safety concerns. His strategies are voluntary behavioral changes, legal restrictions, and safer products. Recommended safety behaviors include the following:

- Learn first aid (stop the bleeding, assure breathing, treat for shock).
- Learn CPR (mouth-to-mouth artificial respiration and heart palpitation).
- Learn to swim; never swim alone.
- Learn self-defense techniques.
- Learn to drive safely (take driver education, use seat belts, practice defensive driving).
- Learn to use firearms safely.
- Learn self-examination techniques to discover cancer in its early stages.
- Learn to avoid excessive radiation (sunshine, X-rays, industrial).
- Learn self-control (e.g., in alcohol use, sexual relationships, stressful situations).

Legal restrictions that have already been implemented in an effort to enhance safety and security include seat belt and speed limit laws, vehicular inspection laws, motorcycle helmet laws, OSHA rules and regulations, gun control laws, and regulation of nuclear energy. Examples of products that have been marketed to improve safety include padded dashboards and bumpers on automobiles, automatic seat belts and airbags, shields on lawnmowers and power saws, easy-to-use home fire extinguishers and first aid kits, child-proof caps on medicines and poisons, and goggles and protective helmets for sports and industrial wear.

To the three strategies recommended by Robertson, we might add the safety campaigns that have become commonplace in industries, schools, and communities. As we have mentioned earlier, *awareness* of risk is a prerequisite to healthy behavioral change. With this in mind, it is important to be aware of the community services at your disposal. These include fire departments, ambulances, and emergency medical centers. The combination of personal preparedness and prompt professional attention is the best insurance we have of minimizing the long-term effects of accidents.

Identify, Clarify, and Enhance Health Values

Still, we know that awareness alone is insufficient to assure healthy behavior. Goodrow (1982) reminded us, "The identification, clarification, and enhancement of personal health values assume an important role in formulating personal health attitudes and resulting behavioral patterns" (p. 19). Using the motorcycle helmet controversy to illustrate this point, he observed the value conflict that exists when laws are passed to regulate safety; we benefit from safer conditions, but we object to the "Big Brother" intrusion of government into our personal lives. Goodrow concluded that safety should be primarily a matter of effective individual decision-making (see problem-solving suggestions in chapter 11) and values clarification strategies (see chapter 1), so that sound judgments are made irrespective of the law. What legislation you support is a reflection of your values.

Sen (1986) wrote a thought-provoking article about the extent to which an individual has the right to take personal risks with his or her safety and security. He described *positive* freedom as the right to be or do what one wishes, so long as it does not infringe on the rights and freedoms of others. *Negative* freedom was defined as "the right not to be prevented by others from doing things one can do" (Sen, 1986, p. 156). Freedom is universally valued, but the concept of negative freedom raises a plethora of values conflicts, especially as they pertain to safety. Two examples of values conflicts are presented in "Examining Your Values" at the end of the chapter (the first is Sen's). The question is not whether we have the right to take risks—we do! The question is, when there are conflicting values and other people are involved, at what point does our responsibility for assuring safety and security outweigh another's freedom to take risks, and who makes that decision?

SUMMARY

Until a person reaches age 40, an accident is more likely to be a cause of death than is any disease. Accidents also cause injuries that result in immeasurable pain, inconvenience, and economic loss. The frequency and severity of accidents can be greatly reduced by those with an internal locus of control and a high value of safety. Accident rates are quite predictable and are closely associated with risk-taking behavior and Type A personality.

Motor vehicle accidents represent the greatest threat to personal safety, especially before age 25. There are three other categories of accidents—home, work-related, and public. Alcohol, which clouds judgment and increases risk-taking, is a precipitating factor in many accidents (perhaps up to half of them) although the official cause may be fire, firearms, drowning, or natural disaster.

Safety is among the most basic of human needs. Most of us value safety but perceive ourselves as less vulnerable to unsafe conditions and behavior than we actually are. Therefore, increased awareness of threatening circumstances is a prerequisite to safer living. Each us can take steps to reduce the likelihood or the consequences of accidents, such as learning to swim, learning first aid and cardiopulmonary resuscitation, and learning to drive defensively. At the same time we should recognize that risk-taking lends excitement to life; some individuals value excitement more highly than safety and are willing to take greater risks.

--------------------- **Examining Your Values** ---------------------

A. Hero decides to drive his car without wearing a seat belt, thus incurring a needless risk (positive freedom).

1. As his passenger, do you have a right to insist that he wear a seat belt because your safety is involved?
2. Would you have the right to insist that Hero wear a seat belt if he were a passenger in your car? Is this an intrusion on his negative freedom?
3. If the law in your state requires the use of seat belts, do you now have a right to insist that Hero wear one in his car? In your car?
4. If Hero were badly injured while driving without a seat belt, and you were a passenger in his car, would you still be morally obligated to administer CPR and first aid? Even if you might be sued for failing to do it properly?
5. If Hero's injuries required hospitalization, and he had no assets, no insurance, and no family, are you obligated as his friend and passenger to help pay his medical bills, even though he ignored your advice to wear a seat belt?
6. Suppose Hero's injuries resulted in permanent incapacity, and he went on Social Security for life at age 21. How do you feel about paying taxes for the rest of your life to support him? Are you "free" to refuse?

B. Your younger sister, age 21, has gone to a party with you and is now obviously "under the influence" but wants the keys to your car so she can take a friend home.

1. Is she free to risk her life in this way?
2. Is she free to risk the life of her friend?
3. Would it make a difference if her friend were drunk or sober?
4. Do you have the right to reduce your sister's negative freedom by preventing her from doing what she wants to do? What gives you that right?
5. At what point (if any) does your responsibility to her outweigh her responsibility to exercise self-control and good judgment?
6. Would it make a difference if she were 20 instead of 21 and not of legal drinking age?
7. Would it make a difference if she were 25 and you were 20?
8. Would it make a difference if she were your only surviving relative or your sole means of support?

C. In general, when does your responsibility for others outweigh their right to risk their own safety or security? At what point does governmental responsibility for the safety and security of its citizens outweigh individual responsibility? Are we not guaranteed "life, liberty, and the pursuit of happiness" by our Declaration of Independence?

CHAPTER 14

Choosing to Improve Health and Quality of Life

Nine tenths of wisdom is being wise in time.

—Theodore Roosevelt

——————— **Self-Examination Statements** ———————

Instructions: Read each statement, then circle the x in the column at the left that most closely describes your belief about that statement. (Use a pencil. After reading this chapter you may wish to come back and change some of your responses on the basis of new information or attitudes.)

SA = strongly agree   **A** = agree   **U** = undecided   **D** = disagree   **SD** = strongly disagree

SA	A	U	D	SD	
x	x	x	x	x	I have sufficient knowledge to enable me to maintain good health most of the time.
x	x	x	x	x	I have a healthy self-concept, one that encourages me to seek a high level of wellness.
x	x	x	x	x	I value good health.
x	x	x	x	x	I believe that good health will help me attain my goals in life.
x	x	x	x	x	I have a positive attitude toward life in general.
x	x	x	x	x	I have a positive attitude toward a wellness lifestyle.
x	x	x	x	x	I intend to make healthy choices most of the time.
x	x	x	x	x	I have developed an internal locus of control as it relates to my health behavior.
x	x	x	x	x	I have a high level of self-efficacy when it comes to performing health behaviors.
x	x	x	x	x	The social norm among my friends is concern for a high quality of life.
x	x	x	x	x	I tend to apply what I learn about good health.
x	x	x	x	x	My health status is good to excellent.

x	x	x	x	x	The benefits of healthy behavior outweigh the barriers or costs.
x	x	x	x	x	Being healthy makes me feel more secure.
x	x	x	x	x	I believe it is healthy to develop a strong social network of family and friends.
x	x	x	x	x	My achievement level rises when I am healthy, which is good for my ego and self-esteem.
x	x	x	x	x	I believe that I am a self-actualizing person.
x	x	x	x	x	I believe the quality of my life is improving.
x	x	x	x	x	It is my intent to improve the quality of my life.

WISE CHOICES—CLOSING THE GAP BETWEEN KNOWING AND DOING

You may recall that in chapter 1 we defined knowledge as what one knows and wisdom as what one does with what one knows. Health books have traditionally been knowledge oriented, but the current trend is to focus on turning awareness into action. The specific action we are concerned with is health behavior. Our goal is to help you close the gap between what you know about healthy behavior and what you do to improve the quality of your life.

Each of us ought to insist on the right to make independent judgments about how to live in order to improve our health and the quality of our life. The seven-step values clarification process (choosing from among alternatives, considering consequences, choosing freely, prizing your choice, publicly affirming your choice, acting on your choice, and consistency of action) and the three-step values education process (values analysis, values consciousness, and values criticism), both of which were described in chapter 1, were intended to help you sort through the myriad of information available to you, accepting some and rejecting whatever is not pertinent to your life at the moment. This requires an objective, insightful mind, the development of which is a never-ending process.

QUALITY OF LIFE INDEX

Ferrans and Powers (1985) developed a Quality of Life Index (QLI) to assist in the decision-making process. Quality of life is very difficult to measure because we all value things differently and because our values change over time. They reviewed the literature, however, and concluded that life satisfaction was by consensus the most important dimension. They differentiated between happiness, which is primarily affective (feeling), and satisfaction, which is mostly cognitive (thinking). The following were among the factors that they included in their QLI because they affect life satisfaction:

- Socioeconomic status
- Physical health
- Personal appearance
- Personal faith
- Perceived stress
- Friendship
- Family
- Marriage
- Life goals
- Self-acceptance
- Depression
- Housing and neighborhood

They used 32 items to measure the level of satisfaction and the importance of each factor. You can assess the quality of your own life by asking yourself these two questions: What is it that I value, that adds satisfaction to my life? What is the relative importance of each value, and how much is it contributing to my life at present? You can then make behavioral changes on a rational basis.

TURNING KNOWLEDGE INTO ACTION

Throughout this book we have emphasized that knowledge is an important prerequisite to healthy behavior but that it is not sufficient to produce significant changes in most instances. What is it, then, that produces such changes? Let us summarize some of the things you can do to make your knowledge have an impact on your health and the quality of your life:

Step 1. The first step is to develop a positive self-image, a healthy self-concept, a high level of self-esteem. Powell (1984) has offered a fitting illustration of the old adage, "You can't soar like an eagle if you live like a turkey" (see the shaded box).

Changing Self-Concept

The most important of all our perceptions is the way we perceive ourselves. There is a story in American Indian folklore that illustrates this truth very clearly. According to the legend, an Indian brave came upon an eagle's egg that had somehow fallen unbroken from an eagle's nest. Unable to find the nest, the brave put the egg in the nest of a prairie chicken, where it was hatched by the brooding mother hen. The fledgling eagle, with its proverbial strong eyes, saw the world for the first time. Looking at the other prairie chickens, he did what they did. He crawled and scratched at the earth, pecked here and there for stray grains and husks, now and then rising in a flutter a few feet above the earth and descending again. He accepted and imitated the daily routine of the earthbound prairie chickens. And he spent most of his life this way.

Then, as the story continues, one day an eagle flew over the brood of prairie chickens. The now aging eagle, who still thought he was a prairie chicken, looked up in awed admiration as the great bird soared through the skies. "What is that?" he gasped in astonishment. One of the old prairie chickens replied, "I have seen one before. That is the eagle, the proudest, strongest, and most magnificent of all the birds. But don't you ever dream that you could be like that. You're like the rest of us, and we are prairie chickens." And so, shackled by this belief, the eagle lived and died thinking he was a prairie chicken.

Our lives are shaped by the way we perceive ourselves. The all-important attitudes by which we perceive and evaluate ourselves tells us who we are and describe the appropriate behavior for such a person. We live and die according to our self-perception. (p. 6)

Note. From *The Christian Vision* by John Powell, S.J. © Copyright 1984 by Tabor Publishing, 25115 Avenue Stanford, Valencia, CA, 91355. Used with permission.

Step 2. The second step is to identify the things you value most in life and decide where health ranks among your values. This will allow you to reduce any cognitive dissonance between your values and your self-concept as a healthy person. When value conflicts arise, you can make decisions based on your priorities, accepting the fact that sometimes there are valid reasons for making the ''unhealthy'' choice.

Step 3. Your values should be the basis for formulating attitudes. If you discover that there is disagreement among your attitudes and values, try to resolve this regardless of whether you change your attitudes or your values. You should find it helpful to employ the seven-step values clarification process described in chapter 1 and summarized earlier in this chapter.

Step 4. Your attitudes should influence how you intend to behave, and they will probably be influenced by your perceptions of social norms and what you think significant others expect you to do. You are most likely to be influenced by peers who have attitudes and values similar to your own. Remember that this is a two-way street and that your attitudes and behavior can also influence those around you, positively or negatively.

Step 5. Intentions are likely to be the best predictors of how you will actually behave. When a difficult choice must be made, commit yourself to an intended action, even if the commitment is only one you make silently to yourself.

Step 6. Making a verbal commitment to another person regarding your intent to change your behavior in the direction of a healthier lifestyle is more likely to lead to the intended behav-

ior. Make a behavioral contract in which you identify your long-range goal and your intermediate objectives, put these in writing, and sign your name to them; this is even more likely to result in the intended behavior.

Step 7. All of the above will predispose you to act. Then you will need to develop some skills that will enable you to do what you intend. These may be behavioral skills such as problem solving or time management, designed to help you cope with the stress that accompanies values conflicts in your life; or they may be such physical skills as learning to swim, monitoring your blood pressure, or measure your percent of body fat.

Step 8. Don't be afraid to make changes in your lifestyle that bring you closer to your goal. Remember that a ''hardy'' person is one who likes challenges and sees changes as more challenging than threatening. It will be helpful if you are also committed to a goal or worthy cause and believe that you can control events leading to it.

Step 9. You will need to develop a social support network that reinforces your intended behavior(s). This may mean cultivating new friendships among persons with similar interests or allowing nonsupportive relationships to fade into the background. This can be among the most enriching and rewarding aspects of your trip toward high-level wellness.

Your progress toward wellness may appear to be slow at first, but as time passes a very satisfying feeling, a feeling of self-actualizing, comes over you when you see the result and like what you see. In this case, the result is you, and you can be exactly what you want to be.

APPENDIX A

Caloric Content of Selected Foods and Beverages

	Quantity	Calories
Beverages		
Apple juice	12 oz	180
Beer	12 oz	150
Beer, lite	12 oz	96
Colas	12 oz	145
Colas, diet	12 oz	—
Cranberry juice	12 oz	240
Cranberry juice, sweetened	12 oz	600
Eggnog	12 oz	510
Ginger ale	12 oz	135
Grapefruit juice	12 oz	140
Grape juice	12 oz	240
Lemonade	12 oz	150
Liquor, 80 proof	1.5 oz	95
Liquor, 90 proof	1.5 oz	110
Milk, white whole	12 oz	225
Milk, chocolate whole	12 oz	315
Milk, 2%	12 oz	180
Milk, skim	12 oz	125
Orange juice	12 oz	180
Pineapple juice	12 oz	210
Prune juice	12 oz	290
Root beer	12 oz	150
Soda/mixers	12 oz	170
Tomato juice	12 oz	70
Wine, table	12 oz	300
Meats and meat substitutes		
Bacon	2 slices	85
Beef, ground	3 oz	185
Beef, pot roast	3 oz	245

(Cont.)

	Quantity	Calories
Beef, rib roast	3 oz	375
Beef, steak	3 oz	330
Beef, corned	3 oz	185
Beef, dried	3 oz	170
Bologna	1 slice	85
Cheese, cheddar	1 cup	455
Cheese, cottage	1 cup	235
Cheese, parmesan	1 cup	455
Cheese, provolone	1 cup	350
Cheese, ricotta	1 cup	428
Cheese, swiss	1 cup	370
Chicken, breast, fried	1	320
Chicken, drumstick, fried	1	90
Crabmeat	1 cup	135
Eggs	1	80
Fishsticks	1	50
Haddock, fried and breaded	3 oz	160
Ham	3 oz	245
Hotdogs	1	170
Lamb chop	3 oz	350
Lamb, roast leg	3 oz	235
Liver, beef	3 oz	195
Lobster	3 oz	100
Oysters	1 cup	160
Porkchop	3 oz	330
Pork roast	3 oz	310
Salmon	3 oz	120
Sardines	3 oz	175
Shrimp, fried	3 oz	190
Tuna	3 oz	170
Turkey, dark meat	3 oz	175
Turkey, light meat	3 oz	150
Veal cutlet	3 oz	185
Fruits		
Apples	1	80
Applesauce w/sugar	1 cup	230
Applesauce w/o sugar	1 cup	100
Apricots	1	15
Apricots, dried	1 cup	340
Avocado	1	370
Banana	1	100
Blackberries	1 cup	85
Blueberries	1 cup	90
Cantaloupe	1	160
Cherries	1 cup	105

	Quantity	Calories
Coconut, shredded	1 cup	275
Dates, chopped	1 cup	490
Fruit cocktail	1 cup	195
Grapefruit	1	100
Grapefruit sections	1 cup	180
Grapes	1	4
Honeydew melon	1	500
Lemon	1	20
Orange	1	65
Peach	1	40
Peaches, canned w/syrup	1 cup	200
Pear	1	100
Pears, canned w/syrup	1 cup	195
Pineapple, fresh	1 cup	80
Pineapple, canned w/syrup	1 cup	190
Plum	1	30
Plums, canned w/syrup	1 cup	215
Prunes, dried	1	22
Raisins, seedless	1 cup	420
Raspberries, red	1 cup	70
Raspberries, frozen and sweetened	1 cup	224
Rhubarb	1 cup	380
Strawberries	1 cup	55
Tangerine	1	40
Watermelon	1 slice	110
Vegetables and beans		
Asparagus	4 spears	10
Beans, green	1 cup	35
Beans, kidney	1 cup	230
Beans, lima	1 cup	170
Beans, navy	1 cup	210
Bean sprouts	1 cup	35
Beans, yellow	1 cup	35
Beets	1 cup	55
Beet greens	1 cup	25
Broccoli	1 cup	40
Brussels sprouts	1 cup	55
Cabbage	1 cup	30
Carrot, raw	1	30
Carrots, cooked	1 cup	50
Cauliflower, raw	1 cup	30
Cauliflower, cooked	1 cup	30
Celery	1 stalk	5

(Cont.)

	Quantity	Calories
Corn, sweet	1 cup	130
Corn, creamed	1 cup	210
Cucumber	1	5
Lentils	1 cup	210
Lettuce	1 head	25
Onions, chopped	1 cup	65
Parsnips	1 cup	100
Pickles, dill	1	5
Pickles, sweet	1	20
Potatoes, baked	1	145
Potatoes, french fried	1 strip	14
Potatoes, hash browned	1 cup	345
Potatoes, mashed w/butter and milk	1 cup	195
Pumpkin	1 cup	80
Radishes	1	1
Sauerkraut	1 cup	40
Spinach	1 cup	45
Squash, winter	1 cup	130
Sweet potatoes, candied	1	175
Tomatoes	1	25
Tomatoes, canned	1 cup	50
Breads, cereals, pastas, and grain products		
Bagel	1	165
Barley	1 cup	700
Biscuits, baking powder	1	105
Bread, brown	1 slice	95
Breadcrumbs	1 cup	390
Bread, cracked-wheat	1 slice	65
Bread, French	1 slice	100
Bread, raisin	1 slice	65
Bread, rye	1 slice	60
Bread, white	1 slice	70
Cereal, branflakes	1 cup	105
Cereal, cornflakes	1 cup	95
Cereal, oatmeal	1 cup	130
Cereal, puffed rice	1 cup	60
Cereal, shredded wheat	1 cup	180
Cereal, sugar-coated cornflakes	1 cup	155
Buckwheat flour	1 cup	340
Cornmeal	1 cup	435
Crackers, graham	1	28
Crackers, saltine	1	12
Macaroni, cold	1 cup	115

	Quantity	Calories
Muffins, blueberry	1	110
Muffins, bran	1	105
Muffins, corn	1	125
Noodles	1 cup	200
Pancakes, buckwheat	1	55
Rice, white	1 cup	180
Rolls, pan	1	85
Rolls, hot dog/hamburger	1	120
Rolls, hard	1	155
Spaghetti w/o sauce	1 cup	155
Waffles	1	210
Wheat flour	1 cup	420
Combination foods		
Burger Chef Super Shef	1	600
Burger King Whopper	1	663
Chicken à la king	1 cup	470
Chicken chow mein	1 cup	255
Chili con carne w/beans	1 cup	340
Chop suey w/beef and pork	1 cup	300
Dairy Queen Super Dog w/cheese	1	593
Kentucky Fried Chicken	9 pieces	1892
Long John Silver's battered fish	3 pieces	477
Macaroni and cheese	1 cup	430
McDonald's Big Mac	1	587
McDonald's Egg McMuffin	1	352
Pizza, cheese	1 piece	145
Pizza, mushroom and cheese	1 piece	200
Pizza, pepperoni and cheese	1 piece	200
Pizza, sausage and cheese	1 piece	250
Pizza Hut's Supreme, thick	3 slices	640
Soup, bean and pork	1 cup	190
Soup, beef and noodle	1 cup	65
Soup, clam chowder	1 cup	80
Soup, cream of chicken	1 cup	180
Soup, cream of mushroom	1 cup	215
Soup, cream of tomato	1 cup	175
Soup, vegetable beef	1 cup	80
Spaghetti w/sauce	1 cup	260
Spaghetti w/meatballs and sauce	1 cup	330
Taco Bell's Burrito Supreme	1	457
Tuna salad	1 cup	350
Yogurt, fruit flavored	1 cup	230

(Cont.)

	Quantity	Calories
Desserts, "luxury" foods, and miscellaneous		
Barbecue sauce	1 cup	230
Brazil nuts	1 cup	1450
Butter	1 stick	815
Butter	1 tbsp	100
Cake, angelfood	1 piece	135
Cake, Boston cream	1 piece	210
Cake, coffee	1 piece	230
Cake, devil's food	1 piece	235
Cake, gingerbread	1 piece	175
Cake, white and frosting	1 piece	250
Candy, caramel	1 oz	115
Candy, chocolate	1 oz	145
Candy, chocolate-covered peanuts	1 oz	160
Cashew nuts	1 cup	785
Cookies, brownie w/frosting	1	90
Cookies, chocolate chip	1	50
Cookies, fig bar	1	50
Cookies, oatmeal	1	60
Custard, baked	1 cup	305
Danish pastry	1 piece	275
Doughnuts, unfilled	1	150
Doughnuts, filled	1	250
Fats, vegetable shortening	1 cup	1770
Hazel nuts	1 cup	730
Ice cream, hard	1 cup	270
Ice cream, soft	1 cup	375
Ice milk	1 cup	185
Jams and jellies	1 tbsp	100
Lard	1 cup	1850
Margarine	1 stick	815
Mushrooms	1 cup	20
Oil, salad (corn)	1 cup	1925
Oil, olive	1 cup	1910
Oil, safflower	1 cup	1925
Olives, green	1	5
Olives, black	1	5
Peanut butter	1 tbsp	95
Peanuts, roasted	1 cup	840
Pecan nuts	1 cup	810
Pie, apple	1 piece	345
Pie, banana cream	1 piece	285
Pie, blueberry	1 piece	325
Pie, cherry	1 piece	350

	Quantity	Calories
Pie, lemon meringue	1 piece	305
Pie, mince	1 piece	365
Pie, pecan	1 piece	495
Pie, pumpkin	1 piece	275
Piecrust	1 whole	900
Popcorn, popped w/oil	1 cup	40
Popsicle	1	70
Potato chips	1	12
Pretzels, large twist	1	60
Pudding, chocolate	1 cup	385
Pudding, vanilla	1 cup	285
Pudding, tapioca	1 cup	220
Salad dressing, blue cheese	1 tbsp	75
Salad dressing, French	1 tbsp	65
Salad dressing, Italian	1 tbsp	85
Salad dressing, Thousand Island	1 tbsp	80
Shake, chocolate	1	355
Shake, vanilla	1	350
Sunflower seeds	1 cup	810
Sugar, brown	1 cup	820
Sugar, white	1 cup	770
Syrup, hot fudge	1 tbsp	65
Tomato catsup	1 tbsp	25
Sour cream	1 cup	495
Walnuts, chopped	1 cup	785
Whipped cream	1 cup	155
Yogurt, plain	1 cup	145

Primary source: *Nutritive Value of Foods*, Home and Garden Bulletin No. 72. Washington, DC: U.S. Institute of Home Economics and U.S. Department of Agriculture.

APPENDIX B

Procedures for BSE and TSE

HOW TO DO BSE

Breast self-examination should be done once a month so you become familiar with the usual appearance and feel of your breasts. Familiarity makes it easier to notice any changes in the breast from one month to another. Early discovery of a change from what is "normal" is the main idea behind BSE. If you menstruate, the best time to do BSE is 2 or 3 days after your period ends, when your breasts are least likely to be tender or swollen. If you no longer menstruate, pick a day, such as the first day of the month, to remind yourself it is time to do BSE.

The next two steps are designed to emphasize any change in the shape or contour of your breasts. As you do them you should be able to feel your chest muscles tighten.

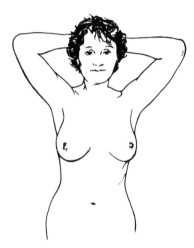

2. Watching closely in the mirror, clasp hands behind your head and press hands forward.

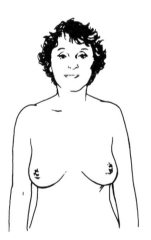

1. Stand before a mirror. Inspect both breasts for anything unusual, such as any discharge from the nipples, puckering, dimpling, or scaling of the skin.

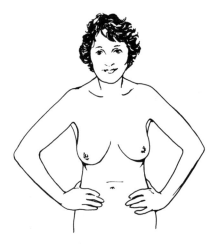

3. Next, press hands firmly on hips and bow slightly toward your mirror as you pull your shoulders and elbows forward.

Some women do the next part of the exam in the shower. Fingers glide over soapy skin, making it easy to concentrate on the texture underneath.

breast. Pay special attention to the area between the breast and the armpit, including the armpit itself. Feel for any unusual lump or mass under the skin.

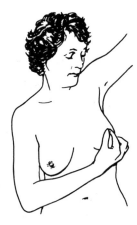

5. Gently squeeze the nipple and look for a discharge. Repeat the exam on your right breast.

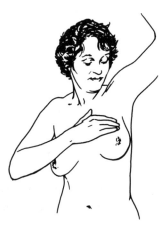

4. Raise your left arm. Use three or four fingers of your right hand to explore your left breast firmly, carefully, and thoroughly. Beginning at the outer edge, press the flat part of your fingers in small circles, moving the circles slowly around the breast. Gradually work toward the nipple. Be sure to cover the entire

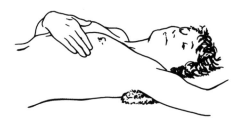

6. Steps 4 and 5 should be repeated lying on your back, left arm over your head and a pillow or folded towel under your left shoulder. This position flattens the breast and makes it easier to examine. Use the same circular motion described earlier. Repeat on your right breast.

TESTICULAR CANCER AND HOW TO DO TSE

Cancer of the testes—the male reproductive glands—is one of the most common cancers in men 15 to 34 years of age. It accounts for 12 percent of all cancer deaths in this group. If discovered in the early stages, testicular cancer can be treated promptly and effectively. It's important for you to take time to learn the basic facts about this type of cancer—its symptoms, treatment, and what you can do to get the help you need when it counts.

Risk Factors, Symptoms, and Procedures

Men who have an undescended or partially descended testicle are at a much higher risk of developing testicular cancer than others. However, it is a simple procedure to correct the undescended testicle condition. See your doctor if this applies to you.

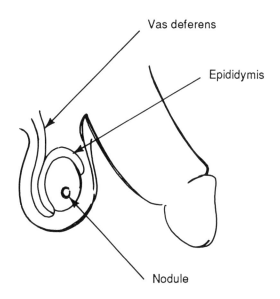

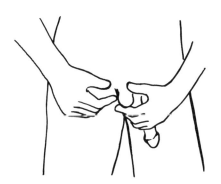

The first sign of testicular cancer is usually a slight enlargement of one of the testes, caused by a hard lump called a nodule, and a change in its consistency. Pain may be absent, but often there is a dull ache in the lower abdomen and groin, together with a sensation of dragging and heaviness.

Your best hope for early detection of testicular cancer is a simple 3-minute monthly self-examination. The best time is after a warm bath or shower, when the scrotal skin is most relaxed.

Roll each testicle between the thumb and fingers of both hands. If you find any nodules you should see your doctor promptly. They may not be malignant, but only your doctor can make the diagnosis. Following a thorough physical examination, your doctor may perform certain X-ray studies to make the most accurate diagnosis possible.

Treatment and Cure

Surgery is usually the preferred treatment, and in certain cases it may be used together with radiation therapy or chemotherapy. Although the 5-year survival rate of all cases of testicular cancer is 68 percent, the most common type of testicular cancer—seminoma—has a survival rate approaching 100 percent in cases detected and treated early.

Note. Information on BSE came from "Breast Exams: What You Should Know" by the National Institute of Health, 1986 (NIH Publication No. 86-2000). Distributed by the National Cancer Institute. Information on TSE came from "For Men Only: Testicular Cancer and How to Do TSE (A Self Exam)" by the American Cancer Society.

Glossary

abortion—The act of ending a pregnancy prematurely by inducing the uterus to expel its embryo or fetus.

accident—A harmful event that results from bad luck, fate, chance, carelessness, ignorance, aggressiveness, or negligence.

accident prone—Tending to have a series of accidents, often due to risk-taking behavior or an external locus of control.

acyclovir—A drug used to reduce the severity of, but not a cure for, genital herpes.

aerobic exercise—Exercise that is rhythmic, continuous, and of sufficient intensity to cause the body to use oxygen to produce the training effect without creating oxygen debt.

affiliation—A close association, attachment, or relationship between a person and another person, a family, or a social group; Maslow identified love/affiliation as one of the five basic levels in the hierarchy of human needs.

AIDS—Acquired immunodeficiency syndrome, a sexually transmitted disease that is often fatal.

alcoholic—A person who suffers from alcoholism, the primary symptom of which is an inability to drink in moderation.

amphetamines—Drugs used to stimulate the central nervous system, combat fatigue, or reduce the appetite (''pep pills'').

anaerobic exercise—Exercise that is either too mild to produce the training effect, or so intense that it must be interrupted due to oxygen debt.

anorexic—The condition of a person suffering from anorexia nervosa, a disease that afflicts primarily adolescent females and is characterized by an obsessive desire to be thin; self-starvation resulting in more than 25 percent loss of original body weight.

arteriosclerosis—A disease caused by hardening of the arteries that results from calcium deposits.

atherosclerosis—A disease caused by clogging of the arteries that results from plaque and other fatty deposits.

attitude—A way of thinking or feeling that is specific to a person, situation, or condition.

attribution theory—A set of principles frequently used by social psychologists to explain the cause and effect of human endeavors (i.e., whether outcomes should be attributed to ability, effort, personality, luck, or other uncontrollable factors.)

autogenics—A form of stress management; the process of sitting or lying quietly and using concentration or mental imaging to produce feelings of calm and control.

azidothymidine (AZT)—A drug that has been used to slow the effects of, but that is not a cure for, AIDS.

barbiturates—Drugs used as sedatives to reduce nervous tension or treat insomnia (sleeping pills); may cause physical dependence.

basal metabolic rate (BMR)—The rate at which the body expends energy while at rest (e.g., for respiration and circulation).

behavior contract—A written, signed agreement designed to facilitate behavioral change by specifying objectives, clarifying a plan of action, and placing responsibility with the learner/client.

biofeedback—A stress management intervention process consisting of using physiological feedback (e.g., skin temperature, pulse rate, blood pressure) to differentiate between a relaxed and stressed state, then controlling those factors to aid relaxation.

birth control—Any method used to prevent a live birth, including abstinence, contraception, sterilization, or abortion.

blood alcohol content (BAC)—The concentration of alcohol in the blood; e.g., .05 BAC puts one legally "under the influence" in most states; .10 represents legal intoxication; .15 may be lethal.

body composition—One of the five components of health-related physical fitness; refers to the percentage of body weight that is fat, as opposed to lean-body tissue (muscle and bone).

Body Mass Index (BMI)—A method of calculating a healthy weight range, which is a BMI of 21-23 for women and 22-24 for men. BMI = weight (kg) / height (meters)^2. (1 kg = 2.2 lbs; 1 meter = 39.37 inches.)

BSE—Breast self-examination, the procedure recommended by the American Cancer Society and most physicians for *early* detection of breast cancer, the key to improving the cure rate.

buffering effect—The positive influence on mental and physical health that is exerted by a social support group or "significant other" in one's life, by softening the shock or blow of a negative life event.

bulimic—The condition of a person suffering from bulimia, characterized by the habit of gorging, then purging food, to control weight.

caffeine—A stimulant found in coffee, tea, cola drinks, and chocolate; excessive caffeine consumption is now thought to be associated with increased risk of coronary heart disease (CHD).

calcium—An essential dietary mineral found primarily in dairy products, citrus fruits, and leafy vegetables; it protects against hypertension and osteoporosis.

calculated risk—A course of action in which there are known hazards, but the perceived benefits outweigh the perceived hazards.

carbon monoxide—One of the three main harmful ingredients in tobacco smoke, it reverses the effects of aerobic exercise by reducing the capacity of the cardiorespiratory system to transport oxygen.

carcinogens—Cancer-producing substances, thought to include asbestos, charcoal soot, nitrites, radiation, and tobacco smoke.

cardiorespiratory/cardiovascular endurance—One of the five health-related components of physical fitness; a measure of the efficiency of the heart, lungs, and blood vessels to deliver oxygenated blood to the muscles to sustain aerobic exercise.

cardiovascular disease (CVD)—Illness in the heart and blood vessels; includes atherosclerosis, arteriosclerosis, coronary thrombosis, and hypertension.

chlamydia—The most common form of sexually transmitted disease in the U.S.; it manifests itself in the form of pelvic inflammatory disease (PID) among females and nongonococcal urethritis (NGU) or nonspecific urethritis (NSU) in males.

cholesterol—A waxy substance found in saturated animal fats, but also manufactured by the liver; in excess, it is a risk factor for atherosclerosis.

cirrhosis—A chronic disease of the liver that is precipitated by excessive alcohol consumption, and one of the 10 leading causes of death in the U.S.

cocaine—An addictive drug that stimulates, then depresses, the central nervous system, leading to further usage; a Schedule I drug because it is illegal and has no current medical application.

cognitive dissonance—A combination of behaviors, attitudes, values, beliefs, or perceptions that are not in harmony, and the resulting feelings of unrest or discord.

complex carbohydrates—The most nutritious and efficient source of human energy; includes fruits, vegetables, and whole-grain products such as breads and cereals, and should constitute 40 percent or more of one's daily caloric intake.

confrontation—The act of openly questioning, criticizing, or opposing the actions or behavior of another person.

contraceptive—Any device used for the purpose of preventing conception (pregnancy) (e.g., a condom, diaphragm, or IUD).

controlled study—A scientific method of controlling the variables of an experiment so that a hypothesis can be tested.

coronary risk factors—Whatever increases risk for morbidity or mortality of coronary heart disease. Some factors—age, sex, race, heredity—are not controllable, but many—smoking, diet, obesity, sedentary lifestyle, stressful lifestyle—are.

coronary thrombosis—A heart attack, caused by a clot (thrombus) in a coronary artery.

CPR—Cardiopulmonary resuscitation, the combination of mouth-to-mouth breathing and closed-chest heart massage used to sustain life in an emergency situation.

defense mechanism—Human means of coping with stressful situations (e.g., repression, regression, rationalization) while avoiding the need to deal directly with the problem.

defensive driving—Anticipating that other drivers will make errors in judgment, or that conditions will create dangers, and taking precautions to prevent accidents before they occur.

deontology—The belief that one ought to act in the most moral way, irrespective of consequences.

diastolic blood pressure—Pressure exerted against the interior arterial walls when the heart is between contractions; always the lower number of a blood pressure reading.

disease prevention—Personal and medical efforts to reduce both the incidence and severity of disease.

diseases of choice—Those caused not by germs or infections, but by habits of one's own choosing—smoking, alcohol, overeating, eating unhealthy foods, and so on.

DRGs—Diagnostic Related Groups, a prospective payment system related to the treatment of Medicare patients. Costs have been estimated for each of 467 diagnoses, and the hospital is reimbursed that amount whether it actually costs them more or less to treat the patient. The intent is to provide an incentive for controlling health-care costs.

drug abuse—Using illegal drugs, or using legal drugs in ways other than intended, when either results in a lower level of health or reduced ability to function.

drug classification schedule—Defines five classes of drugs, ranging from the most potent and illegal (Schedule I) to those that are legal, medicinal, or have low abuse potential (Schedule V).

drug use—Use of legal drugs (e.g., cold tablets or penicillin) for intended purposes.

efficacy—The ability to produce a desired outcome with a given behavior.

emphysema—A disease caused principally by smoking cigarettes, preventing the alveoli in the lungs from efficiently transporting oxygen to the bloodstream.

empirical—Based on observation and practical experience, without regard to science or theory.

enabling factors—Skills and resources that make it possible for a person to develop and maintain a healthy lifestyle.

endorphins—Chemicals produced by the body and released during vigorous physical activity, masking pain much in the same manner as does morphine, and producing a euphoric feeling often described as "runner's high."

epidemiological—Having to do with the causes of distribution of diseases.

ethics—Principles of action or conduct that are consistent with the laws of civilization, and are fair and just for all.

eustress—Positive stress; e.g., graduation, promotion.

euthanasia—A "good death" that ends suffering for a person who is not able to sustain life alone. Active euthanasia or "mercy killing" is illegal, but passive euthanasia, withholding medical services that prolong the life of a dying person, is legal.

exercise—Repetitive physical activity that is planned for the specific purpose of improving or maintaining physical fitness.

external locus of control—Implies that a person's health is largely controlled by others, or by some combination of luck, fate, or chance.

fats—Next to carbohydrates, the best source of energy in foods, and an otherwise essential ingredient of a balanced diet; should be limited to about 30 percent of one's total caloric intake.

fat-soluble vitamins—Vitamins A, D, E, and K are stored in the body's fatty tissues, need not be consumed daily, and can be harmful if taken in megadoses.

fiber—The indigestible portion of complex carbohydrates, it enhances weight control and digestion while reducing the risks from certain forms of cancer and heart disease.

flexibility—One of the five health-related components of physical fitness, the ability to maintain a complete range of motion at each of the joints.

General Adaptation Syndrome—A three-stage reaction of the body to stress, described by Hans Selye as alarm, resistance, and exhaustion.

genital herpes—A highly contagious form of sexually transmitted disease, for which there is no known cure.

handguns—Pistols and revolvers, used primarily to commit crimes and for self-protection, as opposed to being used primarily for hunting or target shooting.

hassles—Experiences and conditions of a daily nature that have a negative impact on one's mental or emotional health; for instance, indebtedness or bad health.

health—A balance of physical, emotional, social, intellectual, and spiritual well-being.

Health Belief Model (HBM)—The theory that healthy behavior is more likely to occur when a person feels threatened by illness, perceives the consequences to be serious, perceives the benefits of action to outweigh the costs and barriers, is given a cue to act, and has a high level of self-efficacy.

health education—The process of informing, influencing, and assisting others so that they will voluntarily assume greater responsibility for adopting and maintaining healthy living practices.

health promotion—A combination of resources and initiatives that allows and encourages individuals not only to reduce disease, but also to enhance their health and well-being through voluntary lifestyle decisions.

heterosexuality—An interest in and preference for having sexual relations with members of the opposite sex.

high density lipids (HDL)—The portion of cholesterol that protects against atherosclerosis by lubricating the interior walls of the coronary arteries, thus reducing accumulation of plaque.

HMO—Health Maintenance Organization, a group of health-care professionals who contract to provide comprehensive services to a voluntarily-enrolled population for a prepaid fee; places the emphasis on prevention of illness rather than its cure.

home accidents—Mishaps in a residence, including those involving falls, fires, and firearms, many of which are related to excessive consumption of alcohol.

homeostasis—The tendency of the human body to resist stress and change, or to adapt to maintain an internal balance.

homosexuality—An interest in and preference for having sexual relations with members of the same sex.

hyperglycemia—Too much glucose (blood sugar), usually as a result of too much insulin being manufactured by the pancreas, or eating too many refined sugars; related to diabetes and obesity.

hypertension—High blood pressure, involving systolic pressure above 160 or diastolic pressure above 95.

intelligence—The capacity to learn.

internal locus of control—Implies that a person's health is largely subject to personal control and can be enhanced by appropriate behavior.

isokinetic—Muscular tension that is constant throughout a complete range of motion, as when using Cybex and Nautilus equipment.

isometric—Muscular tension without range of motion; the irresistible force against the immovable object.

isotonic—Muscular tension that produces concentric (shortening) or eccentric (lengthening) movement of a specific muscle or muscle group, as in calisthenics and weight training.

IUD—Intrauterine device, used to prevent fertilized eggs from implanting in the uterine lining, thus preventing pregnancy.

knowledge—A body of information that has been accumulated by an individual.

Living Will—A document that authorizes medical personnel to practice passive euthanasia when meaningful life is no longer a reasonable expectation.

low density lipids (LDL)—The portion of cholesterol that increases risk of atherosclerosis by clogging coronary arteries in the form of plaque.

maximum oxygen uptake ($\dot{V}O_2$max)—A common measure of cardiorespiratory fitness; the amount of air that can be exchanged by the lungs in a specified period of time (usually 1 minute).

Medicaid—A health insurance program designed for people who can't afford regular medical service, subsidized by state and federal taxes.

Medicare—A health insurance program provided by the federal government to certain persons who have disabilities, and all persons with permanent kidney damage or who are 65 or older.

metabolism—The rate at which the body uses energy.

methadone—A synthetic drug commonly used to treat heroin addiction. It is now known that methadone creates a chemical dependency of its own.

monogamy—Marrying or partnering with only one person, and practicing sexual fidelity to that person.

moral network—See *social network*.

morals—Actions based on core values and ethics, with consideration for how they affect the lives of others.

morbidity—The rate of illness, especially as it pertains to a particular cause or subsection of the population.

mortality—The rate of death, especially as it pertains to a particular cause or subsection of the population.

muscular endurance—One of the five components of health-related physical fitness; the ability of a muscle or muscle group to repeatedly contract, isotonically or isokinetically.

muscular strength—One of the five components of health-related physical fitness; the maximum force that can be exerted in a single contraction of a muscle or muscle group, isometrically, isotonically, or isokinetically.

negative freedom—Not being restricted from taking risks, so long as the risks involved are to self and not to others.

neuroses—The most common forms of mental illness; include anxiety, depression, and phobias (fears).

NGU—Nongonococcal urethritis; has replaced gonorrhea as the most common form of sexually transmitted disease among U.S. males; also referred to as nonspecific urethritis (NSU).

nicotine—One of the three main harmful ingredients in tobacco, it is toxic and addictive; it is the reason smokers find it so difficult to quit.

obesity—An excess of body fat; more than 25 percent of total body weight for men, more than 30 percent for women, or more than 20 percent over one's ideal weight.

osteoporosis—A progressive deterioration of bone that most often affects postmenopausal women; it is hastened by a deficiency of calcium in the diet, and retarded by regular physical exercise.

OTCs—Over-the-counter drugs, so named because they can be legally purchased over the counter without a doctor's prescription.

overload principle—The belief that a muscle (including the heart) will grow in size, strength, and endurance by being systematically placed under increasing levels of stress.

perceived barriers—Reasons given for failing to initiate or adhere to a healthy behavior; for instance, cost, inconvenience, or pain.

physical activity—Any bodily movement that uses energy, regardless of its purpose or intensity.

physical fitness—Measurable attributes that are either health-related (cardiovascular endurance, muscular strength and endurance, flexibility, and body composition) or skill-related (agility, balance, coordination, speed, power, and reaction time).

PID—Pelvic inflammatory disease, an infection of the female genitals that typically emanates from chlamydia and that can cause sterility.

polydrug model—A pattern of drug use that implies that most smokers, users of alcohol, and users and abusers of prescription and illegal drugs use several drugs rather than one in isolation.

positive freedom—The right to do whatever one wishes, as long as it does not infringe on the rights and freedoms of others.

PPO—Preferred Provider Organization, a group of health-care professionals who contract to provide services to a defined group of consumers, often employees and their dependents, for a discounted group-rate fee.

predisposing factors—Beliefs, attitudes, values, self-concept, and other influences that cause a person to be favorably disposed toward healthy behavior.

prevention—See *disease prevention*.

primary health care—Initiatives taken by an individual to maintain good health, even in the absence of disease; includes good hygiene, proper diet, adequate rest, and exercise.

Pritikin Plan—A diet very high in complex carbohydrates and low in consumption of fats and proteins, coupled with regular exercise and avoidance of smoking and caffeinated or alcoholic beverages.

problem drinker—A person who typically consumes more than three drinks per occasion, is legally "under the influence" (BAC of .05 or higher), and has some loss of control over actions or emotions.

problem solving—An approach to stress management that includes identifying a problem, considering alternative plans of action, gathering data, choosing and implementing the preferred plan, and continuing to evaluate choices in terms of results.

progressive relaxation—Learning to relax by alternately tensing and relaxing each major muscle in the body in a controlled sequence; a popular stress management intervention.

promiscuity—Indiscriminate sexual relationships with numerous partners.

proteins—An essential nutrient in a healthy diet that builds and repairs body tissues but should be limited to 10-20 percent of daily caloric intake.

psychoactive drugs—Those drugs that affect thinking or behavior; among them are caffeine, alcohol, nicotine, marijuana, cocaine, heroin, LSD, PCP, amphetamines, and barbiturates.

psychoses—Severe forms of mental illness (e.g. schizophrenia and manic-depression) in which one loses touch with reality.

puberty—The time when secondary sex characteristics (e.g., breasts and facial hair) begin to appear in adolescents.

public accidents—A major category of accidents that excludes highway accidents but includes those associated with rail and air traffic, natural disasters, and acts of crime.

recommended dietary allowance (RDA)—Nutritional standards published by the National Food and Nutrition Board that serve as a guide to planning what we need to consume in the way of vitamins, minerals, and calories.

reinforcing factors—Attitudes of significant others and social norms that create a positive environment conducive to healthy behavior.

residual volume—The air remaining in the lungs after a complete exhalation; it is inversely related to cardiorespiratory fitness.

risk factors—See *coronary risk factors*.

risk-taking behavior—Choosing a course of action where the failure rate is high or the penalty for failure is severe.

Rokeach Values Survey—Includes 18 instrumental (modes of conduct) and 18 terminal (end-states of existence) values that, when rank-ordered, provide insight into one's priorities.

saturated fats—Fats found primarily in red meat and other animal products that usually appear in solid rather than liquid form; high in cholesterol.

secondary health care—Health care provided by health-care professionals, in response to threats of illness or disease.

self-actualization—The process of striving to fulfill one's potential; the highest human need in Maslow's hierarchy.

self-concept—How one sees oneself; feelings of self-worth.

self-confrontation—The act of questioning or critically appraising one's own actions or behavior.

self-efficacy—The belief in one's ability to produce a desired outcome in a specific setting with controlled behavior.

self-esteem—Realistic and deserved self-respect.

serial monogamy—Having a series of sexual or marital partners, but practicing fidelity to each in turn while the relationship lasts.

set point theory—The theory that the human body has a normal weight range that will be maintained despite dieting because the hypothalamus will adjust metabolic rate to conserve energy.

sex roles—Those behaviors and expectations that become culturally associated more with one sex than the other; that are traditionally either male or female.

simple carbohydrates—Simple sugars found in processed foods; often called "empty calories" because of their minimal contribution to energy and nutrition, they should constitute no more than 10 percent of daily caloric intake.

smokeless tobacco—Chewing tobacco, plug tobacco, or snuff, all of which have at least as much harmful tars and nicotine as is found in cigarettes.

social drinker—A person who rarely drinks alone, usually has one or two drinks per occasion, and whose blood alcohol level remains below .05, the legal level for being "under the influence."

socialized medicine—Universal provision of health-care services by the government, irrespective of one's ability to pay, and subsidized by taxes.

social learning theory—A collection of theories based on the view that individual behavior is learned, largely as a result of environmental and social conditions.

social network—Family members, close friends, and colleagues who provide support in times of ill health or other crises.

Social Readjustment Rating Scale—As developed by Thomas Holmes and Richard Rahe, a listing of life events that require significant change in a person's life, producing either eustress or distress.

STDs—Sexually transmitted diseases (e.g., gonorrhea and herpes) that are highly contagious and spread through sexual contacts.

sterilization—The surgical process of making a person incapable of reproduction; a vasectomy for males and a tubal ligation for females.

stress—Any nonspecific response of the body to demands placed on it, that disturbs biological or psychological equilibrium.

surrogate motherhood—The act of bearing a child conceived through artificial insemination, with the intent of relinquishing all parental rights at birth to the man who fathered the child.

synergy—The combined action of two drugs that, when taken concurrently, produce greater than an additive effect; the synergistic effect of alcohol and barbiturates, for instance, can be deadly.

systolic blood pressure—Pressure exerted against the interior arterial walls when the heart is in contraction; always the upper number of a blood pressure reading.

tars—One of the three main harmful ingredients in tobacco, tars contain the chemicals that cause cancer.

tertiary health care—Treatment that sustains life, and without which death would be likely; examples include open-heart surgery and chemotherapy.

THC—Tetrahydrocannabinol, the primary active ingredient in marijuana cigarettes, which produces physical or psychological dependency.

the Pill—An oral contraceptive that has become the most widely used form of birth control because it is both convenient and highly effective.

training effect—Physiological changes resulting from aerobic exercise that make the body more efficient in transporting oxygen to using cells.

TSE—Testicular self-examination, the procedure recommended by the American Cancer Society and most physicians for *early* detection of testicular cancer; the key to higher cure rates.

Type A personality—A person whose behavior is characterized by anger, aggressiveness, hostility, competitiveness, and a compulsion for doing more and more in less and less time.

Type B personality—A person whose behavior is relaxed, who is not easily upset by interpersonal conflicts, and who does not set or accept unrealistic goals.

Type C personality—A person whose behavior is characterized by commitment to something, control over events, and an acceptance of change as challenge—a combination referred to as "hardiness."

unintentional injuries—Injuries typically referred to as accidental injuries, but not those related to attempted suicides, homicides, child and spouse abuse, rape, and other cases of assault and battery.

unsaturated fats—Polyunsaturated (vegetable) and monounsaturated (e.g., olive oil) fats, usually found in liquid form when at room temperature, and containing less cholesterol than saturated fats.

uplifts—Experiences and conditions of a daily nature that have a positive impact on one's mental or emotional health; for instance, having friends and socializing.

utilitarianism—The theory that an action is moral and just if it brings the greatest good to the greatest number of people.

values—Choices of modes of conduct or end-states of existence that guide behavior and make life worth living.

values clarification process—A seven-step process designed to assist individuals in determining their personal values priorities, without regard to social conformity.

values education—The process of guiding individuals toward a set of values that will be rational, socially acceptable, and morally defensible.

vertigo—A dizziness or loss of equilibrium brought about by disorientation or rapid movement: associated with high-risk activities such as auto racing, hotdog skiing, and sky-diving.

vital capacity—The amount of air that can be breathed out by the lungs in one exhalation; it is positively correlated with cardiorespiratory fitness.

water-soluble vitamins—The B-complex vitamins and vitamin C, all of which are incapable of being stored by the body, and therefore should be consumed daily; complex carbohydrates are among the best sources.

wellness—The state of good health that goes beyond absence of disease, including the attitudes and activities that improve the quality of one's life to the highest possible level. This encompasses physical, mental, social, vocational, and spiritual dimensions and is a positive approach to life.

wisdom—Making an intelligent application of knowledge.

References

Abella, R., & Heslin, R. (1984). Health, locus of control, values, and the behavior of families and friends: An integrated approach to understanding preventive health behavior. *Basic and Applied Social Psychology, 5*, 283-293.

Abernathy, H., Borhani, N.O., Hawkins, C.M., Crow, R., Entwisle, G., Jones, J.W., Maxwell, M.H., Langford, H., & Pressell, N. (1986). Systolic blood pressure as an independent predictor of mortality in the hypertension detection and follow-up program. *American Journal of Preventive Medicine, 2*(3), 123-132.

Ajzen, I., & Fishbein, M. (1977). Attitude-behavior relations: A theoretical analysis and review of empirical research. *Psychological Bulletin, 5*, 888-918.

Ajzen, I., & Fishbein, M. (1980). *Understanding attitudes and predicting social behavior.* Englewood Cliffs, NJ: Prentice-Hall.

Ajzen, I., & Timko, C. (1986). Correspondence between health attitudes and behavior. *Basic and Applied Social Psychology, 7*, 259-276.

Albanes, D., Jones, Y., Micozzi, M.S., & Mattson, M.E. (1987). Associations between smoking and body weight in the US population: Analysis of NHANES II. *American Journal of Public Health, 77*, 439-444.

Alles, W., Lambert, G., & Bibeau, D. (1984). DUI education: An ethical imperative. *Pennsylvania Journal of Health, Physical Education, Recreation and Dance, 54*(4), 4-6.

Anesheusel, C.S., & Huba, G.J. (1983). Depression, alcohol use, and smoking over one year: A four-wave longitudinal causal model. *Journal of Abnormal Psychology, 92*, 134-150.

Angier, N. (1981, August). Marijuana: Bad news and good. *Discover*, pp. 44-48.

Anglin, M.D., Kao, C.F., Harlow, L.L., Peters, K., & Booth, M.W. (1987). Similarity of behavior within addict couples. Part I. Methodology and narcotics patterns. *International Journal of the Addictions, 22*, 497-524.

Anokute, C.C. (1986). Epidemiology of spontaneous abortions: The effects of alcohol consumption and cigarette smoking. *Journal of the National Medical Association, 78*, 771-775.

Ardell, D.B. (1979). The nature and implications of high level wellness, or why "normal health" is a rather sorry state of existence. *Health Values, 3*(1), 17-24.

Arnett, R.H., McKusick, D.R., Sonnefeld, S.T., & Cowell, C.S. (1986). Projections of health care spending to 1990. *Health Care Financing Review, 7*(3), 1-36.

Ary, D.V., Lichtenstein, E., & Severson, H.H. (1987). Smokeless tobacco use among male adolescents: Patterns, correlates, predictors, and the use of other drugs. *Preventive Medicine, 16*, 385-401.

Associated Press. (1988). Drunken-driving arrests up 220 percent since '70. *The Christian Science Monitor, 80*(65), 6.

Auto seat belt use. (1986). *The Gallup Report, 247*, 29.

Autrey, J.H., Stover, E.S., Reatig, N., & Casper, R. (1986). Anorexia nervosa and bulimia. *Annual Review of Public Health, 7*, 535-543.

Avery-Clark, C. (1986). Sexual dysfunction and disorder patterns of working and nonworking wives. *Journal of Sex and Marital Therapy,* **12**, 93-107.

Bandura, A. (1977). Self-efficacy: Toward a unifying theory of behavioral change. *The Psychological Review,* **84**, 191-215.

Bandura, A. (1986). *Social learning theory.* Englewood Cliffs, NJ: Prentice-Hall.

Banks, M.H., Bemley, B.R., & Bland, J.M. (1981). Adolescent attitudes to smoking: Their influence on behaviour. *International Journal of Health Education,* **24**, 39-44.

Baron, J.A., Schori, A., Crow, B., Carter, R., & Mann, J. (1986). A randomized controlled trial of low carbohydrate and low fat/high fiber diets for weight loss. *American Journal of Public Health,* **76**, 1292-1296.

Barr, H.L., & Cohen, A. (1987). Abusers of alcohol and narcotics: Who are they? *International Journal of the Addictions,* **22**, 525-541.

Barrett-Connor, E. (1987). Health promotion: Proof of the pudding. *American Journal of Preventive Medicine,* **3**, 2-11.

Barton, L.M. (1986). *Development, implementation, and evaluation of a course in stress management for college students.* Unpublished doctoral dissertation, University of Pittsburgh.

Baumgartner, R.N., Roche, A.F., Chumlea, W.C., Siervogel, R.M., & Gluech, C.J. (1987). Fatness and fat patterns: Associations with plasma lipids and blood pressures in adults, 18 to 57 years of age. *American Journal of Epidemiology,* **126**, 614-628.

Beck, K.H. (1981). Driving while under the influence of alcohol: Relationship to attitudes and beliefs in a college population. *American Journal of Drug and Alcohol Abuse,* **8**, 377-388.

Becker, D.M., Myers, A.H., Sacci, M., Weida, S., Swank, R., Levine, D.M., & Pearson, T.A. (1986). Smoking behavior and attitudes toward smoking among hospital nurses. *American Journal of Public Health,* **76**, 1449-1451.

Becker, M.H. (1974). The health belief model and personal health behavior. *Health Education Monographs,* **2**, 323-473.

Becker, M.H., Maiman, L.A., Kirscht, J.P., Haefner, D.P., & Drachman, R.H. (1977). The Health Belief Model and prediction of dietary compliance: A field experiment. *Journal of Health and Social Behavior,* **18**, 348-365.

Behme, M.T. (1987). Symposium on diet, nutrition and health, University of Western Ontario, May 1987. *Nutrition Today,* **22**(5), 30-35.

Bem, D.J. (1970). *Beliefs, attitudes, and human affairs.* Belmont, CA: Brooks Cole.

Berger, R.A. (1984). *Introduction to weight training.* Englewood Cliffs, NJ: Prentice-Hall.

Berkman, L.F. (1984). Assessing the physical health effects of social networks and social support. *Annual Review of Public Health,* **5**, 413-432.

Berkman, L.F., & Syme, L. (1979). Social networks, host resistance and mortality: A nine-year follow-up study of Alameda County residents. *American Journal of Epidemiology,* **109**, 186-204.

Berkowitz, A.D., & Perkins, H.W. (1987). Recent research on gender differences in collegiate alcohol use. *Journal of American College Health,* **36**, 123-129.

Berne, E. (1964). *Games people play.* New York: Grove.

Berry, E.M., Hirsch, J., Most, J., & Thornton, J. (1986). The role of dietary fat in human obesity. *International Journal of Obesity,* **10**, 123-131.

Best, J.A., & Cameron, R. (1986). Health behavior and health promotion. *American Journal of Health Promotion,* **1**(2), 48-57.

Blair, S.N., Goodyear, N.N., Gibbons, L.W., & Cooper, K.H. (1984). Physical fitness and incidence of hypertension in health normotensive men and women. *The Journal of the American Medical Association,* **252**(4), 487-490.

Bonaguro, J.A., & Bonaguro, E.W. (1987). Self-concept, stress symptomatology, and tobacco use. *Journal of School Health, 57*, 56-58.

Bonita, R., Scragg, R., Stewart, A., Jackson, R., & Beaglehole, R. (1986). Cigarette smoking and risk of premature stroke in men and women. *British Medical Journal, 293*(6538), 6-8.

Borkan, G.A., Sparrow, D., Wisniewski, C., & Vokonas, P.S. (1986). Body weight and coronary disease risk: Patterns of risk factor change associated with long-term weight change. *American Journal of Epidemiology, 124*(3), 410-419.

Botvin, G., & McAlister, A. (1981). Cigarette smoking among children and adolescents: Causes and prevention. In Charles B. Arnold (Ed.) *Advances in disease prevention* (Vol. I). New York: Springer.

Bradstock, M.K., Marks, J.S., Forman, M.R., Gentry, E.M., Hogelin, G.C., Binkin, N.J., & Trowbridge, F.L. (1987). Drinking-driving and health lifestyle in the United States: Behavioral risk factors surveys. *Journal of Studies on Alcohol, 48*, 147-152.

Brantley, P.J., Waggoner, C.D., Jones, G.N., & Rappaport, N.B. (1987). A daily stress inventory: Development, reliability, and validity. *Journal of Behavioral Medicine, 10*, 61-74.

Breslow, L., & Belloc, N.B. (1972). The relation of physical health status and health practices. *Preventive Medicine, 1*, 46-64.

Breslow, L., & Enstrom, J.E. (1980). Persistence of habits and their relationship to mortality. *Preventive Medicine, 9*, 469-483.

Brown, N., Muhlenkamp, A., Fox, L., & Osborn, M. (1983). The relationship among health beliefs, health values, and health promotion activity. *Western Journal of Nursing Research, 5*, 155-163.

Brown, P.M., & Skiffington, E.W. (1987). Patterns of marijuana and alcohol use attitudes for Pennsylvania 11th graders. *International Journal of the Addictions, 22*, 567-573.

Brown, S.A., & Munson, E. (1987). Extroversion, anxiety and the perceived effects of alcohol. *Journal of Studies on Alcohol, 48*, 272-276.

Brownell, K.D. (1986). Public health approaches to obesity and its management. *Annual Review of Public Health, 7*, 521-533.

Bruhn, J.G., & Philips, B.U. (1987). A developmental basis for social support. *Journal of Behavioral Medicine, 10*, 213-229.

Bruns, C., & Geist, C.S. (1984). Stressful life events and drug use among adolescents. *Journal of Human Stress, 10*, 135-139.

Bry, B.H., McKeon, P., & Pandina, R.J. (1982). Extent of drug use as a function of number of risk factors. *Journal of Abnormal Psychology, 91*, 273-279.

Buchalter, G. (1988, February 21). Why I bought a gun. *Parade Magazine*, pp. 4-7.

Burke, R.J. (1984). Beliefs and fears underlying Type A behavior: What makes Sammy run—so fast and aggressively? *Journal of Human Stress, 10*, 174-182.

Burke, R.J., & Weir, T. (1980). The Type A experience: Occupational and life demands, satisfaction, and well-being. *Journal of Human Stress, 6*(4), 28-38.

Burks, N., & Martin, B. (1985). Everyday problems and life change events: Ongoing versus acute sources of stress. *Journal of Human Stress, 11*, 27-35.

Califano, J. (1986). *America's health care revolution: Who lives? Who dies? Who pays?* New York: Random House.

Callois, R. (1955). The structure and classification of games. *Diogenes, 12*, 62-75.

Camargo, C.A., Jr., Vranizan, K.M., Dreon, D.M., Frey-Hewitt, B., & Wood, P.D. (1987). Alcohol, calorie intake, and adiposity in overweight men. *Journal of the American College of Nutrition, 6*, 271-278.

Casperson, C.J., Powell, K.E., & Christenson, G.M. (1985). Physical activity, exercise, and physical fitness: Definitions and distinctions for health-related research. *Public Health Reports, 100*, 126-131.

Castro, G.G., Maddahian, E., Newcomb, M.D., & Bentler, P.M. (1987). A multivariate model of the determinants of cigarette smoking among adolescents. *Journal of Health and Social Behavior, 28*, 273-289.

Chapman, L.S. (1987). Developing a useful perspective on spiritual health: Love, joy, peace and fulfillment. *American Journal of Health Promotion, 2*(2), 12-17.

Chassin, L., Presson, C.C., Sherman, S., Corty, E., & Olshavsky, R.W. (1984). Cigarette smoking and adolescent psychosocial development. *Basic and Applied Social Psychology, 5*, 295-315.

Christiansen, B.A., & Goldman, M.S. (1983). Alcohol-related expectancies versus demographic/background variables in the prediction of adolescent drinking. *Journal of Consulting and Clinical Psychology, 51*, 249-257.

Cigarette smoking is lowest in four decades. (1986). *The Gallup Report, 249*, 2.

Clarke, K.S., & Parcel, G.S. (1975). Values and risk-taking behavior: The concept of calculated risk. *Health Education, 6*(6), 26-28.

Claydon, P. (1987). Self-reported alcohol, drug, and eating-disorder problems among male and female collegiate children of alcoholics. *Journal of American College Health, 36*, 111-116.

Clayton, R.R., & Ritter, C. (1985). The epidemiology of alcohol and drug abuse among adolescents. *Advances in Alcohol and Substance Abuse, 4*, 69-97.

Cocaine: Middle class high. (1981, July 6). *Time*, p.78.

Cohen, S., & Wills, T.A. (1985). Stress, social support, and the buffering hypothesis. *Psychological Bulletin, 98*, 310-357.

Conroy, W.J. (1979). Human values, smoking behavior, and public health programs. In M. Rokeach (Ed.), *Understanding human values: Individual and societal*. New York: The Free Press.

Cooper, K. H. (1968). *Aerobics*. New York: Bantam Books.

Cooper, K.H. (1982). *The aerobics program for total well-being*. New York: M. Evans.

Cooper, K.H., & Cooper, M. (1972). *Aerobics for women*. Philadelphia: M. Evans.

Corbin, C. (1980). *Nutrition*. New York: Holt, Rinehart and Winston.

Corey, M.A. (1987). A behavioral solution to the drunk driving dilemma. *Journal of Substance Abuse Treatment, 4*, 37-40.

Cousins, N. (1977). *Anatomy of an illness*. New York: Norton.

Cowell, S. (1985). AIDS and community health issues. *Journal of American College Health, 33*, 253-258.

Criqui, M.H., Cowan, L.D., Tyroler, H.A., Bangdiwala, S., Heiss, G., Wallace, R.B., & Cohn, R. (1987). Lipoproteins as mediators for the effects of alcohol consumption and cigarette smoking on cardiovascular mortality: Results from the lipid research clinics follow-up study. *American Journal of Epidemiology, 126*, 629-637.

Croft, J.B., Freedman, D.S., Cresanta, J.L., Srinivasan, S.R., Burke, G.L., Hunter, S.M., Webber, L.S., Snook, C.G., & Berenson, G.S. (1987). Adverse influences of alcohol, tobacco, and oral contraceptive use on cardiovascular risk factors during transition to adulthood. *American Journal of Epidemiology, 126*, 202-213.

Cronkite, R.C., & Moos, R.H. (1984). The role of predisposing and moderating factors in the stress-illness relationship. *Journal of Health and Social Behavior, 25*, 372-393.

Danielson, D.A., & Mazer, A. (1987). Results of the Massachusetts referendum for a national health program. *Journal of Public Health Policy, 8*, 28-35.

Davis, J.R., & Glaros, A.G. (1986). Relapse prevention and smoking cessation. *Addictive Behaviors, 11*, 105-114.

Davis, R.M. (1987). Current trends in cigarette advertising and marketing. *The New England Journal of Medicine, 316*(12), 725-732.

Dawber, T.R. (1980). *The Framingham study, the epidemiology of atherosclerotic disease.* Cambridge, MA: Harvard University Press.

Dearborn, M.J., & Hastings, J.E. (1987). Type A personality as a mediator of stress and strain in employed women. *Journal of Substance Abuse Treatment, 3,* 95-101.

DeJoy, D.M. (1985). Attributional processes and hazard control management in industry. *Journal of Safety Research, 16*(2), 61-71.

Dembo, R., Schmeidler, J., & Koval, M. (1976). Demographic, value, and behavior correlates of marijuana use among middle-class youths. *Journal of Health and Social Behavior, 17,* 177-187.

DeMense, K.P. (1985). The life events stress-performance linkage: An exploratory study. *Journal of Human Stress, 11,* 111-117.

Dennison, D. (1984). Activated health education: The development and refinement of an intervention model. *Health Values, 8*(2), 18-24.

Dent, C.W., Sussman, S., Johnson, C.A., Hansen, W.B., & Flay, B.R. (1987). Adolescent smokeless tobacco incidence: Relations with other drugs and psychosocial variables. *Preventive Medicine, 16,* 422-431.

Deren, S. (1986). Children of substance abusers: A review of the literature. *Journal of Substance Abuse Treatment, 3,* 77-94.

Diamond, E.L. (1982). The role of anger and hostility in essential hypertension and coronary heart disease. *Psychological Bulletin, 92,* 410-433.

DiFranza, J.R., Winters, T.H., Goldberg, R.J., Cirillo, L., & Biliouris, T. (1986). The relationship of smoking to motor vehicle accidents and traffic violations. *New York State Journal of Medicine, 86,* 464-467.

Dishman, R.K., Ickes, W., & Morgan, W.P. (1980). Self-motivation and adherence to habitual physical activity. *Journal of Applied Social Psychology, 10,* 115-132.

Dixon, B. (1978). *Beyond the magic bullet.* New York: Harper & Row.

Dixon, J.K., & Dixon, J.P. (1984). An evolutionary-based model of health and viability. *Advances in Nursing Science, 6*(3), 1-18.

Dolecek, T.A., Schoenberger, J.A., Oman, J.K., Kremer, B.K., Sunseri, A.J., & Alberti, J.M. (1986). Cardiovascular risk factor knowledge and belief in prevention among adults in Chicago. *American Journal of Preventive Medicine, 2,* 262-267.

Doll, R., & Peto, R. (1981). The causes of cancer: Quantitative estimates of avoidable risks of cancer in the United States today. *Journal of National Cancer Institute, 66,* 1192-1308.

Douglas, D.B. (1986). Alcoholism as an addiction: The disease concept reconsidered. *Journal of Substance Abuse Treatment, 3,* 115-120.

Downs, W.R. (1987). A panel study of normative structure, adolescent alcohol use and peer alcohol use. *Journal of Studies on Alcohol, 48,* 167-175.

Ducimetiere, P., Richard, J., & Cambien, F. (1986). The pattern of subcutaneous fat distribution in middle-aged men and the risk of coronary heart disease: The Paris prospective study. *International Journal of Obesity, 10,* 229-240.

Eckert, P.S. (1980). Bottoms up: An alcohol abuse prevention model for college campuses. *Health Values, 4,* 222-228.

Edwards, P. (1986). Strategies for a smoke-free world. *Health Promotion, 24*(4), 2-8.

Eiser, J.R., & Harding, C.M. (1983). Smoking, seat-belt use and perception of health risks. *Addictive Behaviors, 8,* 75-78.

Ensor, P.G., Hunkel, B.I., & Means, R.K. (1978). *Personal health: Confronting your health behavior.* Boston: Allyn & Bacon.

Epstein, S. (1985). Intervention models for adaption in a world of chemicals: A values approach. *International Journal of the Addictions, 20*(5), 795-802.

Estep, R. (1987). The influence of the family on the use of alcohol and prescription depressants by women. *Journal of Psychoactive Drugs, 19,* 171-179.

Evans, G.W., Palsane, M.N., & Carrere, S. (1987). Type A behavior and occupational stress: A cross-cultural study of blue-collar workers. *Journal of Personality and Social Psychology, 52,* 1002-1007.

Ewald, B.M., & Roberts, C.S. (1985). Contraceptive behavior in college-age males related to Fishbein model. *Advances in Nursing Science, 7*(3), 63-69.

Faber, M. (1980). [Forward]. *Family & Community Health, 3,* xiii.

Farchi, G., Menotti, A., & Conti, S. (1987). Coronary risk factors and survival probability from coronary and other causes of death. *American Journal of Epidemiology, 126*(3), 400-408.

Farquhar, J.W. (1978). *The American way of life need not be hazardous to your health.* New York: W.W. Norton.

Farquhar, J.W., Maccoby, N., Wood, P.D., Alexander, J.K., Breitrose, H., Brown, B.W., Jr., Haskell, W.L., McAlister, A.L., Meyer, A.J., Nash, J.D., & Stern, M.P. (1977). Community education for cardiovascular health. *Lancet, 8023,* 1192-1195.

Feldman, R.H.L., & Mayhew, P.C. (1984). Predicting nutrition behavior: The utilization of a social psychological model of health behavior. *Basic and Applied Social Psychology, 5,* 183-195.

Ferrans, C.E., & Powers, M.J. (1985). Quality of life index: Development and psychometric properties. *Advances in Nursing Science, 8*(1), 15-24.

Ferrence, R., Truscott, S., & Whitehead, P.C. (1986). Drinking and the prevention of coronary heart disease: Findings, issues and public health policy. *Journal of Studies on Alcohol, 47,* 394-408.

Fifty-five mph national speed limit still favored by large majority. (1986). *The Gallup Report, 249,* 7.

Fishbein, M., & Ajzen, I. (1984). *Belief, attitude, intention, and behavior: An introduction in theory and research* (2nd ed.). New York: Random House.

Flannery, R.B., Jr. (1986). Major life events and daily hassles in predicting health status: Methodological inquiry. *Journal of Clinical Psychology, 42,* 485-487.

Flannery, R.B., Jr. (1987). Towards stress-resistant persons: A stress management approach to the treatment of anxiety. *American Journal of Preventive Medicine, 3*(1), 25-30.

Flay, B.R., (1987). Mass media and smoking cessation: A critical review. *American Journal of Public Health, 77,* 153-160.

Flores, P.J. (1986). Alcoholism treatment and the relationship of native American cultural values to recovery. *International Journal of the Addictions, 20,* 1707-1726.

Ford, A.S., & Ford, W.S. (1981). The need for cooperative health education: Some survey findings. *International Journal of Health Education, 24,* 83-94.

Forsyth, G., & Hundleby, J.D. (1987). Personality and situation as determinates of desire to drink in young adults. *International Journal of the Addictions, 22,* 653-669.

Fortmann, S.P., Haskell, W.L., & Williams, P.T. (1986). Changes in plasma high density lipoprotein cholesterol after changes in cigarette use. *American Journal of Epidemiology, 124,* 706-710.

Foster, C.J., Weinsier, R.L., Birch, R., Norris, D.J., Bernstein, R.W., Wang, J., Pierson, R.N., & VanItallie, T. B. (1987). Obesity and serum lipids: An evaluation of the relative contribution of body fat and fat distribution to lipid levels. *International Journal of Obesity, 11,* 151-161.

Fox, R.A. (1979). An experience with values clarification. *Health Education, 10*(1), 40-41.

Foxman, B., Higgins, I.T.T., & Oh, M.S. (1986). The effects of occupation and smoking on respiratory disease mortality. *American Review of Respiratory Disease,* **134**(4), 649-652.

Frankena, W.K. (1980). *Thinking about morality.* Ann Arbor: University of Michigan Press.

Friedman, H.S., Hall, J.A., & Harris, M.J. (1986). Type A behavior, nonverbal expressive style, and health. *Journal of Personality and Social Psychology,* **5**, 1299-1315.

Friedman, L.A., & Kimball, A.W. (1986). Coronary heart disease mortality and alcohol consumption in Framingham. *American Journal of Epidemiology,* **124**, 481-489.

Friend, T. (1988, February 15). Fit girls become healthy women. *USA Today,* p. 1D.

Frieze, I., & Bar-Tal, D. (1979). Attribution theory. In I. Frieze, D. Bar-Tal, & J. Carroll (Eds.), *New Approaches to Social Problems* (Chapter 1). San Francisco: Jossey-Bass.

Garrison, R.J., Kannel, W.B., Stokes, J., & Castelli, W.P. (1987). Incidence and precursors of hypertension in young adults: The Framingham offspring study. *Preventive Medicine,* **16**, 235-251.

Gerrard, M. (1987). Sex, sex guilt, and contraceptive use revisited: The 1980s. *Journal of Personality and Social Psychology,* **52**, 975-980.

Gerrard, M., McCann, L., & Fortini, M.E. (1983). Prevention of unwanted pregnancy. *American Journal of Community Psychology,* **11**, 153-167.

Gilchrist, L.D., Schinke, S.P., Bobo, J.K., & Snow, W.H. (1986). Self-control skills for preventing smoking. *Addictive Behaviors,* **11**, 169-174.

Gilgun, J., & Gordon, S. (1983). The role of values in sex education programs. *Journal of Research and Development in Education,* **16**(2), 27-33.

Girdano, D., & Everly, G. (1986). *Controlling stress and tension: A holistic approach* (2nd ed.). Englewood Cliffs, NJ: Prentice-Hall.

Glantz, M.D. (1984). *Correlates and consequences of marijuana use.* Rockville, MD: U.S. Department of Health and Human Services, National Institute on Drug Abuse.

Glanz, K., & Damberg, C.L. (1987). Meeting our nation's health objectives in nutrition. *Journal of Nutrition Education,* **19**, 211-219.

Golding, J.F., Harpur, T., & Brent-Smith, H. (1983). Personality, drinking and drug-taking correlates of cigarette smoking. *Personality and Individual Differences,* **4**, 703-706.

Goodrow, B. (1982). The motorcycle helmet controversy: A test of health values. *Health Values,* **6**(5), 19-22.

Goodstadt, M.S. (1978). Alcohol and drug education: Models and outcomes. *Health Education Monographs,* **6**, 263-279.

Gordon, T., & Doyle, J.T. (1987). Drinking and mortality: The Albany study. *American Journal of Epidemiology,* **125**, 263-270.

Gottlieb, N.H. (1982). The effects of peer and parental smoking and age on the smoking careers of college women: A sex-related phenomenon. *Social Science and Medicine,* **16**, 595-600.

Gottlieb, N.H., Lloyd, L.E., & Bernstein, V.R. (1987). Sex and age differences in lifestyle risk: Implications for health promotion programming. *American Journal of Preventive Medicine,* **3**, 192-199.

Green, L.W. (undated). *Health promotion summary.* Unpublished manuscript.

Green, L.W. (1984). Modifying and developing health behavior. *Annual Review of Public Health,* **5**, 215-236.

Green, L.W., Kreuter, M.W., Deeds, S.G., & Partridge, K.B. (1980). *Health education planning: A diagnostic approach.* Palo Alto, CA: Mayfield.

Green, L.W., & Lewis, F.M. (1986). *Measurement and evaluation in health education and health promotion.* Palo Alto, CA: Mayfield.

Greenberg, N.E. (1985). Nicotine, cigarette smoking, and body weight. *British Journal of Addiction,* **80**, 369-377.

Greenglass, E. (1987). Anger in Type A women: Implications for coronary heart disease. *Personality and Individual Differences,* **8**, 639-650.

Grossman, J. (1984). Wellness for all by the year 2000: An old challenge for a new century. *Human Values,* **8**(2), 35-42.

Grube, J.W., Morgan, M., & McGree, S.T. (1986). Attitudes and normative beliefs as predictors of smoking intentions and behaviors: A test of three models. *British Journal of Social Psychology,* **25**, 81-93.

Haas, R. (1983). *Eat to win: The sports nutrition bible.* New York: New American Library.

Haggerty, R.J. (1977). Changing lifestyles to improve health. *Preventive Medicine,* **6**, 276-289.

Haggerty, P.A., & Blackburn, G.L. (1987). A critical evaluation of popular low calorie diets in America: Part 2. *Topics in Clinical Nutrition,* **2**(2), 37-46.

Haines, A.P., Imeson, J.D., Meade, T.W. (1987). Skinfold thickness and cardiovascular risk factors. *American Journal of Epidemiology,* **126**(1), 86-94.

Hardman, R.K., & Gardner, D.J. (1986). Sexual anorexia: A look at inhibited sexual desire. *Journal of Sex Education and Therapy,* **12**(1), 55-59.

Harris, D.M., & Guten, S. (1979). Health-protective behavior: An exploratory study. *Journal of Health and Social Behavior,* **20**, 17-29.

Harris, J. (1985). *The value of life.* Boston: Routledge & Kegan.

Harron, F., Burnside, J., & Beauchamp, T. (1983). *Health and Human Values.* New Haven: Yale University Press.

Hatch, E.E., & Bracken, M.B. (1986). Effect of marijuana use in pregnancy on fetal growth. *American Journal of Epidemiology,* **124**(6), 986-993.

Hayes, D., & Ross, C.E. (1986). Body and mind: The effect of exercise, overweight, and physical health on psychological well-being. *Journal of Health and Social Behavior,* **27**, 387-400.

Hayes, D., & Ross, C.E. (1987). Concern with appearance, health beliefs, and eating habits. *Journal of Health and Social Behavior,* **28**, 120-130.

Hays, R. (1985). An integrated value-expectancy theory of alcohol and other drug use. *British Journal of Addictions,* **80**, 379-384.

Heimbach, J.T. (1985). Cardiovascular disease and diet: The public view. *Public Health Reports,* **100**, 5-12.

Hendricks, P. (1987). Condoms: A straight girl's best friend. *Ms.,* **16**(3), 98-102.

Hendrix, W.J., & Taylor, G.S. (1987). A multivariate analysis of the relationship between cigarette smoking and absence from work. *American Journal of Health Promotion,* **2**(2), 5-11.

Herold, E.S., & Goodwin, M.S. (1981). Premarital sexual guilt and contraceptive attitudes and behavior. *Family Relations,* **30**, 247-253.

Hester, N.R., & Macrina, D.M. (1985). The health belief model and the contraceptive behavior of college women: Implications for health education. *Journal of American College Health,* **33**, 245-252.

Hickenbottom, J.P., Bissonette, R.P., & O'Shea, R.M. (1987). Preventive medicine and college alcohol abuse. *Journal of American College Health,* **36**, 67-72.

Hingson, R., & Howland, J. (1987). Alcohol as a risk factor for injury or death resulting from accidental falls: A review of the literature. *Journal of Studies on Alcohol,* **48**, 212-219.

Hochbaum, G. (1982). Certain problems in evaluating health education. *Health Values,* **6**, 14-20.

Hochbaum, G.M. (1979). An alternate approach to health education. *Health Values,* **3**, 197-201.

Holder, H.D., & Blose, J.O. (1987). Reduction of community alcohol problems: Computer simulation experiments in three counties. *Journal of Studies on Alcohol, 48*, 124-135.

Holmes, T.H., & Rahe, R.H. (1967). The social readjustment rating scale. *Journal of Psychosomatic Research, 11*, 213-218.

Howard, J.H., Cunningham, D.A., & Rechnitzer, P.A. (1986). Role ambiguity, Type A behavior, and job satisfaction: Moderating effects on cardiovascular and biochemical responses associated with coronary risk. *Journal of Applied Psychology, 71*, 95-101.

Howland, J., & Hingson, R. (1987). Alcohol as a risk factor for injuries or death due to fires and burns: Review of the literature. *Public Health Reports, 102*, 475-483.

Howland, J., & Hingson, R. (1988). Alcohol as a risk factor for drownings: A review of the literature (1950-1985). *Accident Analysis and Prevention, 20*, 19-25.

Howley, E.T., & Franks, B.D. (1986). *Health/ fitness instructor's handbook.* Champaign, IL: Human Kinetics.

Hoyman, H.W. (1975). Re-thinking an ecological-system model of man's health, disease, aging, death. *Journal of School Health, 45*, 509-518.

Hubert, H.B., Eaker, E.D., Garrison, R.J., & Castelli, W.P. (1987). Life-style correlates of risk factor change in young adults: An eight-year study of coronary heart disease risk factors in the Framingham offspring. *American Journal of Epidemiology, 125*, 812-831.

Huckstadt, A. (1987). Locus of control among alcoholics, recovering alcoholics, and non-alcoholics. *Research in Nursing & Health, 10*, 23-28.

Hull, J.G. (1981). A self-awareness model of the causes and effects of alcohol consumption. *Journal of Abnormal Psychology, 90*, 586-600.

Hull, J.G., Young, R.D., & Jouriles, E. (1986). Applications of the self-awareness model of alcohol consumption: Prediction patterns of use and abuse. *Journal of Personality and Social Psychology, 51*(4), 790-796.

Hunter, S.M., Croft, J.B., Burke, G.L., Parker, F.C., Webber, L.S., & Berenson, G.S. (1986). Longitudinal patterns of cigarette smoking and smokeless tobacco use in youth: The Bogalusa Heart Study. *American Journal of Public Health, 76*, 193-195.

Iacono, J.M. (1987). Dietary intervention studies to reduce risk factors related to cardiovascular diseases and cancer. *Preventive Medicine, 16*, 516-524.

Insel, P.M., & Roth, W.T. (1985). *Core concepts in health* (4th ed.). Palo Alto, CA: Mayfield.

Jaccard, J., & Becker, M.A. (1985). Attitudes and behavior: An information integration perspective. *Journal of Experimental Social Psychology, 21*, 440-465.

Jacobson, D.E. (1986). Types and timing of social support. *Journal of Health and Social Behavior, 27*, 250-264.

Jamal, M. (1985). Type A behavior and job performance: Some suggestive findings. *Journal of Human Stress, 11*, 60-68.

Jemmott, J.B., III. (1987). Social motives and susceptibility to disease: Stalking individual differences in health risks. *Journal of Personality, 55*(2), 267-298.

Jonah, B.A. (1986). Accident risk and risk-taking behaviour among young drivers. *Accident: Analysis and Prevention, 18*, 255-271.

Jung, J. (1984). Social support and its relation to health: A critical evaluation. *Basic and Applied Social Psychology, 5*, 143-169.

Kandel, D.B., Davies, M., Karus, D., & Yamaguchi, K. (1986). The consequences in young adulthood of adolescent drug involvement: An overview. *Archives of General Psychiatry, 43*, 746-754.

Kandel, D.B., & Logan, J.A. (1984). Patterns of drug use from adolescence to young adulthood: I. Periods of risk for initiation, continued use, and discontinuation. *American Journal of Public Health, 74*, 660-666.

Kane, W.M. (1985). *Healthy living: An active approach to wellness.* Indianapolis: Bobbs-Merrill.

Kanner, A.D., Coyne, J.C., Schaefer, C., & Lazarus, R.S. (1981). Comparison of two modes of stress measurement: Daily hassles and uplifts versus major life events. *Journal of Behavioral Medicine, 4*, 1-39.

Kaplan, G.D., & Cowles, A. (1978). Health locus of control and health value prediction of smoking reduction. *Health Education Monographs, 6*, 125-137.

Kaplan, H.B., Martin, S.S., Johnson, R.J., & Robbins, C.A. (1986). Escalation of marijuana use: Application of a general theory of deviant behavior. *Journal of Health and Social Behavior, 27*, 44-61.

Kasl, S.V. (1984). Stress and health. *Annual Review of Public Health, 5*, 319-341.

Kaslow, R.A., Ostrow, D.G., Detels, R., Phair, J.P., Polk, B.F., & Rinaldo, C.R., Jr. (1987). The multicenter AIDS cohort study: Rationale, organization, and selected characteristics of the participants. *American Journal of Epidemiology, 126*(2), 310-318.

Katz, R.C., & Singh, N. (1986). A comparison of current smokers and self-cured quitters on Rosenbaum's self control schedule. *Addictive Behaviors, 11*, 63-65.

Kellerman, A., & Reay, D.T. (1986). Protection or peril? An analysis of firearm-related deaths in the home. *New England Journal of Medicine, 314*, 1557-1560.

Keys, A., Menotti, A., Karvonen, M.J., Aravanis, C., Blackburn, H., Buzina, R., Djordjevic, B.S., Dontas, A.J., Fidanza, F., Keys, M.H., Kromhout, D., Nedeljkovic, S., Punsar, S., Seccareccia, F., & Toshima, H. (1986). The diet and 15-year death rate in the seven countries study. *American Journal of Epidemiology, 124*(6), 903-915.

Kiburz, D., Jacobs, R., Reckling, F., & Mason, J. (1986). Bicycle accidents and injuries among adult cyclists. *American Journal of Sports Medicine, 14*(5), 416-419.

Kinney, J., & Leaton, G. (1982). *Understanding alcohol.* New York: C.V. Mosby.

Kirscht, J.P. (1983). Preventive health behavior: A review of the research and issues. *Health Psychology, 2*, 277-301.

Kittleson, M.J., & Sutherland, M.S. (1982). Primary prevention and implications for drug education programs. *Health Values, 6*(6), 30-35.

Knowles, J.H. (1977). The responsibility of the individual. *Science, 198*, 1103.

Kobasa, S.C. (1982). The hardy personality: Toward a social psychology of stress and health. In G.S. Sanders & J. Suls (Eds.), *Social psychology of health and illness.* Hillsdale, NJ: Erlbaum.

Kobasa, S.C., Maddi, S.R., & Courington, S. (1981). Personality and constitution as mediators in the stress-illness relationship. *Journal of Health and Social Behavior, 22*, 368-378.

Kobasa, S.C., Maddi, S.R., & Pucetti, M.C. (1982). Personality and exercise as buffers in the stress-illness relationship. *Journal of Behavioral Medicine, 5*, 391-404.

Kohlberg, L. (1981). *The meaning and measurement of moral development.* Worcester, MA: Clark University Press.

Kolbe, L.J. (1985). Why school health education? An empirical point of view. *Health Education, 16*(2), 116-120.

Koop, C.E. (1987). Surgeon General's report on acquired immune deficiency syndrome. *Public Health Reports, 102*, 1-3.

Koop, C.E., & Luoto, J. (1982). The health consequences of smoking: Cancer, overview of a report of the Surgeon General. *Public Health Reports, 97*, 318-324.

Kovar, M.G. (1979). Some indicators of health-related behavior among adolescents in the United States. *Public Health Reports, 94*, 109-118.

Kowalski, R.E. (1987). *The 8-week cholesterol cure.* New York: Harper & Row.

Kozlowski, L.T., Jelinek, L.C., & Pope, M.A. (1986). Cigarette smoking among alcohol abusers: A continuing and neglected problem.

Canadian Journal of Public Health, **77**, 205-207.

Kriegel, R., & Kriegel, M.H. (1984). *The C zone: Peak performance under pressure.* New York: Doubleday.

Kristiansen, C.M. (1985a). Smoking, health behavior, and value priorities. *Addictive Behaviors,* **10**, 41-44.

Kristiansen, C.M. (1985b). Smoking, health behavior, and values: A replication, refinement, and extension. *Addictive Behaviors,* **10**, 325-328.

Kristiansen, C.M. (1985c). Value correlates of preventive health behavior. *Journal of Personality and Social Psychology,* **49**, 748-758.

Kristiansen, C.M. (1986). A two-value model of preventive health behavior. *Basic and Applied Social Psychology,* **7**, 173-183.

Kristiansen, C.M. (1987). Salient beliefs regarding smoking: Consistency across samples and smoking status. *Journal of the Institute of Health Education,* **25**(2), 93-96.

Kristiansen, C.M., & Harding, C.M. (1984). The social desirability of preventive health behavior. *Public Health Reports,* **99**, 384-388.

Krotkiewski, M., & Bjorntorp, P. (1986). Muscle tissue in obesity with different distribution of adipose tissue. Effects of physical training. *International Journal of Obesity,* **10**, 331-341.

LaCroix, A.Z., Mead, L.A., Liang, K., Thomas, C.B., & Pearson, T.A. (1986). Coffee consumption and the incidence of coronary heart disease. *The New England Journal of Medicine,* **315**, 977-982.

Lakein, A. (1973). *How to get control of your time and your life.* New York: New American Library.

Langlie, J.K. (1977). Social networks, health beliefs, and preventive health behavior. *Journal of Health and Social Behavior,* **18**, 244-259.

Langlie, J.K. (1979). Interrelationships among preventive health behaviors: A test of competing hypotheses. *Public Health Reports,* **94**, 216-225.

LaPlace, J. (1984). *Health* (4th ed.). Englewood Cliffs, NJ: Prentice-Hall.

LaRocco, J.M., House, J.S., & French, J.A.P., Jr. (1980). Social support, occupational stress, and health. *Journal of Health and Social Behavior,* **21**, 202-218.

Lau, R.R. (1982). The origins of health locus of control beliefs. *Journal of Personality and Social Psychology,* **42**, 322-334.

Lau, R.R., Hartman, K.A., & Ware, J.E. (1986). Health as a value: Methodological and theoretical considerations. *Health Psychology,* **5**, 25-43.

Lazarus, R.S. (1984). Puzzles in the study of daily hassles. *Journal of Behavioral Medicine,* **7**, 375-389.

Lazarus, R.S., & Folkman, S. (1984). *Stress, appraisal, and coping.* New York: Springer.

LeGrady, D., Dyer, A.R., Shekelle, R.B., Stamler, J., Liu, K., Paul, O., Lepper, M., & Shryock, A.M. (1987). Coffee consumption and mortality in the Chicago Western Electric Company study. *American Journal of Epidemiology,* **126**, 803-812.

Leichtman, R.R., & Japikse, C. (1985). The way to health. *Journal of Holistic Medicine,* **7**, 46-70.

Leon, A.S. (1987). Age and other predictors of coronary heart disease. *Medicine and Science in Sports and Exercise,* **19**, 159-167.

Levin, L.S. (1981). Self-care: Towards fundamental changes in national strategies. *International Journal of Health Education,* **24**, 219-228.

Levinson, D.J., Darrow, C.N., Klein, E.B., Levinson, M.R., & McKee, B. (1978). *The seasons of a man's life.* New York: Alfred A. Knopf.

Lissovoy, G., Rice, T., Gabel, J., & Gelzer, H. (1987). Preferred provider organizations one year later. *Inquiry,* **24**, 127-135.

Luce, C.B. (1983, November 6). Female choices: Marriage, family or career. *Parade Magazine*, pp. 5-7.

Maccoby, N., Farquhar, J.W., Wood, P.D., & Alexander, J. (1977). Reducing the risk of cardiovascular disease: Effects of a community based campaign on knowledge and behavior. *Journal of Community Health, 3*, 100-114.

Macdonald, D.I. (1987). ADAMHA goes into high gear in the prevention, research, and treatment of drug and alcohol abuse. *Public Health Reports, 102*, 122-123.

Maiman, L.A., & Becker, M.H. (1974). The health belief model: Origins and correlates in psychological theory. *Health Education Monographs, 2*, 336-353.

Maiman, L.A., Becker, M.H., Kirscht, J.P., Haefner, D.P., & Drachman, R.H. (1977). Scales for measuring health belief model dimensions: A test of predictive value, internal consistency, and relationship among beliefs. *Health Education Monographs, 5*, 215-230.

Maleskey, G. (1987a). Food factors that stop cancer: Best news, best bets. *Prevention, 39*(10), 88-95, 108-109.

Maleskey, G. (1987b). Your best blood pressure news in years. *Prevention, 39*(11), 24-32.

Maleskey, G. (1988). Walk away from cancer. *Prevention, 40*(2), 28-32, 135.

Mappes, T.A., & Zembaty, J.S. (1987). *Social ethics: Morality and social policy* (3rd ed.). New York: McGraw-Hill.

Mark, A. (1986). Adolescents discuss themselves and drugs through music. *Journal of Substance Abuse Treatment, 3*, 243-249.

Maslow, A.H. (1970). *Motivation and Personality* (2nd ed.). New York: Harper & Row.

Masters, W.H., & Johnson, V. (1966). *Human sexual response*. Boston: Little, Brown.

Masters, W.H., & Johnson, V. (1970). *Human sexual inadequacy*. Boston: Little, Brown.

Matteson, M.T., Ivancevich, J.M., & Gamble, G.O. (1987). A test of the cognitive social learning model of Type A behavior. *Journal of Human Stress, 13*, 23-31.

Matthews, K.A., Cottington, E.M., Talbott, E., Kuller, L.H., & Siegal, J.M. (1987). Stressful work conditions and diastolic blood pressure among blue collar factory workers. *American Journal of Epidemiology, 126*(2), 280-291.

Mayer, J. (1974). *Health*. New York: Van Nostrand.

McArdle, W.D., Katch, F.L., Katch, V.L. (1986). *Exercise physiology*. Philadelphia: Lea & Febiger.

McCary, J.L. (1979). *Human sexuality* (2nd ed.). New York: Van Nostrand.

McDonough, A.B. (1987). Health implications of obesity. *Topics in Clinical Nutrition, 2*(2), 5-13.

McGinnis, J.M. (1987a). Suicide in America—moving up the public health agenda. *Suicide and Life-Threatening Behavior, 17*, 18-32.

McGinnis, J.M. (1987b). A healthy campus—forecasting from the 1990 health objectives for the nation. *Journal of American College Health, 35*, 158-170.

McGinnis, J.M., Shopland, D., & Brown, C. (1987). Tobacco and health: Trends in smoking and smokeless tobacco consumption in the United States. *Annual Review of Public Health, 8*, 441-467.

McKeown, G.E. (1987). Fiber intake in different populations and colon cancer risk. *Preventive Medicine, 16*, 532-539.

McMillan, A., Lubitz, J., & Russell, D. (1987). Medicare enrollment in health maintenance organizations. *Health Care Financing Review, 8*(3), 87-93.

Meisenbach, A.E. (1987). Reflections on the moral dimension of the AIDS epidemic. *Journal of American College Health, 35*, 279-281.

Miles, G.T. (1986). *Daily hassles and uplifts—short form: Item selection and cross-validation*. Master's thesis, Pennsylvania State University, University Park.

Minkler, M., Wallack, L., & Madden, P. (1987). Alcohol and cigarette advertising in *Ms.* magazine. *Journal of Public Health Policy, 8*, 164-179.

Mintz, J., Boyd, G., Rose, J.E., Charwastra, V.C., & Jarvik, M.E. (1985). Alcohol increases cigarette smoking: A laboratory demonstration. *Addictive Behaviors, 10*, 203-208.

Mondanaro, J. (1987) Strategies for AIDS prevention: Motivating health behavior in drug dependent women. *Journal of Psychoactive Drugs, 19*, 143-149.

Morelock, S., Hingson, R.W., Smith, R.A., & Lederman, R.I. (1985). Mandatory seatbelt law support and opposition in New England—a survey. *Public Health Reports, 100*, 357-363.

Morgan, P. (1987). Women and alcohol: The disinhibition rhetoric in an analysis of domination. *Journal of Psychoactive Drugs, 19*, 129-133.

Morgan, W.M., & Curran, J.W. (1986). Acquired immunodeficiency syndrome: Current and future trends. *Public Health Reports, 101*, 459-465.

Morningstar, P.J., & Chitwood, D.D. (1987). How women and men get cocaine: Sex-role stereotypes and acquisition patterns. *Journal of Psychoactive Drugs, 19*, 135-142.

Morrill, R.L. (1980). *Teaching values in college*. San Francisco: Jossey-Bass.

Morris, J.N., Pollard, R., Everitt, M.G., & Shane, S.P.W. (1980). Vigorous exercise in leisure-time: Protection against coronary heart disease. *Lancet, 8206*, 1207-1210.

Mosher, D.L., & Vonderheide, S.G. (1985). Contributions of sex guilt and masturbation guilt to women's contraceptive attitudes and use. *Journal of Sex Research, 21*, 24-39.

Moss, A.R., Osmand, D., Bacchetti, P., Chermann, J.C., Barre-Sinoussi, F., & Carlson, J. (1987). Risk factors for AIDS and HIV seropositivity in homosexual men. *American Journal of Epidemiology, 125*, 1035-1047.

Mueller, D.P., Edwards, D.W., & Yarvis, R.M. (1977). Stressful life events and psychiatric symptomatology: Change or undesirability. *Journal of Health and Social Behavior, 18*, 307-317.

Muhlenkamp, A.F., & Sayles, J.A. (1986). Self-esteem, social support, and positive health practices. *Nursing Research, 35*, 334-338.

Mullen, K.D. (1986). Wellness: The missing concept in health promotion programming for adults. *Health Values, 10*(3), 34-37.

Muller, A. (1980). Evaluation of the costs and benefits of motorcycle helmet laws. *American Journal of Public Health, 70*(6), 586-592.

Naroll, R. (1983). *The moral order*. Beverly Hills: Sage.

Nash, J.D. (1987). Eating behavior and body weight: Psychosocial influences. *American Journal of Health Promotion, 2*, 5-13.

Nathan, P.E. (1987). What do behavioral scientists know—and what can they do—about alcoholism? In P.C. Rivers (Ed.), *Alcohol & Addictive Behavior*. Lincoln, NE: University of Nebraska Press.

National Center for Health Statistics. (1986). *Nutrition monitoring in the United States: A progress report from the joint nutrition monitoring evaluation committee* (DHHS Publication No. PHS 86-1255). Hyattsville, MD: U.S. Department of Health and Human Services.

Neff, C. (1987, January 5). Bosworth faces the music. *Sports Illustrated*, pp. 20-25.

Newcomb, M.D. (1986). Nuclear attitudes and reactions: Associations with depression, drug use, and quality of life. *Journal of Personality and Social Psychology, 50*, 906-920.

Newcomb, M.D., & Bentler, P.M. (1986). Drug use, educational aspirations, and work force involvement: The transition from adolescence to young adulthood. *American Journal of Community Psychology, 14*, 303-321.

Newcomb, M.D., & Harlow, L.L. (1986). Life events and substance use among adolescents:

Mediating effects of perceived loss of control and meaninglessness of life. *Journal of Personality and Social Psychology,* **51**, 564-577.

Newcomb, M.D., Maddahian, E., & Bentler, P.M. (1986). Risk factors for drug use among adolescents: Concurrent and longitudinal analyses. *American Journal of Public Health,* **76**, 525-531.

New guidelines for the prudent. (1987). *Prevention,* **39**(2), 52-54.

Newman, M.A. (1986). *Health as expanding consciousness.* St. Louis: Mosby.

Norman, R. (1986). Health behaviour: The implications of research. *Health Promotion,* **25**(1,2), 2-5, 9.

Novak, M. (1976). *The joy of sports.* New York: Basic Books.

Nuttall, F.Q. (1987). Diet and diabetes, a brief overview: Personal perspective. *Journal of the American College of Nutrition,* **6**(1), 5-9.

O'Donnell, M.P. (1986). Definition of health promotion. *American Journal of Health Promotion,* **1**(1), 4-5.

Oleakno, W.A. (1987). Drinking, smoking and other factors in the epidemiology of unintentional non-motor vehicle injuries. *Public Health,* **101**, 39-47.

Ortega, D.F., & Pipal, J.E. (1984). Challenge seeking and the Type A coronary-prone behavior pattern. *Journal of Personality and Social Psychology,* **46**, 1328-1334.

Oster, G., Colditz, G.A., & Kelly, N.L. (1984). The economic costs of smoking and benefits of quitting for individual smokers. *Preventive Medicine,* **13**, 377-389.

Out in the open. (1987, November 30). *Time,* pp. 80-90.

Paffenbarger, R.S., Wing, A.L., & Hyde, R.T. (1978). Physical activity as an index of heart attack risk in college alumni. *American Journal of Epidemiology,* **108**, 161-175.

Paffenbarger, R.S., Hyde, R.T., Wing, A.L., & Steinmetz, C.H. (1984). A natural history of athleticism and cardiovascular health. *Journal of the American Medical Association,* **252**, 491-495.

Paffenbarger, R.S., Hyde, R.T., Wing, A.L., & Hsich, C.C. (1986). Physical activity, all-cause mortality, and longevity of college alumni. *New England Journal of Medicine,* **314**, 605-613.

Parcel, G.S. (1984). Theoretical models for application in school health education research. *Journal of School Health,* **54**(6), 39-49.

Parcel, G.S., & Baranowski, T. (1981). Social learning theory and health education. *Health Education,* **12**(3), 14-18.

Parker, D.L., Shultz, J.M., Gertz, L., Berkelman, R., & Remington, P.L. (1987). The social and economic costs of alcohol abuse in Minnesota, 1983. *American Journal of Public Health,* **77**, 982-986.

Parra, W.C., & Cates, W., Jr. (1985). Progress toward the 1990 objectives for sexually transmitted diseases: Good news and bad. *Public Health Reports,* **100**, 261-269.

Patterson, B.H., & Block, G. (1988). Food choices and the cancer guidelines. *American Journal of Public Health,* **78**, 282-286.

Pauly, J.T., Palmer, J.E., Wright, C.C., & Pfeiffer, G.J. (1982). The effect of a 14-week employee fitness program on selected physiological and psychological parameters. *Journal of Occupational Medicine,* **24**, 457-463.

Peck, M.S. (1978). *The road less traveled.* New York: Simon & Schuster.

Pekkanen, J. (1984, August). Nasty habits. *Washingtonian,* pp. 30-33.

Pelletier, K.R., & Lutz, R. (1988). Healthy people—healthy business: A critical review of stress management programs in the workplace. *American Journal of Health Promotion,* **2**(3), 5-12, 19.

Pender, N.J., & Pender, A.R. (1986). Attitudes, subjective norms, and intentions to engage in healthy behaviors. *Nursing Research,* **35**, 15-18.

Pennington, J.A.T. (1981). Considerations for

a new food guide. *Journal of Nutrition Education,* **13**(2), 53-55.

Perine, P.L., Handsfield, H.H., Holmes, K.K., & Blount, J.H. (1985). Epidemiology of the sexually transmitted diseases. *Annual Review of Public Health,* **6**, 85-106.

Petersen-Martin, J., & Cottrell, R.R. (1987). Self-concept, values, and health behavior. *Health Education,* **18**(5), 6-9.

Petosa, R. (1986). Emerging trends in adolescent health promotion. *Health Values,* **10**(3), 22-28.

Pierce, E.R., Benke, J.E., Gislason, C.A., & Broski, D.V. (1986). An interview with Secretary Bowen. *Journal of Allied Health,* **15**, 275-287.

Pincomb, G.A., Lovallo, W.R., & Passey, R.B. (1987). Caffeine enhances the physiological response to occupational stress in medical students. *Health Psychology,* **6**(2), 101-112.

Pomerleau, O.F., Scherzer, H.H., Greenberg, N.E., Pomerleau, C.S., Judge, J., Fertig, J.B., & Burleson, J. (1987). The effects of acute exercise on subsequent cigarette smoking. *Journal of Behavioral Medicine,* **10**(2), 117-127.

Powell, J. (1984). *The Christian Vision.* Allen, TX: Tabor.

Powell, K.E., Thompson, P.D., Casperson, C.J., & Kendrick, J.S. (1987). Physical activity and the incidence of coronary heart disease. *Annual Review of Public Health,* **8**, 253-287.

Prevention Magazine Health Academy Series: The American Heart Association's guide to healthy eating. (1987, February). *Prevention Magazine,* pp. 32, 34-36, 38, 40, 42, 44, 46, 48, 50-52, 54.

Pritikin, N. (1979). *The Pritikin program for diet & exercise.* New York: Grosset & Dunlap.

Puska, P., Nissinen, A., Tuomilehto, J., Salonen, J.T., Koskela, K., McAlister, A., Kottke, T.E., Maccoby, N., & Farquhar, J.W. (1985). The community-based strategy to prevent coronary heart disease: Conclusions from the ten years of the North Karelia project. *American Review of Public Health,* **6**, 147-193.

Rachels, J. (1986). *The elements of moral philosophy.* New York: Random House.

Rahe, R.H. (1979). Life changes events and mental illness: An overview. *Journal of Human Stress,* **5**(3), 2-10.

Rambo drugs. (1987). *American Health,* **6**(7), 43-48.

Raths, L., Harmin, M., & Simon, S. (1974). Teaching for value clarity. In B.I. Chazan and J.F. Soltis (Eds.), *Moral education.* New York: Teachers' College Press.

Ratto, T. (1987a). The four food groups revisited. *Medical Self Care,* **41**, 43-45.

Ratto, T. (1987b). The new science of weight control. *Medical Self Care,* **39**, 25-30.

Raveis, V.H., & Kandel, D.B. (1987). Changes in drug behavior from the middle to the late twenties: Initiation, persistence, and cessation of use. *American Journal of Health Promotion,* **77**, 607-611.

Rawlings, K. (Ed.) (1987). The Active Health Report highlights. Canada. *Health Promotion,* **25**(3), insert 1-14.

Reed, D.M., MacLean, C.J., & Hayashi, I. (1987). Predictors of atherosclerosis in the Honolulu heart program. *American Journal of Epidemiology,* **126**(2), 214-225.

Reiss, I.L. (1981). Some observations on ideology and sexuality in America. *Journal of Marriage and the Family,* **43**, 271-283.

Robertson, L.S. (1980). Crash involvement of teenaged drivers when driver education is eliminated from high school. *American Journal of Public Health,* **70**, 599-603.

Robertson, L.S. (1986). Behavioral and environmental interventions for reducing motor vehicle trauma. *Annual Review of Public Health,* **7**, 13-34.

Robinson, J.C. (1988). The rising long-term trend in occupational injury rates. *American Journal of Public Health,* **78**, 276-281.

Rodale, R. (1987a). Editor's Note. *Prevention,* **39**(2), 25.

Rodale, R. (1987b). Prevention should be for everyone. *Prevention,* **39**(2), 27-31.

Rokeach, M. (1968). *Beliefs, attitudes, and values: A theory of organization and change.* San Francisco: Jossey-Bass.

Rokeach, M. (1973). *The nature of human values.* New York: Free Press.

Rokeach, M. (1979). *Understanding human values: Individual and society.* New York: Free Press.

Rosato, F.D. (1986). *Fitness and wellness: The physical connection.* St. Paul: West Publishing.

Rosen, J.C., & Gross, J. (1987). Prevalence of weight reducing and weight gaining in adolescent girls and boys. *Health Psychology,* **6**, 131-147.

Rosenbaum, M., & Murphy, S. (1987). Not the picture of health: Women of methadone. *Journal of Psychoactive Drugs,* **19**, 217-226.

Rosenberg, L., Werler, M.M., Kaufman, D.W., & Shapiro, S. (1987). Coffee drinking and myocardial infarction in young women: An update. *American Journal of Epidemiology,* **126**(1), 147-149.

Rosenman, R., & Friedman, M. (1974). *Type A behavior and your heart.* Greenwich, CT: Fawcett.

Rosenstock, I.M. (1974). Historical origins of the Health Belief Model. *Health Education Monograph,* **2**, 328-334.

Russ, N.W., & Geller, E.S. (1987). Training bar personnel to prevent drunken driving: A field evaluation. *American Journal of Public Health,* **77**(8), 952-954.

Saltzer, E.B. (1978). Locus of control and the intention to lose weight. *Health Education Monographs,* **6**, 118-128.

Schachter, S. (1982). Recidivism and self-cure of smoking and obesity. *American Psychologist,* **37**, 436-444.

Schapell, D., Bell, S.J., & Blackburn, G.L. (1987). A critical evaluation of popular low calorie diets in America: Part 1. *Topics in Clinical Nutrition,* **2**(2), 29-36.

Scheier, M.F., & Carver, C.S. (1987). Dispositional optimism and physical well-being: The influence of generalized outcome expectancies on health. *Journal of Personality,* **55**(2), 169-210.

Schoenborn, C.A. (1986). Health habits of U.S. adults, 1985: The "Alameda 7" revisited. *Public Health Reports,* **101**, 571-580.

Scragg, R., Stewart, A., Jackson, R., & Beaglehole, R. (1987). Alcohol and exercise in myocardial infarction and sudden death in men and women. *American Journal of Epidemiology,* **126**(1), 77-85.

Secretary of Health and Human Services. (1985). *Alcohol and health: Sixth special report to the U.S. Congress.* Rockville, MD: U.S. Department of Health and Human Services.

Seeman, M., & Seeman, T.E. (1983). Health behavior and personal autonomy: A longitudinal study of the sense of control in illness. *Journal of Health and Social Behavior,* **24**, 144-159.

Seffrin, J.R. (1977). Cigarette smoking: Risks, rewards and values. *Health Values,* **1**(5), 197-199.

Selye, H. (1976). *The Stress of Life.* New York: McGraw-Hill.

Sen, A. (1986). The right to take personal risks. In D. MacLean (Ed.), *Values at risk* (pp. 155-169). Totowa, NJ: Rowman & Allenheld.

Shafer, W. (1987). *Stress management for wellness.* New York: Holt, Rinehart & Winston.

Sherwin, R., & Corbett, S. (1985). Campus sexual norms and dating relationships: A trend analysis. *Journal of Sex Research,* **21**, 258-274.

Shilling, S., & Brackbill, R.M. (1987). Occupational health and safety risks and potential health consequences perceived by U.S. workers, 1985. *Public Health Reports,* **102**, 36-40.

Shirreffs, J.H. (1979). Health education and behavior influence/control: Point/counterpoint. *Health Values, 3*, 38-41.

Shisslak, C.M., Crago, M., Neal, M.E., & Swain, B. (1987). Primary prevention of eating disorders. *Journal of Consulting and Clinical Psychology, 55*, 660-667.

Siegel, B.S. (1986). *Love, medicine, & miracles.* New York: Harper & Row.

Siegel, J.M. (1984). Type A behavior. Epidemiologic foundations and public health implications. *Annual Review of Public Health, 5*, 343-367.

Silverman, M.M., Eichler, A., & Williams, G.D. (1987). Self-reported stress: Findings from the 1985 national health interview survey. *Public Health Reports, 102*, 47-53.

Simmons, D.D. (1982). *Personal valuing.* Chicago: Nelson-Hall.

Singh, B.K. (1980). Trends in attitudes toward premarital sexual relations. *Journal of Marriage and the Family, 8*, 387-393.

Singsank, D., & Singsank, D. (1984). *Personal life plan for health and fitness.* Madison, WI: American Health and Nutrition.

Slater, C.H., Green, L.W., Vernon, S.W., & Keith, V.M. (1987). Problems in estimating the prevalence of physical activity from national surveys. *Preventive Medicine, 16*, 107-118.

Smart, R.G., & Murray, G.F. (1985). Narcotic drug abuse in 152 countries: Social and economic conditions as predictors. *International Journal of the Addictions, 20*, 737-749.

Smith, B.C. (1982). A decision making model used to evaluate a smoking cessation program. *Health Values, 6*(5), 31-35.

Smith, T.W., & Anderson, N.B. (1986). Models of personality and disease: An international approach to Type A behavior and cardiovascular risk. *Journal of Personality and Social Psychology, 50*, 1166-1173.

Smoking news update. (1987). *Medical Self Care, 39*, 9.

Snow, J.T., & Harris, M.B. (1985). Maintenance of weight loss: Demographic, behavioral and attitudinal correlates. *Journal of Obesity and Weight Regulation, 4*, 234-257.

Sobolski, J., Kornitzer, M., DeBacher, G., Dramaix, M., Abramowicz, M., Degre, S., & Denolin, H. (1987). Protection against ischemic heart disease in the Belgian physical fitness study: Physical fitness rather than physical activity. *American Journal of Epidemiology, 125*, 601-610.

Solomon, R.C. (1984). *Ethics: A brief introduction.* New York: McGraw-Hill.

Solum, T.T., Ryttig, K.R., Solum, E., & Larsen, S. (1987). The influence of a high-fibre diet on body weight, serum lipids and blood pressure in slightly overweight persons. *International Journal of Obesity, 11*(Suppl. 1), 67-71.

Some teens seem to get the message on drugs. (1988, February). *The Nation's Health*, pp. 1, 20.

Sorensen, G., Jacobs, D.R., Jr., Pirie, P., Folsom, A., Luepker, R., & Gillam, R. (1987). Relationships among Type A behavior, employment experiences, and gender: The Minnesota heart survey. *Journal of Behavioral Medicine, 10*, 323-336.

Sorensen, G., & Pechacek, T.F. (1987). Attitudes toward smoking cessation among men and women. *Journal of Behavioral Medicine, 10*(2), 129-137.

Steele, C.M., & Southwick, L. (1985). Alcohol and social behavior I: The psychology of drunken excess. *Journal of Personality and Social Psychology, 48*, 18-34.

Steiber, S.R. (1987a). What's an HMO? 51% of respondents don't know. *Hospitals Magazine, 61*(3), 78.

Steiber, S.R. (1987b). Right to die: Public balks at deciding for others. *Hospitals Magazine, 61*(5), 72.

Stephens, T. (1986). Health practices and health status: Evidence from the Canada Health Survey. *American Journal of Preventive Medicine, 2*, 209-215.

Stephens, T., Jacobs, D.R., & White, C.C. (1985). A descriptive epidemiology of leisure-time physical activity. *Public Health Reports, 100*, 147-158.

Stewart, M.A. (1985). *Attitude-behavior consistency: A problem for social gerontology.* Unpublished doctoral dissertation, University of Notre Dame, South Bend, IN.

Strecher, V.J., DeVellis, B., Becker, M.H., & Rosenstock, I.M. (1986). The role of self-efficacy in achieving health behavior change. *Health Education Quarterly, 13*, 73-92.

Streufert, S. (1986). Individual differences in risk taking. *Journal of Applied Social Psychology, 16*, 482-497.

Strober, M., & Humphrey, L.L. (1987). Familial contributions to the etiology and course of anorexia nervosa and bulimia. *Journal of Consulting and Clinical Psychology, 55*, 654-659.

Strube, M.J., Berry, J.M., Goza, B.K., & Fennimore, D. (1985). Type A behavior, age, and psychological well-being. *Journal of Personality and Social Psychology, 49*, 203-218.

Suls, J., Becker, M.A., & Mullen B. (1981). Coronary-prone behavior, social insecurity and stress among college-aged adults. *Journal of Human Stress, 7*(3), 27-34.

Suls, J., & Mullen, B. (1981). Life events, perceived control and illness: The role of uncertainty. *Journal of Human Stress, 7*(2), 30-34.

Svendsen, K.H., Kuller, L.H., Martin, M.J., & Ockene, J.K. (1987). Effects of passive smoking in the multiple risk factor intervention trial. *American Journal of Epidemiology, 126*, 783-795.

Swinker, M. (1986). Chlamydia trachomatis genital infections in college women. *Journal of American College Health, 34*, 207-209.

Taylor, H., & Kagay, M. (1986). The HMO report card: A closer look. *Health Affairs, 5*, 81-89.

Taylor, M.E., & McKillip, J. (1980). Immediate health-related consequences of student lifestyles. *Health Values, 4*, 213-216.

Teahan, J.E. (1987). Alcohol expectancies, values, and drinking of Irish and U.S. collegians. *International Journal of the Addictions, 22*, 621-638.

Temple, M.T., & Fillmore, K.M. (1986). The variability of drinking patterns and problems among young men, age 16-31: A longitudinal study. *International Journal of the Addictions, 20*, 1595-1620.

Toffler, A.A. (1970). *Future shock.* New York: Random House.

Toffler, A.A. (1980). *The third wave.* New York: Bantam Books.

Tuomilehto, J., Nissinen, A., Puska, P., Salonen, J.T., & Jalkenen, L. (1986). Long-term effects of cessation of smoking on body weight, blood pressure and serum cholesterol in the middle-aged population with high blood pressure. *Addictive Behaviors, 11*, 1-9.

Umberson, D. (1987). Family status and health behaviors: Social control as a dimension of social integration. *Journal of Health and Social Behavior, 28*, 306-319.

Ureda, J.R. (1980). Effect of contract witnessing on motivation and weight loss in a weight control program. *Health Education Quarterly, 7*, 163-185.

U.S. Department of Health, Education, and Welfare, Public Health Service. (1979). *Healthy people: The Surgeon General's report on health promotion and disease prevention.* Washington, D.C.: U.S. Government Printing Office.

U.S. Department of Health and Human Services, Public Health Service. (1980). *Promoting health/preventing disease: Objectives for the nation.* Rockville, MD: Author.

VanderPlate, C., & Aral, S.D. (1987). Psychosocial aspects of genital herpes virus infection. *Health Psychology, 6*, 57-72.

Wald, N.J., Nauchahal, K., Thompson, S.G., & Cuckle, H.S. (1986). Does breathing other people's tobacco smoke cause lung cancer?

British Medical Journal, **293**(6556), 1217-1222.

Walker, L.R., & Glanz, K. (1986). Psychological determinants of breast self-examination. *American Journal of Preventive Medicine,* **2**, 169-178.

Wallack, L., Breed, W., & Cruz, J. (1987). Alcohol on prime-time television. *Journal of Studies on Alcohol,* **48**, 33-38.

Wallack, L., & Corbett, K. (1987). Alcohol, tobacco and marijuana use among youth: An overview of epidemiological, program and policy trends. *Health Education Quarterly,* **14**, 223-249.

Wallston, B.S., Alagna, S.W., DeVellis, B.E., & DeVellis, R.F. (1983). Social support and physical health. *Health Psychology,* **2**, 367-391.

Wallston, B.S., & Wallston, K.A. (1978). Locus of control and health: A review of the literature. *Health Education Monographs,* **6**, 107-117.

Wallston, B.S., Wallston, K.A., Kaplan, K.A., & Maides, S.A. (1976). Development and validation of the health locus of control (HCL) scale. *Journal of Consulting and Clinical Psychology,* **44**, 580-585.

Wallston, K.A., Wallston, B.S., & DeVellis, R. (1978). Development of the multidimensional health locus of control (MHLC) scales. *Health Education Monographs,* **6**, 161-170.

Wallston, K.A., Maides, S., & Wallston, B.S. (1976). Health-related information seeking as a function of health-related locus of control and health value. *Journal of Research in Personality,* **10**, 215-222.

Walsh, D.C., & Gordon, N.P. (1986). Legal approaches to smoking deterence. *Annual Review of Public Health,* **7**, 127-149.

Washburn, R.A., Adams, L., & Haile, G.T. (1987). Physical activity assessment for epidemiologic research: The utility of two simplified approaches. *Preventive Medicine,* **16**, 636-646.

Watson, G.S., Zador, P.L., & Wilks, A. (1980). The repeal of helmet use laws and increased motorcyclist mortality in the United States, 1975-1978. *American Journal of Public Health,* **70**(6), 579-585.

Wattenberg, B.J. (1985). *The good news is the bad news is wrong.* New York: Simon & Schuster.

Weinberger, M., Greene, J.Y., Mamlin, J.J., & Jerin, M.J. (1981). Health beliefs and smoking behavior. *American Journal of Public Health,* **71**, 1253-1255.

Weinberger, M., Hiner, S.L., & Tierney, W.M. (1987). In support of hassles as a measure of stress in predicting health outcomes. *Journal of Behavioral Medicine,* **10**, 19-31.

Weiss, B.D. (1986). Prevention of bicycle-related head injuries. *American Journal of Preventive Medicine,* **2**, 330-333.

Whaley, R. (1982). *Health.* Englewood Cliffs, NJ: Prentice-Hall.

Wiggins, J.A., & Wiggins, B.B. (1987). Drinking at a southern university: Its description and correlates. *Journal of Studies on Alcohol,* **48**, 319-324.

Wiley, J.A., & Camacho, T.C. (1980). Lifestyle and future health: Evidence from the Alameda County study. *Preventive Medicine,* **9**, 1-21.

Willett, W.C., Green, A., Stampfer, M.J., Speizer, F.E., Colditz, G.A., Rosner, B., Monson, R.R., Stason, W., & Hennekens, C.H. (1987). Relative and absolute excess risks of coronary heart disease among women who smoke cigarettes. *New England Journal of Medicine,* **317**, 1303-1309.

Williams, A.F., & Lund, A.K. (1986). Seat belt laws and occupant crash protection in the United States. *American Journal of Public Health,* **76**, 1438-1441.

Williams, A.F., Peat, M.A., Crouch, D.J., Wells, J.K., & Finkle, B.S. (1985). Drugs in fatally injured young male drivers. *Public Health Reports,* **100**, 19-25.

Williams, F.G., & Knox, R. (1987). Alcohol abuse intervention in a university setting. *Journal of American College Health,* **36**, 97-102.

Williams, G.D., Dufour, M., & Bertolucci, D. (1986). *Drinking levels, knowledge, and associated characteristics, 1985 NHIS findings*. Washington, DC: National Institute on Alcohol Abuse and Alcoholism.

Williams, M.H. (1983). *Nutrition for fitness and sport*. Dubuque, IA: Wm. C. Brown.

Williamson, D.F., Forman, M.R., Binkin, N.J., Gentry, E.M., Remington, P.L., & Trowbridge, F.L. (1987). Alcohol and body weight in United States adults. *American Journal of Public Health, 77*(10), 1324-1330.

Wingard, D.L. (1984). The sex differential in morbidity, mortality, and lifestyle. *Annual Review of Public Health, 5*, 433-458.

Wingard, D.L., Berkman, L.F., & Brand, R.J. (1982). A multivariate analysis of health-related practices. *American Journal of Epidemiology, 116*, 765-776.

Wurtele, S.K., Britcher, J.C., & Saslawsky, D.A. (1985). Relationships between locus of control, health value, and preventive health behaviors among women. *Journal of Research in Personality, 19*, 271-278.

Yamaguchi, K., & Kandel, D.B. (1984). Patterns of drug use from adolescence to young adulthood: III Predictors of progression. *American Journal of Public Health, 74*, 673-681.

Yarber, W.L. (1986). Delay in seeking prescription contraception and the health lifestyle and health locus of control of young women. *Journal of Sex Education and Therapy, 12*(2), 51-54.

Zabin, L.S. (1984). The association between smoking and sexual behavior among teens in U.S. contraceptive clinics. *American Journal of Public Health, 74*, 261-263.

Zuti, W.B. (1984). Health promotion in the social service setting. In J.P. Opatz (Ed.), *Wellness Promotion Strategies: Selected Proceedings of the Eighth Annual National Wellness Conference* (p. 110). Dubuque, IA: Kendall/Hunt.

Zuti, B., & Golding, L. (1976). Comparing diet and exercise as weight reduction tools. *The Physician and Sports Medicine, 4*(1), 49-53.

Index